JUDGMENT
AT
GALLATIN
THE TRIAL OF FRANK JAMES

JUDGMENT AT GALLATIN
THE TRIAL OF FRANK JAMES

GERARD S. PETRONE

INTRODUCTION BY
RICHARD MAXWELL BROWN

TEXAS TECH UNIVERSITY PRESS

This book was set in Aldine 721 and Copperplate Gothic and printed on acid-free paper that meets the guidelines for permanence and durability of the committee on Production Guide lines for Book Longevity of the Council on Library Resources. ∞

Unless stated otherwise photographs belong to the author's personal collection.

Design by Melissa Bartz

Printed in the United States of America

Library of Congress Cataloging-in-Publication Data
Petrone, Gerard S.
        Judgment at Gallatin : the trial of Frank James / Gerard S.
Petrone.
              p.   cm.
        Includes bibliographical references and index.
        ISBN 0-89672-398-4 (alk. paper)
        1. James, Frank, 1844-1915. 2. Outlaws—West (U.S.)—
    Biography. 3. Trials (Murder)—Missouri—Gallatin. 4. James,
    Frank, 1844-1915—Trials, litigation, etc. I. Title.
F594.J24P48 1998
3693.15'52'092278—dc21   98-6746
                                                                CIP

98 99 00 01 02 03 04 05 06 / 9 8 7 6 5 4 3 2 1

Texas Tech University Press
Box 41037
Lubbock, Texas 79409-1037 USA
800-832-4042
ttup@ttu.edu

I dedicate this book to nature's little alarm clocks—
Petey, Lime Rickey, Spunky, Sparkle, and Timmy—my wife's
parakeets, whose noisy chattering at daybreak reminded me to get
up and start writing.

In America,
an acquittal doesn't mean you're innocent,
it means you beat the rap.
—F. Lee Bailey

CONTENTS

PREFACE

On the whole, trials, even murder trials, are disappointingly dull. Justice wends its tedious way through a maze of legal verbiage and courtroom machinations, lawyers argue, witnesses drone on, the audience falls asleep, and jurors wonder when they'll be able to go home.

But a thrilling exception took place in the autumn of 1883 in Gallatin, Missouri, a sleepy little town in the northwestern part of the state. This is where Frank James, surviving member of perhaps the greatest gang of outlaws in the annals of Western frontier crime, was tried for murder of a passenger during a train holdup in nearby Winston in 1881. The proceedings were jam-packed with excitement, and the nation paused to watch with rapt attention.

The Frank James trial was one of the most celebrated criminal cases of last century. In terms of public interest and excitement, the prosecution of western Missouri's infamous son certainly rivaled the contemporary trial of Charles Guiteau, President James A. Garfield's assassin. The proceedings would have soared to even greater heights of public spectacle and sensationalism had the trial been held in any other place than obscure, out-of-the-way Gallatin. Likewise, if the person placed in the prisoner's dock had not been a subject of such public fascination and hero worship as Frank James was, little fuss would have ever been made over the trial.

The trial was highly unusual in a number of respects. To have thirteen distinguished lawyers gather in one courtroom to do battle was excessive by contemporary standards, and the professional associations they formed during the trial were surprising, if not ironic. Two ex-Union officers, for example, were the lead attorneys engaged to defend the ex-Confederate soldier James, two former colleagues in law faced each other as adversaries, and one of the defense counsels and his prime witness, once bitter enemies during the Civil War, now joined hands in a common cause. Another noteworthy aspect of the trial was the role played by the enigmatic Thomas T. Crittenden, governor of Missouri. Although he was responsible for starting the chain of events that led to the breakup of the James gang, his later actions helped to ensure the eventual freedom of Frank James.

The trial, a courtroom epic played out over a two-week period, was marked by old-fashioned country lawyering, moving eloquence of speech, humor, a rich panoply of characters, high drama, and many surprises. It was what writers of the period liked to call "an interesting episode in history." The case was a bare-knuckled fight to the finish by two groups of opposing attorneys, and, despite the damning testimony of Dick Liddil, the former gang member and coconspirator who incriminated Frank James on the charge of murder, the verdict of not guilty shocked the nation.

To many people and especially the press, the James trial was a flagrant miscarriage of justice. Frank James, as it turned out, was aided by more than eminent counsel. Observers attributed the jury's acquittal to strong Southern sympathies for the former Confederate guerrilla who had ridden with Quantrill's raiders, which blinded them to the strong evidence and persuasive legal arguments against James.

How James came to be brought before justice in the first place, however, is a story as dramatic and intriguing as the trial itself. At the age of forty, Frank James—man on the run; mastermind of one of the most notorious band of outlaws to ever roam the Western frontier; revered, admired, and beloved folk hero of thousands of Missourians; the most feared and sought-after criminal in the West; a man who seemed invincible as the target of one of the longest-running manhunts in American history—suddenly stepped off the streets in Jefferson City one day in October 1882, handed his pistols over to Missouri Governor Crittenden, and calmly announced his surrender.

The act stunned everyone. James's decision, however, which on the surface seemed impetuous and irrational (one newspaper called him "crazy"), was in reality a bold and carefully planned, but enormously risky, gamble to escape the hangman's noose. By it James hoped to take a giant leap from life as a murderer and robber with a price on his head to that of a free and respected member of society. It was a long and arduous journey. The following narrative, based on trial records, contemporary newspaper articles, and historical references, describes that journey.

Gerard S. Petrone

Acknowledgments

I wish to thank the following individuals whose kind and unselfish sharing of historical information and images helped in the production of this book: David Carroll of Tinley Park; Illinois, Monte Russell of Stockton, Missouri; and Daryl Wilkinson of Gallatin, Missouri. History professor Roger McGrath of Thousand Oaks, California, also provided valuable advice and encouragement. I am particularly indebted to practicing attorney Michael Cronan of Kansas City, Missouri, and retired law professor James Jeans Sr. of Platte City, Missouri, who edited and contributed to the legal portions of the manuscript. Last but not least, I extend a warm thank-you to an old friend and ex-Missourian, Ed Ridgway of La Mesa, California, for he knows what.

Despite copious publication on the James brothers for more than a century, a huge gap has been the lack of a full-fledged book on by far the least-explored major event in their lives: the 1883 trial of Frank James in Gallatin, Missouri. Until the present admirable treatment by Gerard S. Petrone, the only book on the trial had been an obscure and narrow item of 1898 little seen even by specialists.[1]

The evidence in *Judgment at Gallatin* is strongly to the effect that the bold bank and train robbers, Frank and Jesse James, were also cold-blooded killers. Yet, the Jameses were idolized by an array of law-abiding citizens. This was because Frank and Jesse were the prototypical "social bandits" in American history.[2] As conceived by the distinguished British historian, Eric J. Hobsbawm, social bandits around the world emerged as heroes, because their daring crimes appealed to the social discontents and grievances of those who would never commit such crimes on their own.

In Hobsbawm's widely influential formulation, the model social bandit was the legendary medieval English hero, Robin Hood, who took from the rich to give to the poor. Jesse James astutely cultivated the image of Robin Hood for himself and his compadres. In the classic ballad about the demise of Jesse James there is this verse:

> Jesse James was a lad who killed many a man.
> He robbed the Glendale train.
> *He stole from the rich and he gave to the poor,*
> He had a hand and a heart and a brain.[3]

Indeed, one of the most enduring pieces of folklore about the James-Younger gang is their rescue of a poor widow's farm from the greedy grasp of a rich banker. It never happened. In their larcenies, the Jameses and Youngers took from economically affluent banks and railroads, but they did not give to the needy. They kept the money and lived on it.

Hobsbawm found that the mythic (and sometimes true) image of the "noble robber" from continent to continent consists of the following nine points, all of which fit Frank and/or Jesse James like a glove. The pronoun, "he," that begins each item refers to the generic "noble robber." I have put in brackets my comments on the first seven points:

1. He begins his outlaw career "not by crime but as the victim of injustice." [This Frank and Jesse claimed for themselves.]
2. He rights wrongs. [Widely believed of Frank and Jesse.]
3. He "takes from the rich to give to the poor." [Ditto.]
4. He kills only in self-defense or "just revenge." [Ditto.]
5. If he survives, "he returns to his people" as an honorable citizen. [Frank did.]
6. He is "admired and supported by his people." [True of both Frank and Jesse.]
7. He dies "invariably and only through treason." [True of Jesse, betrayed and slain by Bob Ford.]
8. He "is—at least in theory—invisible and invulnerable."
9. He is not the enemy of the state but of only local or "other oppressors."[4]

In regard to point 1, Frank and Jesse never confessed to any of their crimes, but it was an open secret to family, friends, and vocal supporters like the Kansas City journalist, John N. Edwards, that they committed them. To sympathetic contacts like Edwards—who aired their views in public—the Jameses claimed that after the Civil War ended their bloody service as Confederate guerrillas, Missouri authorities would not let the brothers go straight. Instead, Frank and Jesse turned to robbery out of desperation. As "victims of injustice" they were forced into outlaw careers. In fact, the vast majority of ex-Confederate guerrillas of Missouri became law-abiding civilians without hindrance, but this course the Jameses did not choose. Instead, Frank and Jesse James continued their violent wartime ways, but made their targets banks and railroads instead of federal soldiers.

In regard to the eighth point that the noble robber "is—at least in theory—invisible and invulnerable," many refused to believe that it was Jesse James who was killed by Bob Ford in St. Joseph, Missouri, on April 3, 1882. Impostors who claimed to be Jesse James came forward as late as 1948. The last point—that the noble robber is the enemy only of local or "other oppressors'—fits equally as well: the brothers and their supporters reasoned that by not allowing them to pursue peaceful livelihoods, it was the authorities themselves who plunged Frank and Jesse willy-nilly into a fifteen-year struggle for survival, pitting them against the likes of the railroads and their Pinkerton hired hands.

While Frank and Jesse James pursued outlaw occupations, two situations made them heroes rather than villains to a great portion of the public. First were lingering but deep Civil War animosities. A great many Confederate-minded Missourians revered the Jameses and Youngers because they had been impetuous Confederate guerrillas in the sanguinary struggle against Unionist marauders, U. S. Army troops, and the oppressive anticivilian policy of federal military Order No. 11, a shockingly brutal policy that embittered a generation and is pointedly discussed by Dr. Petrone. To these Missourians still emotionally loyal to the "lost cause" of the Confederacy, the ill-fated but audacious 1876 James-Younger bank robbery in Northfield, Minnesota, was like a gallant guerrilla raid deep into the heart of the enemy country of the North. Few, however, saw the irony that the Northfield fiasco was as disastrous to the outlaws as Robert E. Lee's invasion of Pennsylvania in 1863 was to him.

The second situation involved festering post-Civil War tensions in Missouri that stemmed from the rise of powerful new forces of industry, finance, and commerce. The impersonal, aggressive ways of heedless plutocratic power were rolling over the old rural society with its traditional values of the sort in which the James brothers and many others had been reared. Squeezed by onerous mortgages in the deflationary decades of the 1870s–1890s, aroused dirt farmers seethed over the high rates and high-handed tactics of railroads monopolizing the vital arteries of transportation. Beleaguered agrarians wasted little sympathy on the railroads and banks victimized by the James-Younger gang. These peaceful citizens never dreamed of robbing banks or trains, but they felt a surge of affection for those who did—Frank and Jesse James, chief among them. Historian Richard White points to this sizable segment of the hinterland population as "passive" but ardent supporters of the social banditry of the James brothers. Such supporters may have included the jury in the 1883 trial of Frank James in rural Daviess County, Missouri.

Following his trial in 1883, Frank James did return to a peaceful civilian life in which a great many Missourians revered him as an honorable citizen. Having been a lifelong old-fashioned Democrat, Frank James veered to the left. Within ten years, he joined the radical agrarian third-party movement of the Populists. In the presidential election of 1896, the best hope of the Populists, William Jennings Bryan of Nebraska,[5] led a nationwide crusade against the Wall Street financiers and "robber barons" of the time. Yet, Bryan was defeated by the Republican candidate, William McKinley. Unreconciled to the triumph of McKinley, Frank James announced in 1897, "if ever there is another civil war in this country . . . it will be between capital and labor" and declared himself "as ready to march now" in behalf of labor "as I was when a boy in defense of the South."[6]

The leitmotif of capital vs. labor in the James-Younger story came to the fore in 1875 when Missouri railroads hired the Pinkerton National Detective Agency to hunt down the outlaws. With great success, the Pinkertons spearheaded the corporation crusade against the violent Molly Maguires in the Pennsylvania coal fields. Yet Pinkerton tactics that worked so well in Pennsylvania backfired disastrously in Missouri. Failing to capture Frank and Jesse, the Pinkertons—as described by Gerard Petrone—succeeded only in killing their half brother, Archie, and maiming their mother, Zerelda. The result was a wave of sympathy for the outlaw brothers and their family.

In due course, Frank and Jesse James became a hotly debated factor in bumptious Missouri politics. Pro-railroad and law-and-order elements among the Democrats coalesced with Republicans against the Jameses while the powerful pro-Confederate, anti-railroad wing of the Missouri Democratic Party found ways to excuse the brigandage of Frank and Jesse. The eventual outcome of this political conflict was the crucial anti-James policy of Governor Thomas T. Crittenden so ably recounted in all its complexity by Dr. Petrone.

Meanwhile, the mighty mythology of Frank and Jesse was being forged in the crucible of Missouri public opinion. Leading the widespread popular adulation of the James-Younger gang in the 1870s was—with the shrewd assistance of public-relations conscious Jesse James—a barrage of strongly favorable columns by the talented Kansas City journalist, John N. Edwards, who was virtually a press agent for Frank, Jesse, and their criminal colleagues. Next came romanticized sketches of Jesse James, followed in the early 1880s by a flood tide of dime novels that littered newsstands on into the twentieth century. Immune to the glamorization of the outlaw Jameses was the Postmaster General of the United States who from 1883 to 1889 forced a temporary halt to the dime novels in response to general concern that the lurid paperbacks inspired urban juvenile crime.

Fact was slow to catch up to fancy, for not until the 1920s did Robertus Love produce the first realistic, albeit unduly favorable, biography of Jesse

James. Yet any pretense of realism about Frank and Jesse James was over-whelmed by the smash-hit movie of 1939, *Jesse James*, a technicolor epic filmed in the beautiful Missouri Ozarks. Brilliantly cast as the mythic James brothers were two of the most popular Hollywood leading men of the time. A dashing, darkly handsome Tyrone Power played Jesse James while an appealing, dead-game Henry Fonda took on the role of the older brother Frank. A mixture of much fiction and little fact, the film glorified Jesse James as a heroic social bandit who used outlaw deeds to fight the economi-cally oppressive railroads of Missouri and the Midwest.

Not to be overlooked, however, is that in both life and legend there is, in counterpoint to the social-bandit, the socially conservative hero of the West, represented, for example, by the frontier marshals Wild Bill Hickok and Wyatt Earp.[7] The aspect of the American mind that values order and security responds to the reassuring myth of the intrepid lawman always besting evil, whereas the social-bandit hero appeals to the instinctive American fondness for dissent and distrust of established power.

As we read Dr. Petrone's engrossing tale of the trial of Frank James, the realm of film and fiction, of myth and legend is left far behind. Instead, our pleasure is in a lively but resolutely factual treatment deeply grounded in primary sources. To posterity, Frank James has always been in the shadow of his flamboyant younger brother Jesse. Unlike Jesse, Frank had no desire for the limelight, in which he was squarely centered during the course of his trial for murder, which riveted the attention of Missouri, the Midwest, and the nation in 1883. In Gerard Petrone's vivid, perceptive portrait, Frank James and his trial truly come alive.

An essential contribution to the serious study of the James-Younger epi-sode, *Judgment at Gallatin* negotiates the intellectually perilous mine field of the myth and reality of Frank and Jesse James. Sidestepping the toils of legend, Dr. Petrone never strays from the path of rigorous realism. The re-sult is a delight for the reader—a fascinating trip into the past with reso-nance for the present.

Richard Maxwell Brown

Bibliography

Brant, Marley, *The Outlaw Youngers: A Confederate Brotherhood* (Lanham, Md.: Madison Books, 1992).

Broehl, Wayne G., Jr., *The Molly Maguires* (Cambridge, Mass.: Harvard Univer-sity Press, 1964).

Brown, Richard Maxwell, "Desperadoes and Lawmen: The Folk Hero," *Media Studies Journal*, 6 (winter 1992): 151-161, and "Western Violence: Structure, Values, Myth, *Western Historical Quarterly*, 23 (February 1993): 5-20, for the contrast between social-bandit heroes and socially-conservative heroes.

Brownlee, Richard S., *Gray Ghosts of the Confederacy: Guerrilla Warfare in the West, 1861-1865* (Baton Rouge: Louisiana State University Press, 1958).

Fellman, Michael, *Inside War: The Guerrilla Conflict in Missouri During the Civil Way* (New York: Oxford University Press, 1986).

Eric J. Hobsbawm, *Social Bandits and Primitive Rebels* (Glencoe, Ill.: Free Press, 1959), and *Bandits* (1969; 2nd edition, revised, New York: Viking Penguin, 1985).

Robertus Love, *The Rise and Fall of Jesse James* (1926; reprinted, Lincoln: University of Nebraska Press, 1990), a well-intentioned work sometimes belied by its author's sympathy for the Jameses.

Frank Morn, *The Eye That Never Sleeps: A History of the Pinkerton National Detective Agency* (Bloomington: Indiana University Press, 1982).

Frank R. Prassel, *The Great American Outlaw: A Legacy of Fact and Fancy* (Norman: University of Oklahoma Press, 1993), an exhaustive and perceptive treatment of the American outlaw tradition from colonial times to the recent past.

William A. Settle, Jr., *Jesse James Was His Name: Or, Fact and Fiction Concerning the Careers of the Notorious James Brothers of Missouri* (Columbia: University of Missouri Press, 1966), the best overall book on its subject.

Richard Slotkin, *Gunfighter Nation: The Myth of the Frontier in Twentieth-Century America* (New York: Atheneum, 1992).

David Thelen, *Paths of Resistance: Tradition and Dignity in Industrializing Missouri* (New York: Oxford University Press, 1986).

Paul I. Wellman, *A Dynasty of Western Outlaws* (1961; reprinted, Lincoln: University of Nebraska Press, 1986), chaps. 1-2.

Richard White, "Outlaw Gangs of the Middle Border: American Social Bandits," *Western Historical Quarterly*, 12 (October 1981): 387-408.

Notes

1. Cited and discussed in Dr. Petrone's Bibliography and Note References.
2. Another hugely famed social bandit is Billy the Kid. Among many other American social bandits are Joaquin Murieta, Butch Cassidy, John Dillinger, and Bonnie Parker and Clyde Barrow.
3. Settle, p. 173. Emphasis added.
4. Hobsbawm (1985), pp. 42-43, for the list of the nine items.
5. In 1896 both the Populists and the Democrats nominated Bryan for president.
6. Slotkin, p. 153.
7. Hickok was a deputy U. S. marshal and marshal of Abilene, Kansas. Earp was a deputy U. S. marshal in Arizona.

1 FRANK AND JESSE—THE ROBBING AND KILLING YEARS

As a breed of hero, outlaws in the early American West never seemed to die out. As soon as one brave but misguided hero turned in his spurs and patent leather holsters, vainly gripping his Colt revolver while uttering his dying words, "They got me!" another hero a county or a state away rose in his place to receive the adulation of the public and be celebrated in admiring prose that flowed from the pens of otherwise intelligent and responsible journalists. Few characters of the Old West, however, have captured the imagination and fancy of so many readers for so many years as the James brothers of Clay County, Missouri. Tales of their daring exploits—some true, some false, the rest highly exaggerated—were told and retold countless times, even before their criminal careers drew to a close in 1882. Well over a century later, these romantic heroes still exert a fascination.

The outlaw career of the James brothers, Jesse and Frank, spanning the years 1866 to 1882, is unmatched in the history of the American West. It is far more remarkable than that of their contemporaries: the Youngers, the Daltons, Dave Rudabaugh, Billy the Kid, and all the other desperadoes who terrorized the frontier west of the Missouri River in the late nineteenth century. The James boys had style, flair, and nerve. While most other criminals plied their trade in sparsely settled and lawless country, they stopped crowded trains in civilized, populated regions. They relieved passengers of their valuables, blew up express-car safes and emptied the contents, and then let the trains proceed. Anyone who resisted risked getting a bullet in the face. At other times, the James gang would fly into town on horseback, rob a bank of thousands of dollars, perhaps shooting down an uncooperative cashier, and then ride off like the wind.

Not the least of their accomplishments was the James brothers' uncanny ability to escape capture by the law. For a period of fifteen years, the citizens in Missouri (which newspaperman Carl Schurz once satirically labeled the "robber state"), and particularly the residents of western Missouri, feeling a mixture of sympathy and fear toward the brothers, gave safe haven to them and their gang members. Both brothers enjoyed safety within the ranks of society, living like ordinary law-abiding citizens, by growing beards, adopting aliases, and refraining from small talk with neighbors. "The man who talks is the man who gets caught," Frank James liked to say.

Most of the time it wasn't necessary for Frank and Jesse to run off and hide out in caves or in rugged, uninhabited badlands. It wasn't their preference and it wasn't necessary either. Previous to his last move to St. Joseph, for example, Jesse James took up residence in a house in Kansas City. After participating in the Blue Cut train robbery, he calmly returned home to his wife and child. The next morning he left his house to buy a newspaper, and came back to read accounts of the holdup.

Lives Forged in Violence

The lives of Frank and Jesse James begin before the Civil War. Zerelda Cole, their mother, was born in Scott County, Kentucky, in 1828. After being educated at a convent in Lexington, she married Reverend Robert James, a Baptist minister. On January 10, 1843, at the age of fifteen, she bore a son, Alexander Franklin James, later to be called Frank, or by his mother's favorite nickname, Buck. Two years later the small family moved from Kentucky to Clay County in western Missouri and worked a farm several miles outside Kearney, a station on the Hannibal and St. Joseph railroad. Jesse Woodson James was born there on September 5, 1847.

Reverend James caught gold fever and went west in 1850, lured by his brother, who had written of the fortunes to be found in the goldfields of California. The preacher died there a short time later of unknown causes. Mrs. James remained a widow for six years before marrying Dr. Reuben Samuel, a physician and native of Kentucky, in 1857.

During the 1850s Clay County was not a quiet place. The border between Missouri and Kansas was already aflame with great violence before the Civil War was formally declared. Differences between abolitionists in Kansas and slaveholders in Missouri had long since turned to bitter hatred, then open warfare and the spilling of blood. Under the Union flag, Kansas Jayhawkers (or Red Legs, as they were also called) led forays across the state line, shooting Southern sympathizers, driving off horses, capturing and freeing slaves, and burning down homes and farms.

In reprisal, bands of armed renegades from Missouri inflicted equally brutal attacks on communities in Kansas. They came to be called "border bandits" or "border ruffians." Many of the Missouri raiders were recruited

Photo taken in Nashville in 1864. Left to right: Charles "Fletch" Taylor (ex-guerilla), Frank James, and Jesse James. Frank, seated, wears a fancy studio costume. (Courtesy State Historical Society of Missouri, Columbia. Reprinted with permission.)

from Clay, Ray, and other counties around Kansas City, which later became hotbeds of Confederate sympathy.

As war clouds gathered on the horizon, the Samuels became secessionists and were quite outspoken in their views. The James boys, Frank and Jesse, were growing up. They spent some time in district schools, but records do not indicate how diligent or how successful they were in their studies. When the war broke out in 1861, Frank was eighteen years old and Jesse fourteen. News of the daring escapades of small groups of Confederate raiders in Kansas and Missouri had fired the imagination of many young and impressionable males in Clay County. Frank soon felt the urge to join them.

In the spring of 1862, he was easily persuaded to enlist by William Gaugh, a sixteen-year-old local boy who had gone off to fight with the rebels. As Frank James saddled his horse and rode away with Gaugh, he said good-bye to peaceful pursuits in life and cast his lot with a company of gray-coated volunteers [1]. His commander would be a former school teacher of Canal Dover, Ohio, by the name of William Clark Quantrill.

As the war progressed, hostility toward Southern sympathizers in western Missouri increased. Stationed in the vicinity of Kearney were elements of Union militia called the "home guard" who were well aware that the Samuels had strong pro-South leanings and also that Frank had joined up with Quantrill. A detachment of troops decided to pay a surprise visit one day to the couple's farm not long after Frank left.

The exact nature of the torture inflicted on Dr. Samuel by the Federal troops that day is not known. The most popular account is that the soldiers pulled Samuel from a field where he was plowing with Jesse, dropped a noose around his neck, and threw the other end over a tree limb. The doctor was ordered to tell the militia the location of Frank and Quantrill. When he repeatedly protested ignorance, the soldiers hanged the old man each time nearly to the point of death in a futile effort to extract information. He was left for dead.

Jesse was forced to watch the cruel punishment and, before the troops left, was thrashed with a rope end until his back was bleeding. His stepfather survived, but Jesse James, embittered and bent on revenge, left home at the age of fifteen and enlisted with the Confederates.

Quantrill achieved unprecedented notoriety for his monstrous actions conducted during the war. The rebel guerrilla leader, whose mother once described him after the war as having a "kind and affectionate nature," left

4

Frank James at an early age (ca. late 1860s).

home at the age of sixteen to wander out West for several years. When war erupted, Quantrill enlisted in Kansas in 1861 as a private in a troop of Confederate cavalry. He crossed into Missouri and fought with distinction under General Sterling Price. Price had high regard for this good soldier, whom he described as the "handsomest man in the saddle" he had ever seen and who was understandably idolized by Southern sympathizers in Missouri.

Frank James, ca. 1865. (Courtesy State Historical Society of Missouri, Columbia. Reprinted with permission.)

Quantrill was subsequently put in charge of an independent band of skirmishers whose job was to harass Union lines. It was one of three such companies that operated in Missouri; the other two were led by William Anderson (Jesse James joined his group) and George Todd. When Frank James took his place with Quantrill's marauders, the group numbered about thirty. Among the men were Clell Miller, George Shepherd, and Coleman and James Younger, two sons of a former judge, lawmaker, rebel sympathizer, and stockman from Cass County. After the war, many of these Quantrill veterans would join Frank and Jesse James in criminal pursuits.

The lives of the James boys while they were with Quantrill and Anderson were filled with terrible and bloody deeds, but a full and accurate account of them was never made, nor did the boys ever discuss them publicly after the war. We do know, however, that Frank and Jesse were involved in the massacres at Lawrence, Kansas, and Centralia, Missouri, two of the bloodiest atrocities committed during the entire Civil War.

The Lawrence attack took place in 1863. Lawrence was selected as a target because it was the home of General Jim Lane, a Kansas Red Leg and Quantrill's archenemy. Quantrill and his forces, armed to the teeth and numbering about 350, were given orders to shoot everybody in sight. Galloping into the small Kansas town one September night, they shot down scores of innocent and helpless people in the streets (the official count was around 180), sacked two banks, and burned the town to the ground. The number of civilians personally killed by Frank James was never established, although Jesse reportedly boasted of murdering thirty-six.

The assault on Centralia was equally heinous. This time, in September 1864, it was committed by a force of 100 Confederate guerrillas. Leading the group was the particularly sadistic Quantrill protégé William "Bloody Bill" Anderson, who was known to scalp his victims and dangle the scalps from his saddle as battle trophies.

The troops rode into town at noon, climbed aboard an incoming train, robbed the passengers, and capped the day's activities by shooting to death two dozen unarmed and wounded Northern soldiers going home on leave. The raiders were surprised by a chance appearance of some Union cavalry, who gave chase to the marauders. A short distance out of town, however, Anderson's men suddenly turned on their pursuers with deadly purpose and ended up killing all but a handful of Federals. Some had their throats cut.

As the war wound down in 1865, the brothers split up. Jesse went to Texas with George Shepherd while Frank followed the fortunes of Quantrill who, once the war came to an end, remained a marked man. On June 11, 1865, Quantrill was killed in a pitched battle with Federal forces in Kentucky. For a while, the James boys sank from public view.

Old Habits, New Career

On February 14, 1866, a robbery took place at Liberty, Missouri, causing a flurry of local excitement. The Commercial Bank was robbed of $70,000 by five men, and a bank employee was shot and killed during the melee. The names of the James boys were immediately connected with the holdup.

What was different about the Liberty robbery was that it had been committed by a gang, not a single individual, as was the custom among bank robbers up to that time, and it was brazenly conducted in daylight. This was a new breed of crime. While shootings, robberies, and other acts of lawless violence were an almost everyday occurrence on the wild Western frontier, outlaws had rarely worked in organized groups before this event.

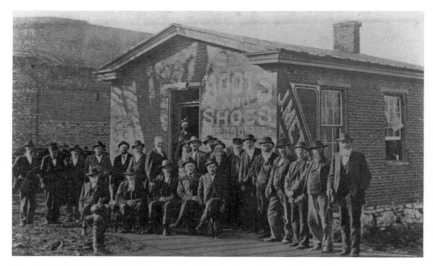

The old bank of Gallatin, Missouri robbed by James boys, December 7, 1869, in which cashier Sheets was killed. (Courtesy Missouri State Historical Society, Columbia. Reprinted with permission.)

Frank and Jesse James had learned their lessons well with Quantrill. Returning home and joining forces with the Younger brothers and other bandits, they made full use of the skills that had allowed them to survive and succeed as wartime guerrillas—riding as a group, making lightning-fast raids, and laying low afterward to avoid capture. The gang subsequently held up a number of banks in Missouri and Kentucky over the next decade, eluding the law with frightening ease.

On December 7, 1869, the gang rode into Gallatin, Missouri, and emptied their six-shooters into the air, driving the inhabitants to cover. While Frank and others stood guard on their horses in the street, Jesse and a companion entered a bank on the public square and looted it of a considerable sum of money. The exact amount was never disclosed; some estimates ran as high as $80,000. One authority was quoted as saying that the wad of bank notes "was a bundle big enough to choke a cow, and all in five-hundred-dollar bills." During the robbery, Jesse, irritated by the cashier's slowness in handing over the cash, gunned down an unarmed employee. Three days later, the slain cashier, John W. Sheets, was laid to rest in the largest funeral service ever seen in Gallatin.

$5.000 REWARD.

A Passenger Train on the Chicago, Rock Island & Pacific Railroad

Was thrown from the track on Monday evening, July 21st, near Adair, Iowa, by obstructions placed upon the track by

SEVEN MASKED MEN,

Who shot and killed the Engineer of the train and robbed the express.

The Chicago Rock Island & Pacific Railroad Co.

will pay a reward of

$5,000

for the arrest and conviction of the seven men who were engaged in the crime, or for the arrest and conviction of any one or more of the number, will pay the proportionate reward of Five Thousand Dollars.

A. KIMBALL, Ass't. Gen'l. Supt. C., R. I. & P. R. R. Davenport, Iowa, July 22, 1873.

Newspaper reward notice of the Adair, Iowa, train robbery (1873).

In September 1872, the gang pulled their most daring heist ever. They rode into the fairgrounds during the state fair in Kansas City in broad daylight and robbed the box office of approximately $9,000.

The James boys took a break from robbing banks and next turned to a new type of crime in America: train robbing. They pulled their first job on July 21, 1873, creating a nationwide sensation.

The gang tore up a section of track, near Adair, Iowa, about fourteen miles west of Council Bluffs, and lay in wait for the fast-flying express. The locomotive, unable to stop, plunged down an embankment, killing the engineer. The passengers were forced to get off the train. As they stood with

9

upraised arms, the robbers rifled the contents of the express and mail cars, making off with several thousand dollars.

Scores of lawmen pursued the James gang with great determination but no success. In desperation, train companies hired the Pinkerton detective agency in 1874 to assist in the national manhunt. Three of their best men were sent out in the field. In rapid succession, all three were brought back dead, each with a bullet in the face or chest. It was the mark of the James gang, some said, to never shoot a victim in the back. One agent, J. H. Whicher, nosing around the James homestead near Kearney disguised as a farmhand, was ambushed and killed by unknown assailants.

Realizing that it was up against a group of wary and clever bandits, the Pinkerton agency let word get out that it was looking for someone in Clay County willing to give information to assist in the capture of the gang. Not long afterwards, a lawyer in Liberty by the name of Hardwicke offered to keep the detectives posted on the gang's whereabouts. He finally sent a wire to Chicago stating that the whole gang would be at the James farm near Kearney on a certain day and night.

The authorities acted swiftly. A force of lawmen including Pinkerton agents raided the James family home shortly after midnight on the night of January 25, 1875. The strike force surrounded the farm house, broke out the windows, and tossed in an explosive charge. The violent explosion killed young Archie Samuel, Frank and Jesse's half brother, and blew off part of Mrs. Samuel's right arm. However, the outlaws were not at home (or escaped unnoticed during the attack, according to some accounts).

By 1875 the state of Missouri was determined to bring in the James gang. A resolution introduced in the Missouri legislature in Jefferson City, in effect, invited the James and Younger boys to go home and refrain from further criminal activities in exchange for a pardon for all past crimes. Upon a vote, the measure was defeated.

In 1876 the gang's long string of good luck finally ran out in one of the most exciting armed holdups to occur in the Old West. On the afternoon of September 7, Frank and Jesse James, three of the Younger brothers, and three other outlaws rode into Northfield, Minnesota, a tiny town of 2,500 inhabitants in Rice County, with the intention of robbing the First National Bank. As Frank entered the building, knife in hand, he demanded keys to the safe from a cashier named Heywood.

Like many bank tellers and express agents in those days, who were entrusted with guarding great amounts of money, Heywood possessed a proud sense of duty and a fierce dedication to his employer. Most such workers were veterans of the war and were not intimidated by, or afraid of entering, situations in which their lives were in great danger. Robbing banks and trains, it must be remembered, were new forms of crime in the 1870s, and managers in the banking and train business had not yet formulated rules for employee conduct during holdups. Basically the individual was left to act or react as he or she thought best, although certainly the last thing that was expected of employees was to comply with a bandit's wishes.

In any case, Heywood refused to hand over the keys to Frank James and reportedly crouched down behind the counter. For his stubbornness, Heywood, like Captain Sheets at Gallatin and others before him, made the ultimate sacrifice in the line of duty. Jesse James leaned over the counter, placed the muzzle of his pistol to Heywood's temple and pulled the trigger, killing him. The same demand was then made of another cashier, A. E. Brinker, who turned and ran, but he, too, was fired upon and hit.

The sound of the gunshots and an alarm sounded by a seventeen-year-old boy who had spotted the gang roused the town into action, and shortly a fierce gunfight broke out. Angry citizens surprised the robbers by firing at them with deadly aim from walls, doorways, and windows. A doctor who occupied rooms across the street shot and killed two of the gang as they sat on their horses.

Frank and Jesse, unaccustomed to such resistance, fought their way out of the bank, mounted their horses, and with the three remaining members of the gang beat a hasty retreat. For days the fugitives rode through unfamiliar territory filled with inhospitable people. Traveling in circles, they were pursued night and day by a posse that at one point numbered 400 well-armed and well-mounted men. They pursuers were spurred on by Governor Pillsbury's offer of a $1,000 reward for each of the robbers, or $5,000 for all of them (assuming they all survived).

Jim Younger had been badly wounded, which slowed down the bandits' progress; his blood was also leaving a convenient trail for the posse to follow [2]. Frank and Jesse wanted to leave him behind (or kill him, according to one account), but Cole and Bob Younger refused to abandon their brother, so the team split up.

Frank and Jesse eventually got away over the Iowa state line and made it back to safety in Missouri. The Youngers were not so fortunate. They headed southwest, chased by the heavily armed posse. After riding in the rain with nothing to eat for two weeks, the outlaws were finally cornered in

A peck of trouble. Previously unpublished album tintype. Left to right: Jesse James, Frank James, and Cole Younger, ca. mid-1870s. (Courtesy Steve Crowley, Westport, CT. Reprinted with permission.)

a wooded swamp 140 miles away, near Madelia, Minnesota, and a deadly shootout took place. Coleman, James, and Robert Younger, all badly shot up by this time, finally surrendered. Cole had eleven bullets in him when he was captured, one of which was lodged behind his right eyeball [3].

The outlaws would have been lynched by a mob if the posse had not hurried the prisoners away under heavy guard to Faribault, the seat of Rice County. In a trial that set a record for speed, all three, upon the advice of their attorneys, pleaded guilty to murder in the first degree and threw themselves upon the mercy of the court. Each was sentenced to life imprisonment and were already on their way to the state penitentiary at Stillwater when the public became aware of the proceedings.

It took two years for the James gang to recover from the Northfield disaster. Recruits, however, were not especially hard to find. There seemed to be no lack of blighted youth in western Missouri who, bored with farm life, handy with a gun, and thirsting for a little adventure and quick cash, were easily drawn to the outlaw brothers.

The fate of Frank and Jesse James would change forever after the Ford brothers, Robert and Charles, who farmed property near Richmond, enlisted under the group's black flag in the winter of 1881. The Fords were quiet and genteel boys when sober, but when angered or intoxicated, which was often, they became, as a Kansas City editor once described them, "the meanest crowd that ever blowed through a nose" [4]. Another young man, who found his way into the fold of the James gang at this time was the restless and trouble-prone James Andrew ("Dick") Liddil of Vernon County. With these new recruits the criminal activities of the James gang continued with a series of three train robberies in Missouri: at Glendale in October 1879, Winston in July 1881, and Blue Cut two months later, in September.

The End Draws Near

By now, all attempts to capture the infamous brothers and their band had ended in dismal failure, and the state of Missouri had become a national embarrassment. Land in the state was worth ten dollars less an acre, people said, because of the James brothers' escapades, and it had become a standard joke that settlers deliberately bypassed Missouri on their way west. Out-of-state presses took delight in running regular journalistic attacks on the state government and made fun of its feeble efforts to curb rampant lawlessness.

Fear of the James gang among the general population finally reached a point where law-and-order advocates insisted upon action and turned the problem into a hot political issue. Stepping propitiously into the public spotlight to confront this vexing problem was Thomas T. Crittenden, the newly elected Democratic governor of Missouri. His four-year term in office, which began in 1881, would become the most tempestuous in the state's history.

Crittenden, forty-seven, was a strong-willed Kansas City attorney, originally from Kentucky, and a former colonel in the Union cavalry and two-term Congressman. Described as a man who "employed no diplomacy in winning friendships and no subserviency in ingratiating himself with men of influence and position," Crittenden was determined to do everything in his power to end the reign of the James gang, which numbered seven at the time, once and for all [5]. His solution was a bold but desperate one: he decided to offer a large cash reward for the capture of the gang.

The governor's plan was initially thwarted by state law, which did not permit the chief state executive to offer more than $300 for each man. He knew this paltry amount would never induce anyone to risk his life by going one-on-one with a gang member, especially Frank or Jesse James, so the quick-thinking politician turned to the railroad owners for financial help. Crittenden called a meeting in St. Louis of the general managers of all the railroads previously victimized by the James gang and, after some not-so-gentle arm-twisting, got them to sweeten the pot by pledging $50,000 for the arrest and conviction of the entire gang, or $5,000 each for the arrest of Frank and Jesse James, and an additional $5,000 each for their convictions.

Such an astronomical amount of reward money, while not unprecedented in American history (twice that much was offered for John Wilkes Booth following Lincoln's assassination), offered a heady incentive to bounty hunters. Despite many historical claims to the contrary, the words "dead or alive" never appeared on the wanted posters [6, 7].

Prompted by the train robbery and murder of two passengers at Winston two weeks earlier, news of the reward was promulgated on July 28, 1881. Surprisingly, the announcement touched off a firestorm of controversy around the state, which was fanned by Republicans eager to make political capital out of the governor's iron-fisted reaction. The venerated Joseph Pulitzer, editor of the *St. Louis Post-Dispatch*, labeled Crittenden a tyrant and consulted lawyers to see if the governor could be prosecuted for inciting what would amount to murder [8]. A Kansas newspaper editor likewise asked, "Can the governor of a state authorize one man to deliberately kill another?" [9]. These opinions were shared by many other Missourians who felt the governor was stepping outside the law by offering what could be construed as an open public contract for assassination. Others considered the act crass, cowardly, and even ungentlemanly.

The groundswell of negative public opinion toward Crittenden had long-term effects. A few years later, President Grover Cleveland refused to give Crittenden a political appointment because of the Missouri governor's clumsy handling of the James brothers [10]. Thus, the reward, conceived with the honorable intention of serving the public good, largely backfired on the state executive. Like a faint but lingering and offensive odor, it followed the governor for the rest of his life. Crittenden, however, never apologized for what he had done.

Initially, the impact of the reward was nebligible. Frank and Jesse remained one maddening step ahead of the law. In the end, however, the huge cash offer paid off, and treachery accomplished what courage, determination, and hordes of sheriffs, posses, and Pinkerton agents could not—the death of Jesse James. But not before other events transpired that brought about the demise of the outlaw band.

On Sunday morning, December 4, 1881, a lethal gun battle occurred about a mile east of Richmond on the Harbison farm, the home of Mattie Bolton, sister of the Ford brothers, and her two children. Robert Ford also happened to be visiting there at the time. Arriving at the farmhouse the night before were two James gang members, Dick Liddil and Wood Hite, who had come to discuss a private matter.

Liddil was a short, thin, plain-looking man with heavily lidded eyes. Wood Hite, on the other hand, was startlingly handsome and fancied himself a ladies' man. In the idiom of nineteenth-century backwoods Missouri, he was considered a "clean straw game." It was said that Mattie loved both men. In Richmond, a jealous Wood Hite crossed paths with Liddil, whose high-pitched voice and quiet demeanor belied a hair-trigger temper.

The tension between the two men at the breakfast table that morning was intense. It wasn't long before a petty argument broke out. In an instant angry words escalated into gunplay. Both men stood up, drew their revolvers, and fired at each other at point blank range.

Mattie ran to the cellar as bullets sprayed the kitchen. Robert Ford, armed and standing in the next room, threw open the door to the kitchen. It was never established with certainty whether the bullets that struck Hite

CHARLES FORD

Charles Ford, Robert's brother. (*Leslie's Illustrated Weekly*, April 22, 1882).

were Liddil's or Ford's, or both men's, but Hite fell to the floor gravely wounded. Liddil escaped serious damage during the free-for-all, taking a single bullet in the leg [11]. Hite died a short time later and his body was buried that night in a nearby pasture. Police Chief Speers of Kansas City, later commenting on the crime scene, stated that the wooden walls and floor of the kitchen had been torn to pieces by the 48-caliber lead slugs.

Wood Hite was Jesse James's closest companion. When word of Hite's killing reached Jesse in Tennessee, he sent word back that he would kill Dick Liddil on sight. Already on the outs with the gang and fearing a deadly reprisal from Jesse more than punishment at the hands of the law, Liddil arranged to surrender to the authorities in exchange for a pardon. Governor Crittenden, figuring that Liddil's assistance would be invaluable in eliminating the James gang, approved the deal, and on January 24, 1882, Liddil turned himself in to the sheriff of Clay County, James R. Timberlake.

Shortly thereafter, authorities conducted secret negotiations with Charles and Robert Ford, who had come forward and announced their intention of securing the reward for bringing in Jesse James. Governor Crittenden accepted their plan. The brothers then went to St. Joseph and moved in with Jesse, his wife, and child.

The Fords knew their man. They had been gang members long enough to understand that it was a risky business to try to take Jesse James when he had his pistols on, asleep or awake. The brothers also knew that if Jesse had any inkling of suspicious intent, they were dead men. Concluding that it was far safer to kill Jesse than to try to take him alive, the brothers stalked him through the winter of 1881 while living under the same roof. There was no margin for error. The time and location of the assassination would have to be carefully planned.

Jesse James seemed to possess nine lives. From his time as a member of the rebel raiders, he had survived a succession of gunshot wounds, including two in the right lung that required months of medical care and recuperation and undoubtedly resulted in a permanently collapsed lung. But on a warm afternoon on April 3, 1882, Jesse James made a fatal mistake: he removed his pistol belt to stand on a chair in his living room to adjust a hanging picture. Standing behind him was Robert Ford, who finally saw his chance. He put a bullet through the back of Jesse's head, killing him instantly.

The single shot from Ford's revolver that, in the words of a popular ballad, "laid poor Jesse in his grave," finally broke the mythical invincibility of the James brothers. Jesse was now gone, but police and public attention immediately shifted to his brother, Frank, whose whereabouts and plans remained a mystery.

Robert Ford, Jesse James's assassin. (*Leslie's Illustrated Weekly*, April 22, 1882).

17

2 RETURN OF THE OUTLAW

Sightings

News of Jesse's assassination by Robert Ford on April 3, 1882, was no sooner flashed to the world from the small town of St. Joseph, Missouri, than people's thoughts immediately turned to his brother Frank. Where was he? What was he up to? And more importantly, when would he avenge his brother's death and who would be his first victim?

No one knew. Frank James had seemingly disappeared in recent years. According to rumor, he had taken part in the Winston and Blue Cut train robberies in 1881, along with Jesse and other gang members. Rumor or not, authorities had issued formal indictments against the elder James for these crimes.

Following Jesse's assassination, a spate of sightings of his famous brother occurred, which were blown up by a press eager to print provocative copy. A typical dispatch of dubious authenticity placed Frank James in Dallas in early April 1882. In the company of two other men, he was allegedly seen buying a train ticket for Independence and overheard to say: "Dick Little [sic] is a damned traitor and an ingrate. He has been protected by Jesse James and the boys. He will not live thirty days to enjoy the lousy dollars for which he sold him" [1].

Other reports of Frank James returning to seek revenge came by way of the supernatural. Spiritualists in Atchison, Kansas, who held a seance on April 16, solemnly reported that they had talked several hours with the ghost of Jesse James. The slain robber confided that Frank would be killed in an attempt on Governor Crittenden's life [2].

Some sightings of Frank were jokes. An Omaha, Nebraska, newspaper claimed Frank James as a recent resident, while a rival journal in Lincoln countered that the former bandit had been and still was "a pitchfork clerk in a Lincoln livery stable" [3].

Cynical commentaries also appeared in the press. "Frank James is safer in Clay county today than Gov. Crittenden is in Jefferson City,"

As newspaper reporters in Kansas and Missouri reveled in the idle, sensational gossip, even more preposterous stories about the notorious bandit surfaced. The morning edition of the *Kansas City Journal* on April 25, for instance, wanted their readers to know that Frank James had been in St. Joseph the afternoon before to visit Jesse's widow at the home of Mr. McBride, her brother-in-law, on Seventeenth Street. At this meeting Frank reportedly turned over "a quantity of securities and some cash, and some more arms and ammunition which are to be sold as relics of the departed Jesse."

According to another rumor, Frank had attended his brother's funeral in disguise, and one person had recognized him there. A few days later, a newspaper in Atchison, Kansas, reported: "It is now positively known that Frank James was in St. Joe on Tuesday (one week after the shooting). . . . He had little to say while here but his lips were compressed, and his face indicated deep determination."

Other reports lent support to the popular notion that the notorious outlaw was loitering around the crime scene with murderous intent. Marshal Murphy of St. Joseph, interviewed on April 14, told a reporter, "Saturday I talked with three men who told me they had seen and talked with Frank James in the streets of St. Joseph that day, but that he left town in the evening." The federal lawman added a final ominous comment: "I think there will be plenty more bloodshed in this business."

The many unsubstantiated reports of Frank's whereabouts fueled the wild speculation and pervasive paranoia that seized the state of Missouri. Frank James, acting independently or accompanied by former gang members, would most certainly wreak horrible vengeance on those who had a hand in killing his brother. It was only a matter of time, people said. Naturally, the Ford brothers, Governor Crittenden, and Dick Liddil, in that order, stood at the head of the list of Frank's likely victims.

Despite having dropped out of sight for the past five years, Frank James's absence only enhanced the powerful mystique that surrounded him. He was still considered a dangerous man and no one relished the idea of being stalked by the shadowy figure of Frank James, whose reputation as a gunslinger with deadly aim had not faded during his exile. A small measure of the fear his lurking presence evoked was expressed by the editor of a St. Louis newspaper who wrote, "The *Globe-Democrat* has not heard of the death of Frank James yet, and until it does, it will reserve its opinions on Jesse, for prudential reasons." [4]

Frank James's most likely targets, the Ford brothers, held up under the strain surprisingly well, at least outwardly. Reporters constantly brought up the subject of Frank's possible revenge during interviews with the brothers, fishing for juicy quotes. The Fords answered with aplomb. They weren't afraid of Frank James, they bragged, and in a way were looking forward to having a showdown with him, knowing full well that their imminent pardons from the governor could further whet Frank's vengeful appetite.

Governor Crittenden, on the other hand, took the matter quite seriously. Even before the public uproar over his role in engineering the killing of Jesse James, which had made him unpopular with many people in the state, the controversial governor had made plenty of enemies during his term in office. Angry political opponents, outraged citizens, and rabid James supporters penned letters threatening the governor's life (many of them signed "Frank James") or reporting the ominous presence of the former bandit in the state capitol. Alarmed, the police instituted precautions to ensure the governor's safety. Following Crittenden's return from the East in mid-April, a detail of guards was drawn every night from the penitentiary and stationed around the grounds of the governor's mansion [5].

On April 27 the *St. Louis Post-Dispatch* published the following:

> Frank James makes his headquarters at Atchison, Kansas, and is said to own a house on the Missouri side of the river a couple of miles below Atchison, where he has been living quietly ever since the assassination of his brother. Those best posted seem to believe that some quiet night in the dark of the moon, he will drop down to Jefferson City and furnish a gaudy piece of news for the afternoon paper.

Irresponsible reporting such as this, undoubtedly false but totally believable at the time, only heightened fears of a possible assassination of Governor Crittenden. On April 8 one unauthorized report, originating under mysterious circumstances in St. Louis and circulated abroad, announced that the governor had been assassinated, presumably by Frank James. The news item was immediately retracted. A telegram sent from Missouri Secretary of State McGrath to an inquiring Associated Press correspondent stated tersely that the sensational message was "nonsensical" and that "the Governor is well." The uneasy calm surrounding the governor's safety was once again restored [6].

There was one man living in Kansas City, however, who knew what was going on inside Frank James's mind and scoffed at the idea that he would avenge Jesse's death. It was one-eyed George Shepherd, erstwhile Quantrill guerrilla and a trusted rider in the James gang. The fellow outlaw predicted, "Frank will come in . . . he's lonely, afraid and discouraged."

Reflection and a Twinge of Guilt

No one knows for sure how or when Frank James, after seventeen years of being on the run, decided to call it quits as an outlaw, but it took no stretch of the imagination to figure out why. There was nothing romantic or exciting about the life Frank James had led on the run. Though he had settled down now, frightening thoughts passed through his mind. The premeditated murder of his brother must have had a profound and sobering impact on Frank. Despite the care he had taken to provide a new life and identities for himself and his small family, it nonetheless exposed his own vulnerability to an assassin's bullet. He knew it was only a matter of time before someone would find out that B. J. Woodson, the quiet-spoken gentleman working a rented farm outside Nashville, was really Missouri's infamous outlaw, Frank James.

To those who knew Frank James best, credit for abandoning his life in the shadows goes chiefly to Ann, his wife. It was a strange match. Ann Ralston was the daughter of a landowner and pioneer resident farmer of Independence, Captain Samuel Ralston, a flaming rebel supporter and man of violent temper who was best known for settling disputes with his revolver [7]. Ann was a wild sort, too. As a youngster, she used to ride her horse through town at breakneck speed for fun. She probably became acquainted with Frank James through her brother, Samuel Ralston Jr., who took up gunslinging at an early age and achieved a minor reputation for pulling off a series of bold robberies in Jackson County between 1868 and 1874.

It was sometime in 1873 that Ann Ralston raised eyebrows in the community by openly consorting with Frank James on the streets of Independence. His occupation, by that time, was well known but not deemed particularly savory, even by Western Missouri standards.

Ann's parents did not approve of the liaison for obvious reasons, but the former belle, considered the fairest in Jackson County, eventually ran off with Frank and married him. Where they went for the event is a matter of conjecture, the site being variously reported as Omaha, Leavenworth, or

Independence. According to the Omaha story, Frank James signed his true name on the marriage certificate and skipped town as soon as the wedding was over before authorities discovered he was there.

Ann was truly in love with the noted desperado and did not marry him simply to spite her father. Her decision ostracized her from family and friends, but she clung to her husband with deep affection. She never approved of his criminal ways, however, and constantly implored him to give them up, hoping they could move to some country where they could lead a quiet, peaceful, and honorable life. Ann bore Frank a son in 1878, which made this alternative even more compelling.

From 1877 to 1881, according to trial records, Frank James lived with his family on a farm in the White's Creek settlement near Nashville, in complete anonymity. Frank was a changed man now and no longer thirsted for the outlaw life. His dreams were of peace and happiness with his family.

Major John Newman Edwards and General Joseph Orville Shelby, both close friends and Confederate cavalry veterans, also played a vital role in encouraging James to turn himself in. Edwards, who served as adjutant to General Shelby during the war, was an influential journalist and itinerant newspaper editor who was widely known around the state for his fiery and controversial editorials. As the James family's closest confidante and advocate, he worked tirelessly and diligently behind the scenes with a succession of governors—McClurg, Woodson, Hardin, and Phelps—before finding in Crittenden some hope of fair treatment under the law for his client, as an alternative to a lynch party.

It was Edwards, with his loud and persuasive literary voice, who first planted in the public's mind the seed of the idea that the James boys were actually victims of Yankee oppression and mistreatment, not the merciless brigands most people believed they were. The newsman glorified their criminal exploits in romantically inspired but fancifully distorted books he wrote and published in the late 1870s. But Edwards reached the height of obsequious apologies in a moving eulogy to Jesse James that appeared in the Sedalia Democrat on April 13, 1882, eleven days after the outlaw's death.

With Crittenden in office, the time was ripe for Frank to act. His plan was to surrender, declare his innocence and, throw himself upon the mercy of the court. James knew full well that, although a stack of criminal indictments faced him, his odds of beating the charges were better than even. Frank James may have been a thief and a murderer in his day, but he was also a shrewd and calculating man. He knew his chances and he trusted his

Joseph Orville Shelby, Missouri's vaunted Confederate war hero. During the trial, truth kept getting in the way of his testimonial support of Frank James. (Courtesy Library of Congress, Prints and Photographs Division.)

luck. That luck, after all, had enabled him to elude swarms of Missouri militia men, Union troops, Pinkerton agents, and sheriffs' posses for nearly twenty years.

And so, Frank James, the living legend, decided to turn himself in. It wasn't romantic and it certainly wasn't heroic after the fashion of the dime novels that depicted gunslingers dying with their boots on and pistols cocked. In fact, the unexpected act seemed totally out of character for someone of Frank James's stature and reputation. No doubt his decision disappointed many people who had come to revere the famous outlaw.

No insight into this momentous decision was ever provided by James himself. In the thirty-two years that he lived following the Gallatin trial, Frank James tended to shun publicity and never divulged details of his past criminal life.

Courting a Criminal

Six weeks after the shooting of Jesse James, news sources in New York City wired across the country and abroad that Frank James was about to turn himself in, causing great excitement. The details were reported on May 31, 1882, by the *New York Times:* R. J. Haines of Kansas City, attorney for Jesse James's widow, was in St. Louis, where he was conducting talks with agents of Missouri Governor Crittenden on behalf of several friends of Frank James, exploring arrangements under which the outlaw might surrender. The meetings were meant to be secret, but a reporter of the *St. Louis Post-Dispatch* recognized Sheriff Timberlake, who had registered at a hotel under an assumed name. Upon questioning, the lawman admitted that he, along with Police Commissioner Craig and attorney Haines, were negotiating a pardon for James. Indeed, the *Post-Dispatch* had published a statement the previous day revealing that Governor Crittenden had been negotiating with Frank James for the past ten days, and predicted that the notorious gunslinger would be pardoned within a week.

News of the imminent event made strong copy. The *New York Times*, on June 1, verified reports that James had entered into final agreements with the Missouri governor. Crittenden was determined to rid his state of the festering remnants of the James gang and was prepared to go to any length to do so. But, by talking about a pardon and displaying a condescending attitude toward the notorious robber, Crittenden was risking serious, perhaps fatal, damage to his political career; his renomination as governor and, later, his appointment to President Cleveland's cabinet, would be at stake.

Then, without warning, James threw a monkey wrench into the plan by demanding unconditional pardons from the states of Minnesota and Texas for any past crimes for which their courts may have wanted to try him. Governor Crittenden, speaking for the state of Missouri, immediately forwarded a pardon to James, accompanied by the following public declaration: "Let us all join in the noble effort to reform this man and to restore him to a peaceful and useful citizenship."

For the Missouri governor, time was now of the essence. It was important to bring Texas and Minnesota into line as soon as possible because he feared that his successor might deliver Frank James to these states on demand, bringing unwanted political embarrassment on himself. Crittenden's hasty comment, however, angered not only officials in the states of Texas and Minnesota but law-abiding citizens everywhere who had not forgotten that blood still stained the hands of the James gang's leader. In particular, the residents of Northfield, Minnesota, still recalled with great sorrow how one of their own (the bank teller Mr. Heywood) had been gunned down in cold blood by the gang in 1876 during a disastrous bank robbery. Their outcry at Governor Crittenden's decision was echoed by many newspapers across the nation.

It soon became clear that the governments of Texas and Minnesota had no intention of following the lead of Governor Crittenden in offering the former bandit friendship and forgiveness. Their refusal to grant pardons brought the negotiations between Frank James and Governor Crittenden to a standstill. The governor now found himself in an uncomfortable political situation.

On June 2, 1882, Crittenden, quoted in the press, expressed surprise at the "bosh some of the papers were publishing concerning the matter." He categorically denied extending a pardon to Frank James, receiving communications from anyone on the subject, and asking the governors of Texas and Minnesota to join him in granting clemency to Missouri's famous outlaw.

Exactly why Crittenden changed his story we will never now. He did state years later, however, that many details of his handling of the Frank and Jesse James affairs were so sensitive that they were never made public for fear of ruining the careers of certain influential people. He also admitted burning every scrap of paper dealing with the matter. Perhaps Governor Crittenden felt some guilt for his role in the killing of Jesse James by offering a bounty for his death. A story went around briefly that the news report of Frank James's surrender was based on false rumors, since it originated in New York City and could not be confirmed locally at the time in Kansas City, Jefferson City, or in Clay County. It seems more likely that Governor Crittenden lied in order to get out of a tight spot.

Frank James's wife also played a role in his being granted a pardon. From out of nowhere she surfaced in Independence on March 26 with her four-year-old son, creating a great deal of local excitement by paying a visit to her surprised parents. It was the first time in seven years that Ann had returned home since she left to marry Frank. As it turned out, Ann had been sent there by her husband to receive correspondence from the governor's office, if needed, before he emerged from hiding.

An essential part of James's plan was to line up expert legal counsel to help him after he surrendered. Major Edwards acted on Frank's behalf to contact prominent criminal trial attorneys around the state who agreed to represent James if the bandit surrendered. One of them was Colonel John F. Philips. While these dealings were confidential, Philips, in his closing argument at the trial, disclosed the details of his hiring. Frank James had no money and offered none, Philips said. Instead, the noted criminal made a pitch for charity, the "one touch of which makes all the world kin," as the attorney described it. Philips accepted. As magnanimous as it might have seemed, Philips would have been a fool to pass up the job, pay or no pay, for the fame it would bring him.

Stop the Breed

The press in Missouri and Kansas reacted to Governor Crittenden's proposed pardon of the West's preeminent gangster with anger and disgust. An editorial sampling follows.

Jesse James was hunted and killed just as he should have been hunted and killed, and if his scarcely less vicious and criminal brother wants to escape the just penalty of his many cruel deeds, let him go to Mexico, or South America, or anywhere else out of this country, in which he has no right to live. (*Atchison Champion,* June 2, 1882)

It would be disgraceful and cowardly to pardon this fellow [Frank James]. Let him pay the penalty of the innocent blood he has shed and the desolate homes he has made. Why, it is revolting to contemplate for a moment the thought of a great State thus humbling herself before a red-handed murderer and assassin. Double the reward for his scalp with the strict injunction that he be taken dead. Stop the breed. Make the example as frightful as possible. (*Great Bend [Kans.] Inland Tribune,* June 2, 1882)

As to Mr. Frank James, we ask that the pending question shall be put fairly. It is not: Shall Frank James surrender to the State of Missouri? but: Shall the State of Missouri surrender to Frank James? (*St. Louis Globe-Democrat,* June 2, 1882)

Official Correspondence

The summer of 1882 came and went. Negotiations between the governor's office and lobbyists for Frank James appeared to have broken down. There is no documentation that sheds light on this period. But judging by the momentous events that were about to transpire, it seems likely that Major Edwards was busy in Jefferson City trying to broker the best possible deal for his illustrious client.

The thread of record picks up again in early October 1882 with a letter written by Frank James and addressed to the governor, dated October 1 and carrying a St. Louis postmark. The notorious Frank James—for a decade and a half one of the most wanted bandits in the state of Missouri and surrounding territories—wrote that he wished to turn himself in to the state and the law.

The text of Frank James's letter was reproduced in various Missouri and Kansas newspapers. Accuracy, however, was not a priority with some editors (and typesetters), who, either by design or accident, changed the punctuation, syntax, and words, sometimes in ways that significantly altered the gist of the letter. (Even the date of the letter varies widely.) As a result, different texts appeared in different newspapers.

The following rendition was published in the *Topeka (Kans.) Daily Capitol* on October 6. While the letter was initiated by James, the author was undoubtedly John Edwards. Few writers could match Edwards's pen for literary depth and flair for the dramatic.

St. Louis, Mo., October 1, 1882

Hon. T. T. Crittenden, Governor:

Your Excellency—Time has demonstrated that however careful a man may follow the path of good citizenship, and however successful I may be in gaining the confidence and respect of those who associate with me daily and hourly in every act, the work of heaping infamy on the name my children are to bear goes steadily on and on.

As it began so many years ago, the greater the crime which startles the people of our Western States, the greater the certainty that it will be attributed to my act, or instigation. However strange it may seem that a man of the reputation I have, should assume to possess either pride or sensibility, I have the hardihood to lay claim to some degree of both.

For years, the one desire of my life has been to regain the citizenship which I lost in the dark days when, in Western Missouri, every man's hand was against his neighbor's, and to have an opportunity of proving, by submission to the most rigorous test, that I am not unworthy. Logically, it is said, that where there's so much smoke, there must be the fire; that although some of the charges made against me may be unjust, are all without foundation, and that the evasion of the officers of the law is not the course of an innocent man.

May I bow to their logic and reply that the man who is now making this appeal, does not do so from the standpoint of a martyr. He comes to you, their representative, to say that though his suffering has been a hundred fold greater than they have any knowledge of, unmeasurably greater than the course which he evaded would have attached to his acts, he recognized that he has no right to complain of his lot. He comes as a man who, conscious of an honest purpose, asks to be permitted to do what an earnest, law-abiding citizen may to remove from Missouri the odium for which, in part, he is responsible.

He comes as a man who, outlaw though he has been, has innocent ones who call him father and husband, and who possesses a love as strong and devoted as was ever found in men whose lives are blameless before the world, and one who is anxious to remove from their closet the skeleton which has so long been its hideous occupant.

If it were not for the fear of the responsibility for that which I did not do, rather than for that which I did, Governor Crittenden, you should never have had to put a price upon my head; but an excited and justly indignant public is not discriminative, and when a man is stripped of the safeguard of that presumptive innocence with which the law theoretically surrounds him, as I would be, he is put to the dangerous necessity of proving a negative.

That fear is still with me, and as I write, it prompts me to abandon my present purposes, and, having for nearly twenty years proved my ability to evade any attempt to capture me, to take my little family and go to some remote section where I can live a quiet life, free from apprehension. That I refuse to obey such an impulse; that I prefer to go back to my boyhood home and face my disgrace in order to live it down; that I am willing to place myself under a surveillance to which no man in Missouri has ever yet been subjected, as must naturally be the case should I return; that I choose this rough course when some other ones offer, I humbly submit, is a proof that I am not so bad as I have been painted, and that the elements of manhood have not been omitted from my nature.

Right terribly, Governor Crittenden, have the offenses against society which have been charged against the James family been avenged? God knows enough blood has been spilled, enough hearts broken, enough lives blighted. God knows that if it is the purpose of the law to prevent crime by making its punishment awful to contemplate, that purpose has been served in a large degree in the ten years of terror and tragedy.

Is its demand for vengeance insatiable? Is "justice tempered with mercy" a mere poetical nothing? Must the great State of Missouri indulge a spirit of revenge, until it has recovered its last ounce of flesh, or laying all considerations of mercy aside, cannot your State, would to God I could say "my State," better afford now that it has vindicated its laws as no State ever did before, to say to its supplicants, "Yes, come in. We will convert your very notoriety into a proper instrument of good order; we will purely, as an unsentimental investment, restore you to citizenship, and give you an opportunity to prove your contrition and further purpose. We will call upon you to utilize your experience and knowledge of wrong doing in the enforcement of the laws which you have in the past been charged with violating. You have won the confidence of all who now condemn you. We point to it all as a proof of our wisdom."

If I were certain that I would not be made a scapegoat, I would never have troubled you with this petition, but would have long ago faced your courts and met your charges; but being once in the toils, I would have had to accept all the chances; and where none would have been interested in my innocence of what might be alleged, many might find it to their advantage to assist in convicting me.

Put yourself in my place for one moment, and then judge of my course in keeping out of the law's clutches. There is another consideration, other than already mentioned, which has weighed heavier in favor of my taking my present step. For five months I have been in constant dread that some rash friend of mine or Jesse's, or some silly person seeking notoriety, might carry out the threats of assassination which have, according to published reports, poured in upon you.

Suppose for one moment that that had occurred, is there a man living who would not have held me responsible for it? And yet, not only were the threats not mine, as you will discover by comparing them with my writing, but the thought of revenge was never for one moment entertained by me.

I have now stated my case, and have, I trust, avoided savor of mawkishness, and I ask, if you cannot consistently with your duty, give me some hope for amnesty under the conditions I have specified. It may strike you that modesty is not the prominent characteristic of this request, but it should be remembered that it comes from a man who is still at large, and the uncertainty of whose whereabouts is unknown, although it need not be the cause of a deal of apprehension.

I do not appeal as a man who, having followed the wrong course until his head is whitening and he is tottering on the verge of the grave, is taught repentance by his incapacity for further iniquity, but as one who is yet young and vigorous and who has reasonable ground to believe that there are many years left him for active service within the pale of society, than those which he has spent outside of it.

I submit that it is not a proper question for your consideration, whether it would not be better to have Frank James a hunter of fugitives than a fugitive? Whether Frank James, humbled, repented and reformed before all the world, will not be an example more fraught with good to the rising generation than Frank James, a mysterious wanderer, or the occupant of a felon's cell, or grave?

This appeal, though anomalous and possibly without a complete precedent, is not the result of a sudden whim, but is born of a determination which has been forming for years, and which has already stood the test of four years of a sober, industrious farm life, as I will have no difficulty in satisfying you of.

I am prouder of the nerve which has enabled me to take this step in behalf of my better nature, than any courageous act of all my past life. I write this letter from St. Louis and leave it here to be mailed. An answer addressed in care of my wife at Independence, Mo., will reach me. I will not say how fervently I pray that it will not be the answer of a Nemesis.

Yours contritely and hopefully,
[signed] Frank James

James's letter is a long, rambling and wordy discourse, haughty, high-flown and dripping with half-apologies, soul-searching questions, and heavy introspective rhetoric. Some passages are so choked with words they are hard to understand. Stripped to its basic message, James was offering to surrender to the state. He was tired of leading a fugitive's life, tired of being blamed for crimes he didn't commit, and tired of living in mortal fear of being killed. James thought it best, therefore, for the good of himself, his wife, child, and the state of Missouri to give himself up.

Frank James confesses vaguely to having been a criminal and wisely skirts the unsavory details of his past life. The outlaw cum laude brazenly asks for terms, possibly amnesty, reminding the governor that not only had he evaded capture for many years, but he is fully capable of continuing to do so in the future. James also has the gall to graciously offer his services to the state as a crime fighter. Midway through the letter, James draws inspiration from his favorite poet, William Shakespeare, by quoting from the *Merchant of Venice* and likening his own sorrowful plight with that of Antonio, whose neck was saved by Portia through her well-known "pound of flesh" speech. There were detractors, to be sure, who would point out that Frank James was nowhere near the man Antonio was. The document is a masterfully contrived instrument of self-service and, with the exception of the closing, it shows that the arch-criminal was remarkably devoid of guilt, shame, or remorse.

While the governor may have felt some admiration, respect, and perhaps empathy for James, the executive's written reply was brief, cool, and to the point. He offered no terms, only a fair and impartial trial under the laws of the state for all charges against him. Crittenden could not promise amnesty without a trial, but he intimated that if Frank James's case justified a pardon, he would give it his attention. It was the best deal the governor could make under the circumstances.

Executive Department, Jefferson City, Mo., October 5, 1882

Frank James:

Sir—Your letter, dated St. Louis, October 1, 1882, has been received, in which you apply to me for an amnesty or a pardon. Under the Constitution of this State, I cannot grant a pardon, even if inclined to, before conviction of some crime.

Whether you can be convicted of any violation of the law, it is not for me to say. That the courts of the State will determine in the proper way when you are before them. I think it wise in you to abandon the life you are charged with leading, and in surrendering to the legal authorities of the State or the county in which you are located.

If innocent of those charges, then you will have an opportunity to prove it to the world. If guilty, the law dictates the punishment. If you surrender, you, as any other man charged with crime, shall and will have a fair and impartial trial.

The intelligence and character of the course of this State are ample guarantees of such a trial without any assurances from me, one not based upon nor governed by the prejudice or the sympathy of the people, but under the judicial forms of just and well-established laws. Determined as I am to see the laws enforced against all grades of crime, I am nonetheless convinced of the importance to society of having every man within the grasp of the law protected in his rights, however lawless he may have been when he yields voluntarily and submissively to that law, and appeals to it and to me for justice and mercy.

You may be innocent or you may be guilty of all the various crimes charged to you. That the courts will determine, as before said, and after the voice of the courts is heard, then, if it becomes necessary, I will decide what my action shall be.

Yours truly,
Thomas T. Crittenden

Frank James considered the governor's letter carefully. Although it held out no guarantee of clemency, it could also be construed to mean that no drastic measures would be taken against him if he surrendered. And so the former outlaw proceeded with his plan.

On Tuesday, October 3, James boarded a Missouri Pacific train in Independence. At Sedalia he was joined by Major Edwards, and together they traveled on to Jefferson City to ring down the curtain on the final act of Frank James's outlaw career.

Surrendering in Style

When the train carrying James and Edwards rolled into the depot in Jefferson City, Missouri, on the morning of Thursday, October 5, 1882, the two men stepped off. Without bothering to mount the depot platform, they climbed the nearby hill and walked leisurely into town to their destination, the McCarthy House. Entering the hotel at an early hour, they found the office deserted. The men registered as John Edwards of Sedalia, and R. F. Winfrey, of Marshall, Missouri. When the desk clerk made his appearance, just as the two gentlemen had finished registering, Mr. Edwards introduced his companion to the clerk who assigned them a room.

Around nine in the morning, the two guests ventured out of the hotel and strolled through town. Mr. Edwards, well known in the city, met numerous acquaintances, to whom he introduced his friend Mr. Winfrey, none ever suspecting who the stranger really was. The two men returned to the hotel at noon, took lunch, and spent the remainder of the afternoon there lounging in the lobby and reading newspapers.

It was about five o'clock in the afternoon when they again emerged from the hotel. They walked over to the capitol grounds, up the hill, through the door of the governor's mansion, and down the hall to the private offices of Governor Crittenden.

The governor, who had been given a few hours' notice of the momentous visit, felt a great sense of satisfaction and relief at the prospect of finally ending his long battle with the outlaw band. In his elation, Crittenden could not resist playing up the moment by injecting a touch of drama. He therefore summoned a number of state officials to his office under the pretense of an impromptu social gathering to witness the historic event.

The group that assembled that afternoon in the executive office, unaware of what was about to happen, included State Supreme Court Justice

STRANGE SURRENDER.

That of Frank James, the Outlaw,
Yesterday.

His Letter of Repentance - Loneliness in
Crime the only Cause Assigned
for His Action.

Frank James Surrendered.

KANSAS CITY, October 5.—Frank James surrendered to Governor Crittenden at Jefferson City at five o'clock this evening, and will be brought here tomorrow morning and delivered to the Jackson county authorities. Gov. Crittenden telegraphs that officers will leave to-night with the prisoner. Officials here express some surprise at James' action, as no overtures had been made on their part toward a surrender. and having in various ways lost all of his old confederates, concluded it useless to attempt to longer live in outlawrey, preferring to trust to the lenience of the law in voluntarily giving himself up.

JAMES' LETTER TO CRITTENDEN.

KANSAS CITY, October 5.—The Times' Jefferson City special has the following letter:

St. Louis, Mo. October 4.

To Hon T. T. Crittenden, Governor:

Your Excellency—Time has demonstrated

Facsimile portion of an article that ran in the *Topeka Daily Capital*, October 6, 1882.

John Ward Henry; Phil E. Chappel, state treasurer; John Walker, state auditor; and Adjutant General Waddell. The gentlemen passed the time in idle conversation as they awaited the arrival of the food and libation; the governor was waiting for something else.

Finally, Major John N. Edwards presented himself to the outer office of Finis R. Farr, the governor's secretary. He introduced to Farr his mysterious companion, a short, slight-of-build man with dark hair, a droopy, sandy-haired mustache, thin face, blue eyes, and prominent cheekbones. Farr later remarked that the stranger's most striking feature was his piercing eyes, which seemed to follow every move around him and never seemed to blink. Accompanied by the governor's secretary, the two men strode into the governor's office.

The men assembled in the governor's office that afternoon may or may not have noticed a pile of papers resting on the floor behind the door where James and Edwards had entered. They were the remaining copies of the printed posters, issued by the governor the preceding year, offering rewards for the capture and conviction of Frank and Jesse James.

During a visit to Denver the next month, an amused Crittenden told what happened at the meeting. It seems that few, if any, of the officers of the state really heard or otherwise took note of Major Edwards's introduction of Frank James. The group continued to talk among themselves, paying little attention to the mild-mannered visitors [8]. It wasn't until Frank James suddenly pulled back his coat, unbuckled his pistols, and handed them to the governor that the group suddenly realized who the stranger really was. The governor's little joke achieved complete surprise.

The famous encounter between Crittenden and Frank James was the subject of a few well-written newspaper reports. The following is an account published in the *Kansas City Times* on October 6.

> The hands of the clock on the south wall of the office were close upon the hour of five, when, the expectant ears of those present heard the sound of footsteps entering the rotunda of the building. A moment later the well-known figure of Major John W. Edwards appeared in the open doorway.
>
> As he advanced into the room, he was followed by a man nearly six feet in height, of slender, yet neat and trim build, who walked erect and with a quiet, easy and self-possessed gait to the middle of the room. Stopping in front of the Governor, Major Edwards said: "Governor and gentlemen, this is Frank James. He is here to give himself up."
>
> This brief introduction brought face to face the Executive of Missouri and the noted outlaw whose name had been a terror in this State, and is familiar throughout our land, if not the whole world. It was a scene without a precedent in the annals of the State, and to all present was intensely interesting and dramatic.
>
> To all appearances, Frank James was the coolest and least unnerved man in the room. While Major Edwards was introducing him, his countenance was as quiet and calm in its expression as if the business in hand was no concern of his. He advanced a step toward the Governor, and dexterously unbuckled a belt from around his lithe body, and holding it to the Governor, said: "Governor, I am Frank James. I surrender my arms to you. I have removed the loads from them. They are not loaded. They have not been out my possession since 1864. No other man has ever had them since then. I now give them to you personally. I deliver myself to you and the law."

Governor Crittenden received the proffered belt, pistol and cartridges, and with characteristic courtesy requested Frank James to be seated. He said that he was very glad to meet him, particularly in this manner. Frank James answered that he had come in and surrendered himself because he desired to do as he had done for years, that is, live the life of a law-abiding citizen. He hoped to prove that he was not so bad as he had been painted.

Although he had been living the life of a quiet, orderly and law-observing man for four years, he well knew that everything criminal and bad that had been committed in late years, had been credited to him.

"Governor," said he, with more earnestness in his tone than he had hitherto shown, "if some one were to assassinate you, although I might be able to prove myself entirely innocent, I would not be able to convince the people that I was guiltless of the crime. They have been in the habit of attributing all manner of crimes to me, and are ready to believe anything they hear."

Reference being made to the time he had been in the State, he said he had not been in Missouri for over a year previous to the Sunday of September 24, when he reached St. Louis. Governor Crittenden said: "I have received over a bushel of letters from you, or from those purporting to be you. I have received them not only from three or four different men on the same day, but from several different states."

"Yes," answered the outlaw, "that proves that any crime, no matter by whom, is likely to be laid to me. I have surrendered because I wish these to end and prove, as I can, that for these four years I have been a law-abiding citizen, and that I have been painted blacker than I am. I do it for my wife and child's sake. I am in your hands to do with me as you see best."

As soon as the conversation ended between Crittenden and Frank James, the office buzzed with excitement. Adjutant General Waddell, startled at the revelation of Mr. Winfrey's true identity, said to the former bandit, "Why, I met you today at dinner, but I had no idea who you were." Frank James's pleasant and engaging manner instantly made a favorable impression on everyone in the room. Particularly captivated was Judge Henry who was moved to exclaim: "He has won my sympathy already. If I were Governor, I would pardon him right away."

Farr was instructed by Crittenden to deliver James to the sheriff of Jackson County at Independence, but arrangements had not yet been completed so the fugitive was permitted to remain in town overnight. The secretary then escorted James and Edwards to a carriage that returned them to the McCarthy House.

It was not long before news of Frank James's surrender spread to every corner of the city. Streams of curious people hurried to the McCarthy House to see and chat with the famous criminal. Until nearly eleven o'clock that evening, Frank James held a reception for the visitors who crowded his hotel room. A delegation from Calloway, Missouri, pledged their wholehearted support for him and considered it an honor to be allowed to take him by the hand. They assured him that if the decision were left to the people of Calloway, Frank James would be a free man. So ended Frank James's first night as a prisoner of the state of Missouri.

Sentimental Journey

From St. Joseph in the north to Springfield in the south, from the Mississippi River in the east to the Missouri in the west, there were few people in the state of Missouri during the first week of October 1882 who were not talking about Frank James. In streetcars, hotel lobbies, and shops, at breakfast tables, and on street corners, the sole topic of conversation was Frank James, and specifically how he would fare in the hands of the authorities. Opinions varied. While many people favored immediate lynching, others thought that the outlaw should receive some form of amnesty or special treatment for turning himself in, which they deemed a courageous act.

In accordance with a dispatch issued by Governor Crittenden the night before, a party comprised of Jackson County prosecuting attorney Wallace, Marshal Murphy (who carried the arrest warrant), Sheriff Timberlake, and Commissioner Craig, left Jefferson City early on the morning of Friday, October 6, with Frank James in tow. They were headed for the jail in Independence, the Jackson County seat. It was a 120-mile journey. As the train swept through the timbered country, Frank James spent most of his time staring out the window. Pointing at the heavily wooded hills, he remarked: "That's good bushwhacking country. I knew every foot of that ground. Many a time have I watched from that hill and seen the soldiers pass up and down."

At every stop along the way, people crowded the platforms and peered through the windows, or boarded the train and filed down the aisle, to catch a glimpse of the famous bandit who had defied the law. At Pleasant Hill, a big, brawny, heavily whiskered man threaded his way through the crowd and, spotting James, extended his hand through the open window:

"Frank! Is it really you?" he exclaimed.

The ironic nature of Frank James's return to society was captured in this cartoon of *The Judge*, December 9, 1882. (Courtesy Periodyssey Collection, Richard Samuel West, Northampton, MA. Reprinted with permission.)

"Yes," replied James, eyeing the man carefully, "but I don't quite remember you."

"You don't? Why, I am Bill Waymore. I guess you know me now."

As soon as he said his name, a big smile spread across James's face.

"Why, Bill, how are you? Of course, I remember you, but it is so long since we met that I could not have recognized your face. How is your brother Matt and your sister?"

Afterwards, James informed reporters that he and Waymore had soldiered together with William Quantrill. Nostalgic scenes like this were repeated over and over in the next few days. In fact, the train trip from Jefferson City to Independence more resembled a hero's parade than the routine transportation of a prisoner. At various stops along the way, Frank stood on the rear platform and waved to the crowd that had come to see him. The *Kansas City Journal* complained: "The triumphal ride of Frank James from the state capital to Independence was ample evidence that the red-handed murderer and train and bank robber is not without friends among the Missouri moss-backs. Had the train stopped long enough he would have been given an ovation at nearly every station."

At the depot in Independence, a large group of spectators stood waiting for the train to arrive, and the announcement that it was delayed two hours did little to dampen their enthusiasm. To while away the time, a reporter tried to interview Mrs. Samuel, Frank James's mother. The outspoken matriarch was in a surly mood, however, and met his questions with abrupt and sarcastic replies. The reporter took his cue and cut short the interview. Frank James's wife, dressed plainly in black with a bit of color in her bonnet, also proved a taciturn subject for the reporter. She stated briefly that Frank's surrender was a "good thing" and hoped that she and her husband could settle down to farm life some day.

The accompanying officers of the law were next to be questioned regarding the importance and meaning of Frank James's surrender. Commissioner Craig felt that James undoubtedly did it in the full hope of receiving general amnesty for crimes committed in the state of Missouri, being "tired of skulking about the country with a price set on his head." The policeman noted that the surrender was the result of negotiations begun several months previously.

Finally, at 10:30 in the morning, the train pulled into the station. The platform was lined with an expectant mass of people. Frank James's wife and four-year-old son, her father (Colonel Ralston), and Mrs. Samuel had arrived early and formed a privileged and prominent contingent in the crowd.

One of the first men to alight from the train was Farr. Close behind him was the slender figure of the train's famous passenger, Frank James. He was dressed in a black coat and vest with light striped pants and a black-and-white straw hat. He also wore a diamond stickpin and a heavy gold watch and chain.

The former fugitive jumped down to the ground and threw his arms around Mrs. Samuel's neck. The old lady, her eyes wet with tears, shouted "My son! Oh, my dear son!" and clasped him to her bosom. Frank James turned and embraced his wife warmly. Then pulling the little boy up in his arms, the prisoner pushed his way through the mass of people, followed by the small James entourage and a few reporters, until they reached a horse-drawn carriage at the far end of the platform.

A huge crowd had gathered in the streets, slowing the vehicle's progress to the courthouse. Eager citizens reached through the windows to shake hands with the celebrated visitor. Recognizing many, Frank called them out by name as he clasped their hands.

Frank held his little boy in his lap as his wife, sitting beside him, placed her arm around Frank's waist. The outlaw showered the child with kisses and talked to him constantly in a low, soothing voice as the carriage crept through the streets.

During the trip, a reporter asked Frank James, "What are your intentions for the future?"

"It is to settle down to a quiet farming life, just as I have been doing," James answered.

"Do you anticipate much trouble in the courts?"

"I cannot tell. Not if I obtain justice."

At the courthouse, the public commotion made it impossible to formally charge James, and he was taken to the Merchants Hotel to spend the night. The criminal court in Independence would not be in session again until the next month, but Judge White was expected to hold a special hearing on James's indictment the following week. Until then, James would be held in the county jail in Independence.

The James party arrived at the Merchants Hotel and took their rooms. The former bandit registered as "Frank James, wife and child," remarking that this was the first time in sixteen years he had signed his real name.

Immediately a spirited bidding for the outlaw's handwritten registration followed, but the landlord held firm and refused to allow the hotel register to be cut up by enthused autograph seekers. The Jameses were soon joined by Major Edwards.

That night a huge reception was held at the hotel. In a scene identical to the previous night in Jefferson City, Frank James was the center of attention as dozens of old acquaintances applied for admittance to his hotel room, including, as the *St. Louis Globe-Democrat* reported the next day, some of the "wealthiest, most popular and influential men waiting to shake his hand." A group of Independence bankers who, only a short time before had trembled at the very names of the James brothers, had come forward to post a $100,000 bail bond for the man who had robbed one of their institutions in 1868. Also attending the reception was Governor Crittenden and his wife.

While his wife and mother conversed in the room, Frank strolled out into the hall after a while and talked with Major Edwards. It had been an exhausting day and James had refused to see any more visitors. Hundreds of them, including some city officials, were cordoned off at one end of the hall and craned their heads to see what the infamous Frank James looked like. They were eventually forced to leave the hotel, disappointed at not having satisfied their curiosity.

Later that evening, a crowd much larger than normal took supper in the hotel dining room, hoping to spot over their tables the figure of Frank James. But the former bandit fooled them by quietly entering the dining hall after the guests had departed to take his meal. After dinner, Frank held a short reception in the hotel parlor and then was taken to jail by Marshal Murphy after a tearful parting with his family.

The reception the townspeople gave Frank James that day in Independence was a warm and generous one. Many felt they were welcoming an old and familiar friend rather than a celebrated stranger or a vanquished criminal, for it was in Jackson County that the James gang—Frank and Jesse, Clell Miller, George Shepherd, Ed Miller, and the rest—often sought refuge while on the run from the law. The desperadoes were seen frequently in Independence, and there were few city and county residents who were not acquainted with them and who did not recognize them on sight. For Frank James, going to Independence was much like coming home.

By now much of the press in Kansas had had quite enough of the servile attention being lavished on Frank James. Attempting to bring the arch-

41

criminal and his surrender into proper focus, the editor of the *Atchison Daily Globe* expressed the following opinion on October 9, 1882:

> Circumstances alter cases. Had Frank James committed only one murder, he would have been shunned and abhorred by everybody. Or had he been detected in an attempt to steal a horse, the best society of Missouri would have spurned him.
>
> Even had he been guiltless of any crime—had he remained on a farm at Kearney and became [*sic*] a useful citizen, the men who are now proud to know him would have passed him without a sign of recognition. But as he developed not only into a thief but a train wrecker, bank robber and wholesale murderer, honest men are insanely anxious to receive a condescending nod of recognition from him.
>
> His special champion and friend, Major Edwards, would not speak to a man whose worst crime had been the robbing of a hen roost. His old friends and neighbors in Clay county would hunt down and lynch a man who had been guilty of theft, robbery, arson and murder as one whose friendship it is an honor to acknowledge.
>
> There is something strange about this. When we reflect that Frank James is the most hardened criminal in the United States, we cannot help wondering why he is not taken out of the jail at Independence and lynched.

A Sounder Sleep

The newspaper stand outside Bunnell's, at the corner of Broadway and Ninth Street in New York City, carried the morning editions. On October 6, 1882, the *New York Herald,* like other city dailies, announced the surrender of Frank James. But, as was the custom of New York presses in those days, they contented themselves with publishing the brief Associated Press news telegrams, which divulged few details.

Bunnell's was a museum, but not an ordinary one as we know it today. It was a "dime museum," a privately owned institution that housed a collection ("aggregation," the handbills said) of oddities and freaks of nature such as bearded ladies, living human skeletons, two-headed calves, and the like, in the tradition started by the famous entrepreneur and showman P. T. Barnum. These halls of wonders attracted a constant flow of thrill-seeking audiences.

At Bunnell's during that first week in October was a show featuring the Ford brothers of Missouri. Put on six times a day, the show drew large crowds. When the patrons took their seats in the small auditorium packed with the eager faces of men, women, and children (mostly the latter), they saw three men step onto the stage. The long-haired one in the middle, the lecturer, like the interlocutor in a minstrel show (also known in the West as a "lightning calculator," whose function was to feel out the crowd), announced in a deep voice and with great fanfare:

"Ladies and gentlemen! I now have the honor and the pleasure to introduce to you the celebrated Ford brothers of Missouri. The one on my right is Charles, aged 24; the one on my left is Robert, aged 20. (murmurs from the audience)

"Robert is the one who shot and killed the most famous desperado of modern times, Jesse James. (cheers from the small ones) The morning papers of today reported the surrender of Frank James. Mr. Robert Ford has just received a dispatch from the chief of police of Kansas City, confirming his news, and stating that Frank James is now in jail in that city. (more cheers)

"Mr. Robert Ford will now give you an exhibition of his skill with firearms."

The young man then took a large navy revolver in his left hand, aimed and fired it five times in rapid succession at a target about twenty-five feet away on the stage, making a bull's-eye with each shot. The crowd cheered loudly as the Ford brothers, without having uttered a single word during the entire performance, disappeared into the wings.

Also on exhibit at Bunnell's were two horses, a roan and a bay. An affidavit signed by the Fords stated that these were the horses ridden by the James brothers a distance of seventy miles on the night of the Winston train robbery in 1881. While many spectators viewed the two fine animals with awe, more discerning ones may have suspected that the horses were actually rented from a nearby livery stable for the occasion and innocent of any complicity with the Missouri train robbers.

The Ford boys spent the fall of 1882 on tour. Playing first in Chicago and Cincinnati, their act moved on to New York City for two weeks, then to Brooklyn for one week. The brothers earned $500 a week, a tidy sum in those times. No doubt the Fords slept with both eyes closed now, comforted by the thought that their nemesis was safely behind bars in Independence two thousand miles away.

The Celebrated Prisoner of Independence

Cincinnati, O., April 7, 1882—The following appears in an afternoon paper: A preserving company, notorious as the manufacturers of ozone, having tried to purchase the body of Guiteau [President Garfield's assassin] and failed, being too modest in their bid, telegraphed last night to Mrs. Samuels, the mother of Jesse James, offering her $10,000 for her son's body, together with a certain percentage of the receipts which shall accrue to the company through the possession of the corpse

The purpose, of course, is to preserve the body by inclosing [sic] it in a box and subjecting it to the fumes of burning sulphur and ozone and then exhibit it throughout the United States. Mrs. James has been told that $100,000 could be made in less than two years, and it is believed that the fine offer made will insure success. The ozone preparation has been tried, and it is said to keep bodies wonderfully life-like. (*Kansas City Evening Star,* April 4, 1882)

The news that Frank James was now in custody spread like wildfire throughout the state, stirring the population to action. The urge of the common man to see, perhaps touch, or even talk to the larger-than-life outlaws was overpowering. People from far and near traveled to Independence, to pay homage to the famous folk hero at his temporary home and shrine, the county jail.

The scene in Independence on Sunday, October 6, 1882, was one of pandemonium. Overnight the quiet town had been transformed into a circus-like camp, teeming with people from morning to night. Many of them old friends, wartime companions, or acquaintances, they swarmed in from the adjoining countryside to catch a glimpse of the famous prisoner.

In the jailhouse crowd a number of young ladies pressed forward to shake the bandit's hand through the bars with dainty, gloved fingers, smiling and feeling flattered by the honor. Children clinging to their mothers' skirts peered at the caged desperado with open-mouthed curiosity. Autograph hawkers circulated among the crowd soliciting applications for samples of the fugitive's handwriting.

The most celebrated prisoner to ever take up residence in the Independence jail was given special treatment. Frank's cell was narrow and cramped, but it was made as comfortable as possible. As a local newspaperman commented: "Frank James is living about as comfortable as any feller in the state. His cell is furnished with an elegant Brussels carpet, the walls are decorated with pictures, and such furniture as he has room for, is the best sort [9]. The prisoner slept on a simple mattress on the floor, but a rocking chair was placed outside in the corridor for his personal use. His cell door remained unlocked and he was free to walk about the upper floor, or go downstairs, at will. In fact, nothing prevented him from marching right out the front door of the jail.

Over 500 onlookers besieged the jail on the first day. They were permitted to enter the building and file down the hall on the upper floor, where they could look directly into Frank's cell. The prisoner chatted amiably through the iron bars with his many callers. At one point, he told them of a benefit soon to be staged in Independence. The news was taken seriously by many people eager to "help out a train artist in bad circumstances" (as one newspaper reported). When they began to demand tickets, James was forced to explain that the idea was a joke.

Among James's many visitors at the jail were newspaper reporters who were eager to question him on the subject of Robert Ford. Frank surprised everyone by stating that he had no desire to shoot it out with his brother's assassin. He explained: "I see Bob Ford says if he ever sees me, one of us has got to die. Well, I have no desire to kill him and if anybody dies, I guess it will be me. To tell the truth, I don't want to meet Bob at all" [10].

In addition to freedom of movement, Frank James enjoyed other special privileges while in jail. His wife brought him newspapers every morning, which he read with interest, especially those with overly imaginative reports of his career. He found amusement correcting minor historical inaccuracies that had crept into them. Meals were supplied by the chef at a nearby hashery and delivered to Frank's cell. James's wife and child remained with him all day, and he wrote a number of letters to friends and received a visit from his mother once as well.

On October 9, 1882, Governor Crittenden announced in St. Louis that he would not turn over Frank James to any other state for prosecution as long as criminal charges existed against James in Missouri. He was not going to let Frank slip from his grasp.

Perhaps by now the tremendous outpouring of public sympathy and the gawking that had marked the first two days of Frank James's new life was growing tiresome. After all, his very survival for the past fifteen years had depended on maintaining a nameless, faceless existence. While Frank may have basked in the public glow for a while, being in the limelight was simply not his style. It was not safe either. His high profile made him more vulnerable to anyone who might wish to take a shot at him.

But if the public attention focused on Frank James's return to society seemed extraordinary, it was nothing compared to the bizarre public feeding frenzy that followed Jesse's death.

Hundreds of souvenir hunters descended like locusts on the James family home in Kearney and carried off the greater part of it in their zeal to acquire mementos of the late departed outlaw. The house was wrecked so badly, in fact, that the owner, a widow named Henrietta Salzman, sued the state of Missouri for $2,600 in damages. The old lady, however, was not averse to capitalizing on the moment and started charging twenty-five cents a head to let people wander around the property and inside the house.

Jesse's home in St. Joseph, scene of the assassination, was likewise stripped bare. Shingles were torn from the roof and bark ripped from trees on the property. The old rag carpet stained dark red with Jesse's blood was pulled up, cut into pieces, and passed out to young ladies in town, who proudly pinned the scraps over their hearts in tribute to the dead hero [11].

Jesse's belongings and household effects were sold to raise money for his wife. Chairs, plates, saucers, knives, forks, an old jackknife, and other sundry items—a junky lot not intrinsically worth ten dollars—realized two hundred dollars because of the name of the prior owner [12]. Even Jesse's dog, described by the press as "a worthless cur," was hammered down for an outrageous sum of fifteen dollars and then resold at a profit to a merchant in Springfield, Illinois, who used the animal for publicity purposes [13]. It had also become a joke for people in Atchison, Kansas, to send off old hats, boots, and coats supposedly worn by Jesse James when he was shot to friends in the East, who cheerfully paid exorbitant express charges for them. [14].

The list of those who capitalized on Jesse's death is a long one. Jesse's widow and Mrs. Samuel were offered book deals to tell about Jesse's life; the widow James went on a lecture circuit, charging admission to tell stories about her late husband; and theatrical plays were staged here and there reenacting Jesse's assassination [15-18]. A murderous criminal in life, Jesse James became, through these celebrations, almost saintly after his death.

The Unconventional Hero

Of all the surprises attendant to Frank James's emergence from hiding, the most remarkable was his physical appearance. People familiar with the dashing, swashbuckling exploits of the James boys were disappointed

Artist's sketch of Frank James, made during interview. *Kansas City Star,* October 8, 1882.

when they first laid eyes on him. The fabled outlaw did not at all resemble the manly and heroic image painted of him.

Up close in flesh and blood, the notorious James, whose very name had sent shivers of fear down the spine of every express messenger and bank teller west of the Mississippi, now almost resembled an invalid. He looked as if a stiff breeze would blow him over. Even former army comrades did not recognize him until he was pointed out.

Frank James had been through a lot. His body had been pierced twice with minié balls and it bore the numerous scars (seventeen, it was said) from his many scrapes with the law and actions during the war. Yet despite his decrepit physical condition, James repeatedly boasted that he could "ride further and stand more than any other man in the state." He was also proud to say that he could starve himself longer than anyone else, and his appearance seemed to bear this out.

Because of his cadaverous look, it was assumed that Frank James, despite his protestations of good health, was a victim of consumption and that death awaited him just around the corner. He appeared to be, as one reporter once facetiously described him, "a professional man inclined to consumption—anything but a train robber." Another reporter, for a newspaper in Kansas City, described him this way:

> Robbed of all the glamor of romance, denuded of the trickery of imagination, Frank James is an ordinary, not overly bright-looking man—certainly not one who would be selected from a crowd for his distinguished appearance or intelligence. Whatever he may have been, he is today a weak, broken-down, haggard wreck of a man, the handwriting of death and disease on his face, and none of the insignia of the conventional hero about him.

The press delighted in bashing Frank James now that the outlaw was behind bars. Reporters poked fun at the sad-looking specimen of a man who huddled meekly in his jail cell—thin, stooped, almost wasted in appearance, with a hollow chest and sallow, sunken cheeks. He hardly lived up to his legend as Missouri's prince of robbers.

Appearances, however, were deceiving. Had any of the press members met up with Frank James when he was doing what he did best, they would have formed an entirely different impression of him. Police Commissioner Henry H. Craig of Kansas City, who had kept a locomotive fired up and ready to go at an instant's notice to track down the James gang after their latest caper, would have avowed that Frank James was the most cunning criminal he ever pursued. The same could be said of Sheriff Timberlake of Clay County and Allan Pinkerton, as well as every other sheriff or posse member in the region who had been left in Frank's dust. And the bank tellers he had met eye to eye would have vouched for his remarkable self-control. His ability to remain calm and collected in times of great stress had served him well as a soldier and an outlaw. Now it would help him through yet another life-or-death ordeal, the trial he was about to face.

One Last Detail

Just as the infamous criminal had made his surrender, a rash of ghastly murders broke out around the United States. One particularly vicious robbery and murder took place in Waupaca, Wisconsin, on October 8, 1882. A banker was ambushed by a concealed assassin who almost blew the victim's head off with a barrage of bullets. To those familiar with the James gang, it looked like some of Frank's old work. Had the outlaw not been in jail, many believed, he would undoubtedly have been blamed for the hideous crime. [19]

News that the prisoner would be transferred to jail facilities in Kansas City caused a great stir. An expectant crowd of thousands filled Union depot and lined Grand Avenue in Kansas City, only to disperse in disappointment when they received word that the authorities had changed their minds and decided to hold the prisoner in Independence for the time being.

Prosecuting attorney Wallace, county marshal Murphy, and Sheriff Timberlake met in Independence, presumably to arrange bail for Frank James. It was strongly believed that the former bandit was capable of paying his bail, but if he couldn't, a number of influential men in Kansas City had already indicated a willingness to stand his bond. One Kansas newspaper claimed that "the best men of Jackson county" were willing to post Frank's bail because they were the same ones who, as providers of safety and shelter, "have been his security for the last fifteen years."

Frank never did spring for bail during his days as a prisoner, which surprised many, given the enormous amount of money he must have accumulated during his robbing years. James apparently lacked the necessary funds. He admitted later that he considered himself enough of a financial burden to his friends and supporters without asking them for bail money too.

With the famous prisoner safely behind bars, there remained now the task of trying Frank James for his past crimes. While public prosecutors felt confident that they possessed enough evidence to convict him, others outside the legal establishment did not share this optimism. Prevailing public opinion in Missouri held that the legendary Frank James would never suffer punishment at the hands of the law, no matter how incriminating the evidence. One odds-maker reportedly stood in the corridor of the Centropolis Hotel in Kansas City and offered a bet with one-to-two odds that Frank would ever be convicted. He found no takers.

The editor of the *Atchison (Kans.) Daily Globe*, tracking the Frank James story closely, also had grave doubts. Brooding over news of the governor's prospective pardon earlier in the year, the seasoned journalist printed the following cynical but amazingly prophetic opinion on May 25, 1882, a good four months before Frank James had turned himself in and well over a year before he went to trial at Gallatin.

> In case Frank James surrenders himself, where can a witness be found to identify him as connected with any murder or robbery? Those of his outlaw comrades who are dead, cannot; those in the penitentiary would not, if they could; the only remaining two, Liddil and Cummings, cannot do so if they wish to, without convicting themselves also. It is therefore most probable that the unconditional surrender of Frank James will expose him to no consequences more serious than one or two futile attempts to convict him

legally, after which he will be free to lead an entirely new life if so disposed, and prove by the example he hereafter sets to his own and to his brother's children that there was some justice after all in the plea that the James boys were the victims of circumstances, and their outlaw career to some extent a matter of compulsion.

3 THE TRIAL AT GALLATIN

Making a Case

After the public and editorial rejoicing had died down following the surrender and jailing of Frank James in the fall of 1882, the job of bringing him to justice began in earnest. The man who took on the case against Frank James was a fiery, thirty-four-year-old Kansas City attorney, William Hockaday Wallace, a courageous, determined, and incorruptible defender of justice.

Wallace was the crusading public prosecutor of Jackson County and a rising star in the Missouri criminal justice system. He was a man of principle who was not afraid to risk public or political disfavor in the performance of his duties. A self-proclaimed "law enforcement Democrat," he had declared war on those who defied the law in the state of Missouri, as well as complacent public officials who were willing to curry favor with criminals. Some idea of Wallace's strict belief in law and order can be found in his denunciation of the assassination of Jesse James: "It was one of the most cowardly and diabolical deeds in history."

Wallace was also a confirmed moralist and prohibitionist. He supported local blue laws forcing closure of saloons, pool halls, and theaters open on Sunday. His uncompromising stand, delivered with the fervor of a tent revivalist, made him many friends but almost as many enemies.

While still professionally wet behind the ears, the ambitious Wallace, in his third year as prosecuting attorney of Jackson County, had already delivered on a pre-election campaign promise to rid "poor old Missouri" of the nationally embarrassing blight of the James and Younger clans. Wallace would later be criticized for taking on the James case, the biggest of his career, because the venue was in another county and, by strict definition, outside his legal jurisdiction.

It was clear that the scrappy attorney from Jackson County wanted the privilege of trying Frank James himself. While there were surely other prosecutors around as capable as Wallace of handling the technical aspects of the case, not many would have matched the thoroughness with which he

William Hockaday Wallace, the Jackson County prosecutor whose tireless fight to bring Frank James to justice was thwarted by bad luck and the criminal's powerful mystique. The two men eventually became good friends. (Courtesy State Historical Society of Missouri, Columbia. Reprinted with permission.)

prepared for a trial, and certainly no one could surpass his capacity for electrifying speech.

William Wallace was a Southerner. Born on a farm in Clark County, Kentucky in 1848, he was brought to Missouri at such an early age he always considered himself a Missourian. His father, the Reverend Joseph W. Wallace, was a Presbyterian minister who settled near Lee's Summit in Jackson County. The Civil War uprooted the Wallace family and forced them to relocate to Fulton. Young Wallace was able to continue his education there and later graduated from Westminster College with honors in 1871. He supported himself by teaching school and working for a newspaper in Independence before deciding on a career in law, which he studied under his uncle and former state attorney general, John A. Hockaday, at Fulton.

William Wallace was admitted to the bar in 1873, practiced law with George Buchanan in Independence for five years, and then moved to Kansas City in 1880. He first achieved statewide prominence in 1877 when he successfully defended Henry Cathey, a poverty-stricken man accused of murdering Nicholas Crenshaw, a wealthy man who had been dallying with Cathey's wife. Cathey had loaded a double-barreled shotgun and gone to Crenshaw's house, where he called him outside and killed him. The first trial ended in a hung jury; at the second, Cathey was acquitted. The victory brought the young attorney instant acclaim.

In the fall of 1880, while James A. Garfield was stumping for president of the United States, another political office of far less prominence was being contested in Jackson County, Missouri. One of the candidates was William Wallace, then thirty-two years old. A dark-horse candidate, he delivered straight-talk speeches that captured the attention of the voting public. The main plank of Wallace's platform was a bold one. Bring me Missouri's bandits, he said, and I will either swing them from a rope or set them busy painting buckets in the state penitentiary for the next twenty-five years. Wallace was the only candidate for office brazen enough to issue a public challenge to the James and Younger gangs, calling them out by name, one by one. While the action might have seemed tantamount to a death wish, Missourians welcomed a tough attitude toward the outlaws, and Wallace won the election.

The next year, 1881, Wallace successfully prosecuted Bill Ryan, a member of the James gang who was arrested in Nashville, Tennessee. Wallace immediately had Ryan transferred to Jackson County, where he was charged for participating in the Glendale (Mo.) train robbery in 1879. Mouths dropped when people learned that one of the James gang was actually going to trial.

The public prosecutor received numerous warnings and death threats on the eve of the trial and was told by many that no jury would ever convict Ryan. Undaunted, Wallace went ahead. When the case was called at

Independence, it had come down to a battle between law and order on the one hand and lawlessness on the other.

The courtroom was filled with Ryan's friends, many of them armed. At night, rockets were fired off in the woods near town. They were said to be secret signals to Ryan from members of the gang, telling him that rescue was imminent. But Wallace was so thorough and convincing in presenting the case against Ryan that the gang member was found guilty and received a twenty-five-year sentence in the penitentiary. The verdict amazed everyone, including Wallace.

Wallace's victory proved that it was possible to convict a member of the James gang in the state of Missouri. Would he be fortunate enough to win two courtroom victories in a row?

The Jackson County prosecutor now sat down with his staff to examine the case against Frank James. What he saw was an uphill battle fraught with legal obstacles, not the least of which was the state's lack of credible eye-witness testimony. Without this, Wallace would have to build his case on circumstantial evidence. While Wallace could make such a case stick with lesser criminals such as Ryan, convicting someone of the stature and popularity of Frank James on circumstantial evidence was an entirely different matter.

By the end of 1882, the number of formal indictments facing James stood at two: complicity in the slaying of Pinkerton detective Whicher in 1874 and involvement in the Independence bank robbery of 1878. The Whicher case was reviewed closely but a lack of eyewitness evidence, plus the fact that memories of the event had grown dim with time, made it legally tenuous. The robbery case, too, was weak for the same reasons. It was just as well. Wallace much preferred to concentrate on the charge of murder, for a murder conviction would land James on the gallows, or at least fetch him a life term in the state pen. The public prosecutor was determined to deliver the full weight of the law to Frank James.

On January 23, 1883, the prosecution and defense teams gathered in Kansas City to hear formal charges read against James and to set a trial date. The prisoner was transported by train from Independence to appear before the judge. Wearing a neat business suit, Frank James looked relaxed and confident as he bore the scrutiny of hundreds of onlookers who had jammed the courthouse to witness the proceedings.

Wallace addressed the court. After a diligent search, he began, the state had been unable to secure enough evidence to establish the defendant's involvement with either crime; hence the state was forced to dismiss both cases.

His words fell like a bombshell on the audience. Audible gasps were heard. Frank James, shifting in his chair, nodded his head in approval, as if in vindication.

After a pause, Wallace continued: "But now, I will present an indictment against Frank James for participating in the Blue Cut train robbery of September 7, 1881." Then he elaborated on the charge.

The new indictment caught everyone by surprise, including James's attorney. After his client entered a plea of not guilty, the defense counsel asked for a lengthy period of time in which to prepare his case. A brief discussion followed. It was decided that the case would be continued at the next criminal court session in Kansas City beginning on May 4, and bail was set at $3,500. James was returned to jail in Independence that evening [1].

By all appearances, the Blue Cut charge, which involved robbery, not murder, was a deliberate stall for time. Prosecutor Wallace needed to gather enough evidence to charge James with as many murders as he could. He focused his attention on the Winston train robbery in 1881 where not one, but two killings had been committed. Another murder indictment was added against James for the gunning down of Captain Sheets in the Gallatin bank holdup of 1868.

The state's strongest case, however, rested with the Winston robbery and specifically the shooting of Frank McMillan, the unlucky train rider whose curiosity during the holdup cost him his life. To aid in this prosecution, the public prosecutor could, with luck, muster three powerful witnesses, all former gang members, to testify against Frank James: Clarence Hite, Dick Liddil, and Bill Ryan.

Liddil and Hite had participated in the Winston job and could swear that Frank James was not only in on the robbery but had shot McMillan too. Ryan, if he could be induced to talk, could establish James's presence in the state at the time of the robbery and implicate James in planning the raid. By the time of the trial, however, Clarence Hite had died of consumption, and Ryan refused to testify against his former partner in crime, thus materially weakening the state's case. That left it up to Liddil.

Despite his testimonial value to Wallace, Liddil was paradoxically the state's strongest and weakest link. He had previously turned state's evidence on a murder rap in exchange for a pardon, and his intimate knowledge of the gang had proven indispensable in running down and

55

apprehending the last remaining fugitives. While his testimony against Frank James was crucial, his credibility was highly suspect. To some people, notably James's attorneys, the convicted horse thief was obviously a man without scruples.

Liddil's criminal life began as a young man. A meek-looking, baby-faced youth with a squeaky voice, he left home when he was seventeen, after his mother died, and wandered from place to place in search of a profession and mission in life. Liddil eventually found both in robbing and stealing, but he showed no particular talent at either. Caught with another man's horse in Vernon County in 1874, he was arrested and served three and a half years in the state penitentiary for his bungled effort. It was in Jackson County in 1869 that the lad first met members of the James gang, but it would be a full ten years before Liddil joined up with them. His first job with Frank and Jesse was the Glendale (Mo.) bank robbery in October 1879.

At the time of Frank James's trial, Liddil was in prison awaiting sentencing for his involvement in a robbery on March 11, 1881. Alexander Smith, federal paymaster of a river improvement project at Muscle Shoals, Alabama, had been waylaid by a group of three armed men and robbed of five thousand dollars. Five months later, Liddil had been arrested and indicted for taking part in the robbery. Also named in the indictment were Frank and Jesse James and Bill Ryan. At his trial in Huntsville, Liddil claimed that he was in Kentucky at the time at the time of the robbery. The jury found him guilty but recommended clemency. The judge delayed Liddil's sentencing until the next term of court.

Liddil's impending imprisonment in Alabama, as far as law authorities in Missouri were concerned, could not have come at a worse time. Because his ability to testify against Frank James was now doubtful, officials in Missouri sought to obtain a federal pardon from President Chester A. Arthur. Clay County Sheriff Timberlake, Kansas City Police Chief Craig, William Wallace, Governor Crittenden, and U.S. Senator Francis Cockrell all wrote letters requesting a pardon for Liddil, explaining that he was an indispensable witness for prosecuting Frank James. The same request formed the basis of a petition signed by presiding Judge Henry Bruce of Liddil's Huntsville trial, members of the jury, various officers of the court, and several marshals.

There was one loud voice of disapproval, however, from the federal district attorney, William H. Smith. He objected to the idea of pardoning one criminal to prosecute another, and his opinion was shared by U.S. Attorney

Dick Liddil, the controversial state's witness whose testimony against Frank James at Gallatin failed to move a biased jury. (Courtesy Jackson County Historical Society Archives, Independence, Missouri. Reprinted with permission.)

General Benjamin Brewster, to whom the President had referred the request. Brewster, despite extreme pressure from Senator Cockrell, refused to recommend the pardon, and the chief executive, in the end, refused to grant one.

Judge Bruce then took matters into his own hands. On April 10, 1883, he released Liddil from custody on his own recognizance without a sentence. A bond was posted by Police Chief Craig and Sheriff Timberlake, which allowed Liddil to return to Gallatin and testify against Frank James.

As fortunate as Wallace was to have Liddil as a witness, Liddil's criminal past was impossible to hide or gloss over. It would prove to be a constant obstacle in the attorney's relentless pursuit of Frank James's conviction.

Time was running out for the public prosecutor and he had to go with his best case. Wallace therefore instructed the prosecuting attorney of Daviess County, William Hamilton, to charge Frank James with Frank McMillan's murder. By prior arrangement and mutual consent, Hamilton

William Decatur Hamilton, prosecuting attorney of Daviess County and assistant to William Wallace. In 1899 he became state representative in the Missouri General Assembly. (Courtesy State Historical Society of Missouri, Columbia. Reprinted with permission.)

officially invited Wallace to Gallatin and empowered him to direct the case against Frank James. While the action was undoubtedly irregular and brought well-founded criticism upon the two attorneys, it was not illegal.

At the last hearing on the Frank James trial in Kansas City, the prosecution pulled out all the stops. The final list of indictments against James included the murder of McMillan during the Winston train robbery in 1881, accessory to the murder of conductor Westfall in the same holdup, and the murder of cashier Sheets in the Gallatin bank robbery in 1868. The Blue Cut robbery charge had been temporarily dropped.

As expected, the defendant pleaded not guilty to all three counts. His trial for McMillan's murder was set for the third Monday in June, 1883. Since the crime (all three, in fact) had taken place in Daviess County, Gallatin, the county seat, was selected as the site of the trial. The indictment was returned by a grand jury in Daviess County in May 1883, and the trial was continued to August 21, 1883. The stage was set. It was now time for the law to deal with Frank James.

The Winston Train Robbery

In the Old West, most gangs of train robbers consisted of four to eight men, although occasionally there was a man with enough nerve who worked alone. The usual method was to stop the train, overwhelm the crew, and uncouple the express car from the rest of the train so it could be moved to a remote spot far up the track where the safes could be blown open and the contents plundered in safety. Resistance from the engineer or crew members generally resulted in death.

Well mounted and with relays of horses previously arranged, train robbers experienced little difficulty in escaping the poorly organized posses found in sparsely populated regions. Train robbery, however, was considered the most dangerous form of crime, and statistics would show that nearly three-quarters of those who engaged in it eventually died doing so.

Contrary to popular belief, the James brothers were not the first outlaws to rob a train. But they were among the first, and certainly the first ones to deliberately wreck a train in order to rob it, which they did in daring fashion on July 21, 1873, near Adair, Iowa. Train robbing became a specialty of the James gang, and, for the better part of the next decade, they pursued this new and lucrative criminal pastime with great regularity and extraordinary success.

The particular holdup at Winston, the one that brought Frank James to trial at Gallatin, was little different from those preceding it and following it. However, due to a miscalculation on the robbers' part, they had held up the wrong train. The take was paltry, only $700, which netted less than $150 for each of the five robbers. But two harmless bystanders had been shot down in cold blood. Based on testimony given at the trial (a few details are contradictory), here is what happened on that fateful summer night in Missouri, July 15, 1881:

The sun was just setting in the west when a passenger train slowly edged its way out of the huge iron barn at the Union Depot in Kansas City and took its place alongside others ready to depart from the busy rail hub. It was a night express of the Chicago, Rock Island, and Pacific Railroad, made up of a Pullman sleeper, three coaches, a smoking car, and a baggage car, bound for Davenport, Iowa.

Ordinarily, twice a week large amounts of cash, ranging from $4,000 to $8,000, were transported on this line from St. Louis to Gallatin. The cash was consigned to the Farmers' Exchange Bank in Gallatin. But tonight, unbeknownst to the world and of absolutely no concern to anyone except express agents and would-be robbers, the amount carried on board was much smaller than usual. It was stowed in a safe in the baggage car. The main shipment of cash was scheduled later that night on a run of the Wabash line.

Engineer Addison E. Wallcott, driver of the train, opened up the throttle, pulled out of the Kansas City yard, and steamed northward over the tracks. Night had already fallen when the train reached the southwestern corner of Daviess County, about sixty miles north of Kansas City. It had a stop to make in the tiny town of Winston, located about halfway between Gallatin and Cameron on a high stretch of prairie.

It was about nine o'clock when the train, keeping good time, slowed on its approach into Winston. Its headlight gleamed brightly in the darkness as the whistle's shrill blast in the cool night air announced the train's impending arrival to a small crowd of people standing on the station platform. Among those waiting to board the express that night in Winston was a group of stonemasons employed at a nearby quarry who were involved in building a train trestle. At week's end, they were returning home to Colfax, Iowa, a stop an hour or two farther up the line. Among these workers were John Penn, Frank McMillan, and McMillan's father, Thomas.

Nobody took any particular notice of five young men who were also waiting on the platform for the night train. Strangers were not an uncommon sight in a place like Winston. There were always itinerant ranch hands and drifters passing briefly through these parts. Three of them stepped quietly into the smoking car, the other two onto the front platform of the baggage car.

John Penn and the two McMillans also climbed aboard and joined the male crowd in the smoking car. It was full. About thirty to forty gentlemen sat in the warm, comfortable atmosphere enjoying conversation and camaraderie. It was Friday night and they were all going home. No one on the train that night, save the five strangers, ever suspected the horrible fate that was to befall them shortly.

After the last passenger had boarded, William Westfall, the conductor, stood on the metal steps of a car, leaned far out in the night, and swung his red lantern in a slow, graceful arc, signaling Wallcott in the cab to start the train moving. The engineer rang a bell in response to the lantern, and the locomotive, hissing loudly and belching huge clouds of steam that enveloped the station platform, slowly chugged its way up the track and out of

Winston. Westfall then entered the smoking car and walked slowly down the line of men, dutifully punching tickets and returning the stubs in the men's hatbands. It was an old railroading tradition.

The train had just pulled clear of the Winston station when there was a commotion at the front door of the smoking car. The glass windows were smashed in, the door burst open, and three men sprang into the compartment. "Hands up!" they shouted. Two of them aimed revolvers at the assembled passengers. Paralyzed with fear, they raised their hands high in the air.

The train robbers were not masked, but they all wore long linen dusters with the collars turned up high and slouch hats pulled low over their faces. All were bearded and had white neckerchiefs tied loosely around their necks. The two armed intruders moved swiftly through the car, brandishing their weapons and eyeing the passengers carefully.

The third bandit remained at the front door. He pulled down on the tasseled rope dangling from the ceiling in the forward corner of the smoking car and sliced it off with his knife. The rope operated an emergency stop signal and whether he meant to or not, the robber simultaneously tripped the signal, which was automatically transmitted to the engineer.

Wallcott, standing in the cab of the locomotive, heard the emergency bell and, perhaps thinking it odd that it should sound so soon after leaving the station, pulled hard on the long steel handle that activated the air brakes, causing the train, which had not yet reached full speed, to slow down. The train had just ground to a halt when the engineer suddenly heard a loud voice behind him command, "Go ahead!" Wallcott obeyed and got the train moving again, but since the brakes were still set, the engine lost speed and stopped at a point about a fifth of a mile outside of Winston.

Once more Wallcott heard someone scream at him from out of the night: "Go ahead, you son of a bitch!" This time the engineer turned around to see who was barking orders. As he squinted vainly into the darkness of the coal tender, two good-sized men jumped down off the pile of coal and landed right in front of him. Each pointed a pistol in his face.

They demanded that Wallcott get the train moving. Not about to be intimidated, even while looking down the length of two gun barrels, the engineer replied, "I can't! The brakes are down."

Infuriated, one of the armed men picked up a lump of coal and smashed it into Wallcott's head, ordering him to start up the train or else be killed. The engineer reluctantly complied with the gunman's wish and released the brakes. The engine, coming to life under a full head of steam, lurched forward.

For some reason, the robbers' attention was momentarily diverted. The engineer and the fear-stricken fireman standing behind him made a sudden break for freedom. They sprang out of the cab onto the narrow wooden running board alongside the boiler and inched their way forward while hanging on for dear life to the iron grab bar over their heads. The bandits fired their guns toward the two men, but not at them, trying to scare them into returning. At the sound of the shots, however, both men dropped to the ground. Uninjured, they were able to climb aboard one of the passenger coaches a few moments later.

Meanwhile, in the smoking car, the armed pair of bandits walked down the corridor until they spotted the blue-coated figure of conductor Westfall. The taller gunman fired at him. The bullet tore into Westfall's arm, causing the wounded man to spin around and stagger through the car to the rear door. The robber pursued him, firing repeatedly until a bullet hit the train official in the head. Mortally wounded, Westfall began to slump to the floor. The taller bandit caught him under the arms and, with the aid of his partner, dragged the conductor through the rear door of the car and dumped him on the platform outside. Westfall's body slid off the platform into the darkness.

The two men quickly retraced their steps to the front of the smoking car, firing shot after shot into the ceiling and turning the close atmosphere of the car acrid with the smell of gunpowder. The passengers huddled for their lives on the floor and behind the seats. All three robbers left the smoking compartment via the front door.

At this juncture, John Penn and Frank McMillan, seeking to put distance between themselves and the bandits, rose up and sprinted out the back door of the car, where they squatted down low on the steel platform out of sight. The two men heard about six more shots and the robbers shouting over and over, "Down! Down!"

When the wild shooting finally stopped, there was an interlude of silence punctuated only by the clicking of the rails and the creaking of the car. Penn, obsessed with curiosity, stood up to peer into the smoking car. Just then a bullet crashed through the back door, showering the stonemason with wooden splinters and shards of glass. He had looked long enough to see one of the robbers standing at the far door of the car, shooting to the inside through the broken window.

Penn and McMillan heard a man cry out in distress from the besieged smoking car. McMillan exclaimed, "That's father's voice!" McMillan rose up to look into the car. A shot rang out, and a bullet plowed into McMillan's skull above the eye. The stonemason fell backward and tumbled off the platform to the ground.

All this time, the rolling carriages of steel propelled themselves forward into the night along a deserted stretch of track. The train was fast approaching the robbers' prearranged stopping place about a mile north of Winston. There, in a thicket of trees, the raiders had tied up their horses earlier that evening before walking down the line to Winston.

The plan was to halt the train, open the safe, and ride off on horseback with the loot. It would be at least an hour before the news reached Gallatin seven miles away, and even longer before the sheriff could round up a posse and start tracking them down.

It was a good plan, a safe plan, allowing a generous head start on the law, but no one in the robbing party had counted on the sudden and unexpected departure of the engineer and the fireman from the locomotive. Momentary panic seized the two gunmen in the cab as they stood facing each other, realizing that neither one knew how to stop the runaway train. Their worst fears were rapidly becoming reality as the locomotive sped on. Overshooting the horses and having to set out on foot in the dark was not part of the scheme. But just in time another member of the gang suddenly materialized out of the night and stepped into the cab. He pulled the lever and applied the brakes. The train slowed and, screeching its wheels, came to a halt.

The bandits now set about their appointed tasks in robbing the train. All three men dropped to the ground and made their way to the baggage car behind the coal tender. Inside the car was Frank Stamper, baggage master, who had been puzzled by the sudden starting and stopping of the train. He pushed open the heavy wooden door and leaned out to have a look, lantern in hand. From out of nowhere, a man holding a drawn revolver, grabbed Stamper by the leg and pulled him the ground.

Two of the robbers then climbed into the baggage car. They discovered Charles N. Murray, express agent of the United States Express Company, who was trying to hide behind some sample trunks. The robbers asked him where the safe was and demanded the key. Ordered to open the safe, Murray complied and handed over several packages of bills to the outlaw.

The small bundle apparently surprised the robber, who asked repeatedly if that was all the money there was. Yes, the frightened express man replied. Then the raiders told Murray that they had killed the conductor and were going to kill him and the engineer too. Murray was ordered to get on his knees. When he refused, one of the robbers pistol-whipped him into unconsciousness.

Meanwhile, Stamper, after having been thrown to the ground, had picked himself up and managed to escape to the rear of the stalled train, where he boarded the ladies' car. He informed the passengers that a holdup was in progress and began looking for Westfall. During the commotion, Stamper heard shots being fired in the smoking and baggage cars.

Finally, silence enveloped the idled train, and the crew and passengers stirred themselves into uneasy activity to determine if the robbers had gone. Within the space of fifteen minutes, although it had seemed an eternity to many aboard the train, the robbers had done their terrible deeds. Now they had vanished into the night.

John Penn joined a small party of men who left the train and started walking down the tracks toward Winston to find the injured. They ran into a handcar filled with railroad workers, who lent a hand in the search. It wasn't long before the men discovered the lifeless body of McMillan about a half mile from the depot and then a little further on, lying on the north side of the track near a section house, that of the second dead victim, conductor Westfall.

★ ★ ★

For all the testimony given at the Gallatin trial concerning the events that transpired that night, the story of the Winston train robbery was never fully told. A historical postscript was added many years later when a man named Webster Davis, employed at the Department of the Interior in the nation's capitol, came forward. While the details, undisclosed at the time, had no bearing whatsoever on the outcome of the trial, they proved conclusively that the James gang knew it had held up the wrong train. Davis's story was published in the *Washington Post* on March 19, 1899.

When he was a young lad of seventeen, Davis had worked as an assistant to Captain John Ballinger, Gallatin's postmaster, who also doubled as the town's express agent. The post office occupied a little frame house on a corner of the public square and had two large glass doors facing the street. There was a small steel safe in the back room where valuable express shipments were stored. During the day, Mr. Ballinger sold stamps at a small window in the front of the building.

Davis was responsible for waiting up at night for express deliveries that came in by train. If the train was on time, Davis locked up the parcels in the safe and went home. However, if the train was late, which happened often, the assistant slept on a cot in the back room and waited for the delayed shipment.

On the night of the Winston robbery, the young man was on duty in the express office waiting for a late train. It was around midnight when news of the holdup and double murder reached Gallatin, throwing the community into a frenzy. Even at that late hour, men gathered on street corners and excitedly discussed the horrible event while the sheriff rounded up a posse. In a short time, a heavily armed group of horsemen galloped out of town, headed southeast for Winston.

After the posse left, things calmed down. Davis was sitting quietly in the dark when he heard the sound of hoofbeats clattering up the street. Looking through the glass doors, he saw three men on horseback rein up in front of the post office. Davis did not recognize any of them. The strangers were well armed and it looked as if they had ridden a long distance; their horses were panting hard and the animals' coats were lathered with white foam. As one of the riders dismounted, the thought immediately occurred to the highly suspicious Davis that these men might be the train robbers, who had come to take the money due to arrive on a later train that night, the same shipment Davis was waiting for.

The only weapon the clerk had in the office was a shotgun. It was certainly adequate for the occasion, and he was determined to shoot right through the glass doors if the men attempted to force entry. Besides, Davis held supreme advantage: the room was dark and the men didn't know he was inside.

The man on foot slowly approached the front door. He had just placed his hand on the handle when, as if perfectly scripted for a cheap crime novel, he suddenly stopped and cocked his ear to listen. From afar came the thunderous sound of horses running.

Alarmed, the three strangers exchanged words, and with a single bound the one at the door sprang onto his mount. All three turned their horses around and took off at breakneck speed. The noise had come from the posse, which had picked up the trail of the robbers on the main road and followed it back into Gallatin.

65

Two years passed. At the Frank James trial, Davis got the surprise of his life when he was introduced to Dick Liddil, who happened to be quartered at Postmaster Ballinger's home. A smile of instant recognition broke out on Liddil's face.

"We've met before," Liddil remarked.

"You've got the advantage of me," Davis protested. "I never met you before in my life."

"Liddil explained: "Do you remember the two men coming into the post office on the day of the Winston train robbery? One of them had some letters that he wanted to mail and he handed you ten cents. You gave him three stamps and a penny. He pushed the penny back toward you and said, 'I'm no one-cent man, my boy.'"

"You laughed," Liddil continued, "and said that the law required you to give the exact change. The man put the letters in the box and the two walked out of the post office. Do you remember that?"

Davis thought hard and then nodded his head in agreement as details of that incident slowly returned to his memory. Liddil's final comments chilled Davis to the core:

"Well, the man with the letters who spoke to you was Jesse James and the man at his side was myself. That night we held up the train at Winston. After the robbery, Frank, Jesse, and myself rode into town to break into the post office to see if the currency had come in on the Wabash train. We rode up to the building and Jesse got off his horse to try the door, but before we could do anything, the sheriff's posse closed in on us and we had to skedaddle."

After the impact had sunk in on Davis, it was Liddil's turn to be surprised when Davis replied. "And a good thing it was for Jesse James," he said with a laugh, "for I was inside the door with a double-barreled shotgun, and in all probability I would have killed him if he had tried to get in!"

Had the posse come along a minute or two later, it is quite possible that Webster Davis, the seventeen-year-old junior office clerk of Gallatin, Missouri, would have become an instant celebrity and enjoyed everlasting fame as the man who shot down Jesse James. Instead, the Gallatin posse chased the Winston train robbers around the county for miles, but the pursuit ended as had all previous pursuits of the James gang, in failure.

The Wooden Halls of Justice

To reach Gallatin, a small village tucked away in the hills of Daviess County, in northwest Missouri, you had to go by rail north from Kansas City on the Rock Island line, past Cameron. The trip took about five hours. Gallatin, the oldest town in Daviess County and located at the junction of two great railroads, was home to around seventeen hundred inhabitants in 1883 and the seat of government for some twenty thousand more. The town was laid out in 1837 and named for Albert Gallatin, a Swiss-American statesman and former secretary of the treasury. The county was named for Colonel Joseph Hamilton Daviess, an eminent but eccentric Kentucky lawyer and Indian fighter who was killed at Tippecanoe.

The normally peaceful atmosphere of Daviess County had been shattered during its history by the Black Hawk War in 1831, an uprising against Mormon settlers in 1838, and, most momentous of all, the Civil War. Daviess County was predominantly pro-Union when the war broke out and raised the first regiment of cavalry for the Missouri State Militia. On October 27, 1864, a detachment of Daviess County cavalry, under the command of Major Samuel P. Cox, had a brief but violent skirmish near Albany, in Ray County, with "Bloody Bill" Anderson, the famed Confederate raider and bushwhacker, which resulted in Anderson's death and scattering of his troops.

Not surprisingly, few Southern soldiers were recruited in Daviess County. Those residents who responded to the rebel cause left town singly or in small groups to points south, where they joined Confederate units raised from other parts of the state. While no official Civil War battles were fought on county soil, bitter hatred of Confederate sympathizers and ex-soldiers living in the county resulted in occasional brutal acts of violence, and even murder, inflicted upon them.

Justice was first delivered in Daviess County in July 1837 when a circuit court convened at the cabin of E. B. Creekmore. The grand jury deliberated in a nearby hazel thicket and, within an hour, returned an indictment. Their job done, both court and jury disbanded on the spot.

The train route from Kansas City to Gallatin traveled through the Missouri River flatlands and rose to tree-covered hills. The train deposited passengers at a tiny depot nestled in a rocky, wood-sheltered hollow about a half mile away from the town. The depot, local historians were proud to point out, marked the site where John Splawn, the first permanent settler of Daviess County, built his cabin.

Commercial travelers and other people of importance, of course, rode into town in horse-drawn vehicles, while the average person walked. The route on foot was by way of a crooked limestone goat path that coursed through tree-lined glens, which eventually led into town. There foot traffic followed the dusty and weed-strewn streets lined with warped wooden sidewalks to the public square, the center of business, social life, amusement (and justice) in Gallatin.

Despite its diminutive size, Gallatin was the home of a small group of distinguished men in the state. Among them were U.S. Senator Farlay; Colonel James McFerran, a member of the state convention in 1861; Dr. John Cravens, chief surgeon in Sterling Price's Confederate army; Alexander M. Dockery, U.S. congressman-elect in 1883; and the Honorable Joseph H. McGee, former registrar of lands and now U.S. marshal for the western district of Missouri.

Gallatin was a poor community and lacked the sumptuous hospitality and gilded hostelries of large metropolitan areas. Guests accustomed to such elegant places as Chicago's Palmer House or New York's Delmonico's restaurant would not find their equivalent at Gallatin, or anywhere close. Accommodations were considered adequate, albeit spartan, and certainly good enough for the average Missouri tourist.

The town had experienced occasional booms (and a devastating fire around 1838), as shown by its eclectic country-village architecture, which included many brick residences and businesses. Among them was the Daviess County courthouse, which stood on the public square. Built solidly of brick in 1843, it had fallen into a terrible state of disrepair and was overgrown with weeds. Periodic proposals to build a new one had been voted down by distrustful citizens who, aware of past misadventures with fraudulent railroad bonds in other parts of the state, had acquired an abhorrence of community indebtedness.

The Frank James trial was originally scheduled to be held in the courthouse, but it was not large enough to hold the clamoring throngs of people who poured into the hilltop hamlet to watch the trial of the century. After the preliminary indictments had been read, the court adjourned to the nearby wooden opera house, which, while rickety, had seating capacity for four hundred people.

The interior of the opera house was simple and drab. To out-of-towners gazing idly about the room, it was obvious that the hall had recently been the scene of a military ball. The withered remnants of faded evergreen wreaths and festoons hung from the rafters and the walls. On one wall were painted the cryptic letters "N. G. M., Co. A, 2d Regt" and pasted over the wall were several small American flags.

A little stage at one end painted a dingy blue opened to the rear. Here tables were set up for the judge and newspaper reporters. In front of the stage a platform was built up to the same level to seat the jury and witnesses, all of whom faced the prisoner. Only the lawyers sat with their backs to the audience. Separating the participants from the rest of the auditorium was an obtrusive picket fence, described by a newspaperman with the single word "strong." Presumably, it would act as a deterrent to any rowdier members of the public who packed the hall. No one knew what disturbances might arise once the trial started.

The Face of Evil

Throughout the trial, Frank James sat next to the chief defense counsel, Charles P. Johnson. Noble Prentiss, a well-respected but highly impressionable reporter for the *Atchison (Kans.) Daily Globe*, had come to the trial to cover the story. Sitting near James, he conducted a personal study of the defendant and conveyed his unflattering impressions to his readers, as follows:

> [James] was a remarkable figure throughout. Quite slender, emaciated in fact, with long, slender arms and legs, and a slender waist, conveying, one would say, rather the idea of a professional man; but the face was one among ten thousand, and one never to be forgotten— long, thin, worn, not with disease but with watchfulness, long travel, suspicion and anxiety; with a restless, thin-lipped mouth that was never still; a short, sharp chin that rose and fell and occasionally seemed to close up and almost disappear under the thin, sickly-looking, yellowish mustache, so that mustache, lips and chin were blended into one.
>
> Grey eyes with changing shades that betrayed various feelings, but never kindness; and, most remarkable of all, a long, large nose that dominated over his face; not a Jewish nor a Greek nose, but a nose, by itself, not exactly human; a nose like a fox's or a wolf [*sic*]. Straight back, sloping at an angle, almost as great as that of the nose, was a forehead, smooth, white and broad

which, had it been upright, would have been a fine feature, but it lay down, so to speak, after the cruel fashion one sees in cats, leopards, tigers, wolves and the baser and crueler sorts of carnivorous animals.

Across the forehead was a long, thread-like scar, perceptible only on close inspection, and said to have been made in childhood. There was, to make the face more singular, deep depressions below the temples. The mass of the rather small head was behind and above the ears; but not immediately behind them, so as to give the thick neck common in the lower order of criminals; on the other hand, the neck was long, slender and sinewy, and quite fair and displayed by a turn-down collar.

The complexion was hard to describe; it was doubtless bleached from confinement and might become bronze from exposure to the sun. The thin, fine brown hair and the color of the mustache indicated a blond; there were dusky spots, as if the man had a black skin dimly showing through a white one.

The face was one to be studied and studied again, and might then tell very little. His occupation, for instance, could hardly be guessed. A half dozen suggested themselves to the writer, and were discarded. But whatever they were, the idea of dishonor, treachery and wickedness was associated with each.

A confidence man; a sneak gambler (to which the long, slender fingers gave credence); a wandering dentist, using chloroform to debauch his female patrons; an intermittent schoolmaster of limited education and villainous tendencies; a shover of counterfeit money, but not a maker of it; a clerical dead-beat.

There was nothing bold or brave, or manly or open about the face; nothing of the hero, even of the cheapest sort about it. And yet, when the singular combination of mouth, nose, mustache and chin, of which we have spoken, a shadow of infernal cruelty stole over the whole countenance, to the roots of the hair and the edges of the ears.

Whether the journalist was exercising his creative writing skills out of boredom or was truly overcome with awe, Prentiss's belabored and hardly objective description was lapped up by readers. Yet as preposterous as his copy was, Prentiss had unknowingly highlighted a critical point that was virtually ignored by everyone during the trial except the defense attorneys. Frank James's defense hinged on the idea that witnesses for the state were mistaken in identifying the defendant. Frank James did indeed have a face in ten thousand. In particular, it was his nose—disproportionately large and bony—that immediately captured attention, as Prentiss pointed out in such graphic detail. Old photographs of the outlaw make this fact abundantly clear. Another distinguishing feature, one that Dick Liddil liked to point out, was James's temples, which were deeply hollowed and often shadowed. For most people, to see Frank James's face once was to never forget it.

However, through the carefully constructed testimonies of the defense witnesses, James's attorneys performed a nonsurgical facelift, transforming the face of the outlaw until it could no longer be distinguished from other members of the robbing crew who gathered at Winston. This amazing act of courtroom legerdemain proved indispensable in discrediting the state's witnesses, who came forward and swore that they had seen Frank James before, during, and after the robbery.

The Legal Dramatis Personae

The Frank James trial brought together under one roof one of the largest collections of attorneys to ever fight a criminal case in history. The state of Missouri's team of six attorneys was presided over by William H. Wallace, the special prosecuting attorney. His aides included William D. Hamilton, present prosecuting attorney of Daviess County; Judge Joshua F. Hicklin of Gallatin (ex-prosecuting attorney of Daviess County); and Colonel John H. Shanklin, Marcus A. Low, and Henry Clay McDougal, all partners in a law firm with offices in Gallatin and nearby Trenton.

Assembled to defend the famous outlaw at Gallatin were eight of the best trial lawyers and defense specialists in the region, headed by former Missouri lieutenant-governor Charles P. Johnson of St. Louis. Johnson was a criminal lawyer whose fame extended well beyond the borders of the state. The other members of the prestigious defense team included Colonel John Finis Philips, a past president of the Missouri Bar Association and an experienced and highly competent civil and criminal trial lawyer in Kansas City; William M. Rush Jr. of Gallatin (a former two-time Daviess County prosecutor, who was appointed to make final jury selection for the defense); James H. Slover of Independence; John M. Glover of St. Louis; Colonel Christopher Trigg Garner of Richmond, in Ray County, Missouri; and Joshua W. Alexander of Gallatin.

The eighth member of Frank James's legal staff was one of the most unforgettable characters in the history of Missouri after the Civil War. Henry Clay Dean, the "sage of Rebel Cove," was a gate-crasher who had hastened to Gallatin from his farm in northeast Putnam County, Missouri, to volunteer his legal services for Frank James. A highly intelligent man, Dean was sixty-one at the time of the James trial, a native of Virginia who had moved

Charles P. Johnson, lead attorney for
Frank James's defense at Gallatin.

to Missouri in the 1860s. He had been a chaplain for the U.S. Senate, a
Methodist preacher, a lecturer and author by profession; by nature he was
an agitator and political gadfly. Somewhat late in life, Dean discovered that
only a thin line separated a good preacher from a good lawyer. Figuring
that he could put his persuasive speaking abilities to better (and more profitable) use at the bar, the man of God became a man of law and managed to
establish a modest national reputation for himself as a defense specialist.

Dean's magnetizing presence in court, however, was often betrayed by
his almost slovenly personal appearance. In 1861, a young, up-and-coming
Missouri author named Mark Twain, who saw Dean deliver a speech in
Keokuk, Iowa, described him as follows in *Life on the Mississippi:* "It was
the scarecrow Dean, in foxy shoes down at the heels; socks of odd colors;
damaged trousers, relics of antiquity and a world too short, exposing some
inches of naked ankle; unbuttoned vest, exposing a zone of soiled and
wrinkled linen; and shirt bosom open, a bobtailed coat, which left four

Henry Clay Dean, the "sage of Rebel Cove." Snubbed by his defense colleagues at Gallatin, he resigned from the case. (From a sketch, *Kansas City Star,* September 9, 1906).

inches of the forearm unprotected." All in all, he had the appearance of "an escaped lunatic."

But the lawyer in shabby clothes claimed to have never lost a capital case in his life. He won his cases in closing arguments, his specialty, but you wouldn't know it to see him at work up in court. Dean displayed little interest in witnesses and their testimonies and kept his examinations brief. However, at summation time, he was able to recall every scrap of evidence with extraordinary accuracy and delivered his argument persuasively, with withering blasts of sarcasm or pleadings so tender and imploring that they moved jurors to tears.

As something of a loose cannon, Dean proved to be an embarrassment to Johnson's group. Whether this was due to professional jealousy or disapproval of Dean's unusual style is unclear. Early in the trial, he was quoted as saying that he intended "to make a speech, and one that could be 'heard for more'n a half mile.'" Perceived as a liability, he was ignominiously

Colonel John F. Philips (Photograph by M. B. Brady. Courtesy State Historical Society of Missouri, Columbia. Reprinted with permission.)

banished to one end of the defense bench and virtually ignored by his colleagues. The colorful lawyer from Putnam County would never get his chance to speak.

Of those gathered to defend the accused, the most powerful and persuasive voice belonged not to leader Johnson or Henry Clay Dean, but to Colonel Philips, whose sudden appearance at Gallatin, surprising even his co-counsels, made him the object of much public controversy. Philips, at the time of the trial, sat on the Missouri State Supreme Court Commission. The commission was, in effect, an appellate tribunal, the only system of court appeals existing in the state of Missouri at the time.

Jurisdiction of the Missouri Supreme Court, with the exception of certain writs, was very broad, and the list of cases up on appeal was always a long one. The commission was created to handle this overload. Commissioners were paid the same salary as Supreme Court justices and were empowered to hear and rule on petitioned cases. But it was expected that commissioners would not engage in private practice; because of this it had been mutually agreed by all members of James's defense team that Philips would retire from the case.

When Philips showed up unexpectedly on the first morning of the trial, the propriety of his defending James immediately came under sharp attack from certain newspapers in the state. They considered Philips's action, at best, an "exhibition of bad taste." However, Philips had accepted the offer to defend James before his appointment to the commission, and, as Philips explained later in his closing argument, nothing in the state constitution or bylaws of the commission made it illegal or improper for him to take the case. His conscience was clear.

The chief guardian of justice holding sway at the Frank James trial was circuit judge Charles H. S. Goodman of adjoining Gentry County. Goodman, a middle-aged man, was an Ohioan by birth who had pushed his fortunes as a "good lawyer" in Missouri. The press described him as an imposing presence behind the bench (actually a plain table), wearing a heavy black beard and mustache and casting a "bilious, rather threatening eye" over the court. The no-nonsense judge would rule with an iron fist and assert the dignity of the court throughout the proceedings. However, before the trial was over, he would make a decision, in a fit of panic, by which he single-handedly guaranteed its failure.

Day 1   The Trial Gets Underway

Selecting a jury for a criminal trial in late nineteenth-century America, especially in the quiet backwaters of northwest Missouri, bore little resemblance to the slow, in-depth, and calculating process of today. The court and attorneys made no exhaustive examination of prospective jurors. The innermost recesses of their minds were not probed for hidden prejudices or biases, nor were inquiries made into their religious beliefs, membership in subversive organizations, or personal opinions regarding the defendant. Certainly there were no professional consultants around to help find "favorable" jurors with the aid of detailed psychological profiles.

Instead, a few specific questions were asked for the record concerning the prospective juror's age, address, occupation, financial situation, and political party affiliation. Sometimes a brief statement of personal history was also requested. Then the candidates were basically asked, "Can you be fair and make a decision based on the facts in the case?" If they answered yes to this question, they qualified, pending further evaluation, of course. The method was simple and direct.

However, as a means of finding impartial members of the general public, the method was fraught with danger. No one understood this problem better than William Wallace. Before he first set foot in Daviess County, the public prosecutor knew it would be difficult, maybe impossible, to seat a jury that would be fair in its judgment of the legendary outlaw.

At ten o'clock sharp, on Monday, August 20, 1882, the case of Frank James versus the state of Missouri was officially called. Since attorneys on both sides were not prepared to announce themselves ready for trial, the court adjourned until two o'clock. By the time the court reconvened, a crowd, that had been building steadily in size since noon, had poured into the tiny courthouse and quickly filled it to capacity. Those unable to find a seat went outside and gathered around the windows, standing four and five deep in the courtyard.

"Bring in Frank James," ordered the judge. Everyone present watched as the defendant entered the courtroom. James, wearing a black Prince Albert coat, led his five-year-old son into the hall, followed by Daviess County sheriff George Crozier. As James passed the bar, he nodded to counsels Rush and Alexander and took a seat at the end of the defense table.

Shortly, James's wife, who had arrived in Gallatin over the weekend, joined him. His son sat between Frank's legs. The touching scene inspired a newsman to write later with wry insight, "Quite a family group which, if photographed, would undoubtedly sell well." The rest of the defense team, momentarily minus Henry Clay Dean, soon appeared and sat down at the same table.

Daviess County prosecutor Hamilton stood and announced that the state was ready to go to trial. William Rush then stated that all the witnesses for the defense had not yet arrived and asked for a continuance. This the court granted until one o'clock the next day, after a round of trivial bickering among the opposing attorneys, which set an acrimonious tone that would not only persist throughout the trial but worsen.

Before the court adjourned, Judge Goodman ordered Sheriff Crozier to impanel one hundred jurors (called a *venire*, in legal terms), who would be examined the next day before commencing the thinning process. The unexpected delay also gave Judge Goodman the opportunity to address the audience and lay down ground rules for the trial. He got right to the point. Order, the judge warned, would be preserved at all costs, and, accordingly, "any person detected in the court room with weapons on, will be surely, swiftly and to the full extent of the law punished."

The judge went on to announce that in order to accommodate the large throngs of spectators, the trial would be conducted in the opera house. To ensure fairness admission would be by ticket only, the sheriff being responsible for handing out no more than four hundred each day.

By Monday evening, a large delegation of witnesses arrived from Ray County on the Rock Island freight, including several county officials called by the defense. Charles Ford and his father were also in town. (Ford had run into a little trouble with the law en route to Gallatin. While waiting for a train at Plattsburg, the ill-famed gunslinger was arrested for carrying a concealed weapon. After posting a two-hundred-dollar bond, he was scheduled for a hearing a week hence. His presence at Gallatin, until better objects of curiosity and fascination arrived, caused a mild sensation and a large crowd followed Ford wherever he went.)

By this time, the tiny community had been overrun by "a heap of folks," estimated at about a thousand, who had come from all over to witness history. Hotels were filled to capacity, and residents rented rooms in their homes to accommodate the overflow and pocket some quick money. While a few of the town visitors were curious bystanders, most were either friends or sympathizers of the James boys or had come in the hope of seeing the outlaw hanged from the end of a rope. Everyone had an opinion; there was little middle ground.

Among those in attendance were a number of dangerous and desperate men, and the threat of bloodshed before the trial reached an end was a distinct possibility. Acts of violence had occurred before in the area, many of them attributed to the James gang, so it was not surprising that Gallatin became an armed camp. In particular, bad memories of the bank holdup in 1868, in which cashier Sheets was cruelly killed by the James gang, had never faded away. Wild rumors passed from mouth to mouth of old scores to be settled and plots to rescue the prisoner. Adding to the general anxiety was the imminent arrival of Dick Liddil, regarded by friends of the defendant as nothing more than traitorous scum. If anybody's life was not worth a plug nickel in Gallatin at the time, it was the state's main witness.

And it wasn't just the brutish element that sensed danger in the little town; reasonable, prudent, and sober men did too. One of note was prosecutor Wallace, who admitted afterwards that he carried a pistol throughout the entire trial.

Gallatin was sitting on a powder keg. As a precautionary step, Sheriff Crozier swore in a special force of deputies to ensure law and order. Presiding judge Goodman, also mindful of the volatile atmosphere in town, was determined to run a speedy trial.

The press was out in force. The following newsmen, representing the major papers in Missouri and Kansas, had arrived in town to cover the trial: Frank O'Neil and Fred W. Snyder of the *St. Louis Republican*, H. W. Sawyer of the *St. Joseph Gazette*, H. C. Martin Williams of the *Kansas City Daily Journal*, Quintian Campbell of the *Kansas City Daily Times*, and John A. Robinson, stenographer and law reporter from St. Louis. In addition, a handful of journalists representing small-town weeklies in Kansas and Missouri passed in and out of Gallatin over the next two weeks. Accounts of the trial were published daily in most large-circulation papers, while sporadic reports appeared in the others.

One newspaper, the *Kansas City Times*, got off to a bad start by taking a few gratuitous digs at Gallatin and its substandard accommodations, basically lamenting the poor choice of venue for such an important trial. The insensitive remarks insulted and angered the local populace.

Noticeably absent in the press corps at the beginning of the trial were journalists from large East Coast and Midwest papers. Distance, plus the long-standing disgust of the out-of-state editorial citadel for "poor, old Missouri" and her stock of criminals, undoubtedly discouraged these papers from dispatching reporters to Gallatin. However, some of these same newspapers, which for years had gushed over the sordid careers of Frank and Jesse James, did publish wire service releases periodically during the trial, proving that the nationwide fame of Frank James was too irresistible to ignore. Later, as the trial took on sensational proportions, a few East Coast newsmen trickled into Gallatin to observe the proceedings (the *Philadelphia Press*, for example, was represented).

In the courtroom, trouble with the jury selection began almost immediately and escalated amid charges of jury tampering and judicial misconduct. The crisis threatened the viability of the trial itself as well as the substance of the state's case. Much of what happened on the first day occurred behind closed doors and was never reported in newspapers. Thus, a factual reconstruction of the events is difficult.

The day's events, however, were recalled many years later, by the state's prosecutor, William Wallace. He was sitting in front of prosecutor Hamilton's office overlooking the courthouse yard, which was jammed with people, when he noticed Sheriff Crozier, who was busy summoning the jury. Crozier repeatedly pulled a piece of paper from his pocket and looked at it and then approached various men standing on the sidewalk. Suspicious, Wallace confronted Crozier and accused the lawman of stacking the jury with Gallatin townspeople, rather than calling on county residents, whom the prosecutor believed would be less sympathetic to the defendant. Crozier's reply was something to the effect that he intended to get a good jury without going to the country.

Angered at the sheriff's insolence, Wallace returned to Hamilton's office and related his encounter with the sheriff to the Daviess County prosecutor. Both attorneys agreed to prepare an affidavit and file a motion at once with the court, citing improper conduct on the part of Crozier. They formally requested that the court depose the sheriff, declare a mistrial, and start all over again. To replace Crozier, Wallace and Hamilton suggested the county coroner, Dr. D. M. Claggett. (According to another account, several Gallatin citizens came forward armed with proof that Crozier had impaneled the jury from a list given to him by defense counsel Rush and said they were willing to sign an affidavit to that effect.)

When news of the state's plan spread around town, it stirred up a hornet's nest among the town's anti-James forces. The disagreement centered around the fact that Dr. Claggett was an ex-Confederate and therefore was not to be trusted with the important task of summoning a jury. The debate over this sensitive issue ran hot and heavy, but the headstrong Wallace refused to back down.

Finally, Judge Goodman, catching wind of the state's proposal, hurried to Hamilton's office to confirm the rumors. He started off by noting the sheriff's concern that Gallatin had become a heavily armed camp and that the public's safety was in danger. So great was his concern that the lawman had proposed issuing an order to confiscate all sidearms in town. Goodman then got to the point. If the prosecutors intended to go through with the affidavit, it was sure to spark gunplay. The judge would not have blood on his conscience.

Wallace replied that the state had no choice; justice was in jeopardy. Unswayed, Goodman eyed the men coldly and stated his position clearly: "Gentlemen, I am not in the habit of announcing my decisions beforehand, but if you file such a motion I will certainly overrule it in order to prevent bloodshed." The blunt warning, meant to intimidate the young attorneys, was not just irregular under the circumstances but clearly improper. His words jarred the prosecutors. Wallace, in a fit of rage, returned to his hotel, packed his bags, and announced to his colleagues that he was going home. He wished to have nothing further to do with a trial that he saw as quickly degenerating into a farce.

Hamilton and the others implored Wallace to stay. He was the only one who knew all the evidence, they said. After all, it was Wallace and Wallace alone who had traveled thousands of miles around the state of Missouri, personally interviewing witnesses and arranging their testimonies at Gallatin. With Wallace, the state had a fighting chance; but without him, practically no chance at all.

The impassioned pleading worked. The cynical Kansas City prosecutor agreed to stay and remain in charge of the state's case, but not before he had cleansed his conscience by declaring, "We [will] simply try Frank James before the world; that the verdict of the jury, being selected, [is] already written."

Day 2   Thinning the Ranks

By Tuesday, August 21, it seemed as if the world was converging on Gallatin, as more and more visitors continued to pour into town, eager to attend the trial and catch a glimpse of the redoubtable Frank James. Attorneys of both sides passed the morning hours holding consultations and telling stories. Several of them played Seven-up, a popular card game of the era. The most exciting news of the morning concerned Major Edwards, who had just arrived and led a sizable delegation of Frank's friends to the jail, where they paid the defendant an informal visit. Most of the group were old war comrades, whom James greeted warmly.

The court convened at one o'clock in a house packed with spectators, soon to be disappointed. Judge Goodman cleared the courtroom and instructed the sheriff to place deputies at the door of the opera house. Only attorneys, reporters, and jurors would be admitted. The one hundred subpoenaed jurymen entered as their names were called off. Of these, fifty-two were reportedly Democrats, forty-six were Republicans, and two were Greenbackers. Not all of the attorneys had made their way into court yet, a situation that annoyed the punctual-minded judge, who called for the tardy counsels and proceeded to start the examinations.

The exact means by which the original panel of one hundred jurors was pared down to forty is unclear. We know that the men were broken down into groups of eight, brought before the court, sworn to answer questions, and then examined. Accounts differ as to whether attorneys on either side were allowed to make peremptory challenges of the jurors (dismissals for no stated reason) at this stage. The most authoritative account holds that, under rules set down by the court, attorney challenges were not permitted yet; those jurors found by the court to be ineligible to serve were excused, and the rest kept. In this manner, the list of forty was filled by the time sixty names had been called.

Day 3   Death Threats and Other Assorted Problems

On Wednesday, August 22, as the mundane process of jury selection continued, a strange quiet settled on the little town. Most idle conversation centered around the jury selection. Speculation ran high as to who would make the final cut and earn eternal bragging rights for having played an important role in history.

By sunset, though, the calm was abruptly shattered when the community learned that two of its most prominent citizens, Harfield Davis and Alexander Irving, witnesses for the state, had received threatening letters in the mail. The blunt and sinister one-line message, posted in Gallatin that morning and written in a coarse hand, read:

> You better be careful about your evidence against Frank James.
> [signed] A Friend

Excitement reigned as the news passed quickly around town. Both men had taken part in the pursuit of the James gang following the Gallatin bank holdup in 1868. Irving later joined a three-man posse that had two shootouts with the gang at the Samuel's farm near Kearney, the James homestead, before losing the robbers' trail. Davis had also made a sizable donation to the reward for the gang's apprehension.

The town's law-abiding citizenry reacted with righteous indignation at the letters which they considered a blatant attempt at intimidation. James sympathizers undoubtedly found humor in the incident and snickered quietly under their hats. Opposing attorneys, however, shook accusing fingers at each other.

A special meeting of the legal teams was held that evening to discuss the matter. Both sides bitterly denounced the anonymous letters. The prosecution placed the blame on friends of the defendant and held the defense accountable. Not so, said James's counsels, flatly denying the charge. They countered that the threats were a deliberate act on the state's part to poison public opinion against their client. It was obvious that a meaningful and equitable resolution could not be reached, and the meeting adjourned.

Late arrivals at Gallatin on Wednesday were Henry Clay Dean, who was expected to make opening remarks for the defense; General Shelby, who registered at the Palace Hotel; and Clifford Saunders, newsman for the *St. Louis Post-Dispatch*.

Day 4   The Jury Is Selected

On Thursday, August 23, the tension in town generated by the threatening letters was showing signs of abating, but the incident had made one thing ominously clear. Deep and powerful feelings for and against the defendant ran just underneath the calm surface of the community, and the letters demonstrated how quickly these emotions could be provoked into action. Fears of violence at Gallatin were not exaggerated.

At one o'clock, William Rush appeared briefly in court to announce that the defense was still examining jurors. Finally, after eight peremptory challenges from the state in the morning, followed by twenty from the defense in the afternoon, the candidates of the jury were reduced to twelve "good men and true," the peers who would judge the guilt or innocence of Frank James.

The report that the jury would be introduced at four-thirty circulated through town with electric speed, and by three-thirty the opera house was already full. Many women were present, some of whom took seats on the stage that had been reserved for them. At 4:15 the buzz of voices in the audience was stilled the moment the defendant was ushered into the courtroom and sat down at the defense table. Frank James looked debonair in the same suit of black he had worn previously, with a black tie pierced by a gold stickpin that held a large pearl. James also wore a small plain gold ring on the little finger of his right hand, fitted so tightly that it would have to be filed to be removed.

The judge reopened the hearing and asked counsels if they were ready to make announcements. After an affirmative reply, Sheriff Crozier stood and read off the names of the twelve jurors. As each juror was called, he stepped forward and sat down in the jury box. After all were seated, they were given the jurors' oath by a clerk of the court.

A description of the jury members was published in the *Kansas City Daily Journal*. [Bracketed spellings reflect records of the Historical Society of Missouri, Columbia; see photograph on page 184.]

Lorenzo W. Gillreath [Gilreath], aged forty, is a resident of Liberty township, a Democrat and a farmer in fair circumstances financially, and a sensible, good man.

James J. Snyder, thirty-five years old, is a Democrat and a farmer, living in the south part of the county, and owns some property.

Oscar Chamberlain, aged twenty-six years, is a Democrat, a farmer and proprietor of a livery stable in Jamison, a small town on the Wabash road.

Jaseu Williams [Jason Winburn], aged forty years, is a Democrat and a farmer living in the south part of the county, has a fair farm and some property.

E. [B.] H. Shellman, aged thirty-eight years, is a Democrat, a farmer and saw mill man, and lives in the west part of the county, near Winston, where the robbery took place.

James R. [Jos. B.] Smith, aged twenty-seven years, is a Democrat and a farmer in comfortable circumstances; lives just north of Winston.

James W. Boggs, forty-four years old, is a Democrat and a farmer and lives one mile west of Gallatin.

Charles R. Nance, forty-eight years old, is a farmer and a Democrat, and lives in Civil Bend. He is also a stock feeder and shipper in fair circumstances financially.

Benjamin J. [F.] Feurt, twenty-five years, is a Democrat and a farmer in fair circumstances for a young man. He lives on Civil Bend.

William F. Richardson is a Democrat and a farmer, and lives near Winston. He has been in good circumstances, but met with reverses some years back. [Richardson was later selected as foreman of the jury.]

William L. [R.] Merritt, twenty-four years old, is a Democrat and a young farmer, living four miles east of Gallatin. He is a good scholar and a fine young man of excellent character.

Richard E. Hale, aged twenty-three years, is a Democrat and a young farmer in fair circumstances. He lives in the south part of the county.

All the jurors were farmers by trade. Most were young men, the oldest being forty-eight, and all were regarded as good citizens. Reportedly two were war veterans, both having served in the Confederate army.

To a man, the jurors were Democrats—a surprising result given that the intermediate list of forty jurors included twenty-five identified as

Democrats, thirteen Republicans, and two Greenbackers. The fact that no Republicans made the final cut boded ill for Wallace because, during the war, many Democrats in this neck of the woods, like the James brothers, had turned up wearing coats of rebel gray.

Some observers found another, equally important implication in the all-Democrat jury. A Kansas City newsman wrote, "The fact is known that the Republicans were among the most intelligent of the venire." Another member of the press summed up the quality of the jury, when it was first announced, with the lukewarm comment "probably a fine average jury."

The list of witnesses was presented to the court—eighty-nine for the state, thirty-nine for the defense. Of the prosecution's witnesses, fifty had responded and were sworn in. Approximately one-third of the defense's witnesses had answered summonses and were likewise sworn in. They included members of the Samuel family and General J. O. Shelby, a Confederate cavalry leader and close friend of the James boys. Governor Crittenden had been also subpoenaed by the defense, presumably to substantiate Frank James's surrender.

Examination of the witnesses was to start the next morning. Two weeks was the estimated running time, and counsels on both sides were expected to dig in and fight for every inch of ground.

Day 5   The Prosecution States Its Case

The trial got underway at eight o'clock on Friday morning, August 24. Many ladies, more than had been present the day before, were in attendance, with the overflow again seated on the stage. Judge Goodman insisted that room be made for them, even if some gentlemen had to leave. The large number of women who gathered to observe the trial, the elite of Daviess County society, struck the press as odd, but not extraordinarily so. "This trial is like nearly all similar trials," one journalist noted, "the accused having sympathy of a very large portion of the tender sex." So eager were the women seated on the stage to get a better look at Frank James that a railing had to placed in back of the judge's and reporters' tables to contain them.

The rumor of the day once more concerned the jury. It seems that the entire panel had spent the night in the custody of Sheriff Crozier. Assuming they were fraternizing, gossipmongers and street-corner clairvoyants speculated that a guilty verdict was out of the question; a hung jury was most likely and even acquittal was possible.

Thomas T. Crittenden, governor of Missouri, whose mysterious actions behind the scenes played a critical role in ensuring Frank James's freedom. (Courtesy State Historical Society of Missouri, Columbia. Reprinted with permission.)

Talk was also buzzing about Dick Liddil, the prosecution's main witness. He had arrived the night before in the custody of Maurice Langhorne, deputy marshal of Jackson County, and was put up at the home of Gallatin's postmaster, John Ballinger. That Liddil was a man with something to fear was evident the next morning when he appeared on the streets of Gallatin with two long revolvers strapped to his hips.

No one worried that John Ballinger had been entrusted with the safekeeping of such an important witness. Despite outward appearances to the contrary, Mr. Ballinger was more than a humble public servant. From 1862 to 1865, he had served as captain in the Missouri militia and commanded a company of cavalry raised in Daviess County. But it was afterwards, when Ballinger was elected county sheriff, that he had gathered a formidable reputation by helping to bring an end to the notorious Reno gang of Indiana. These nefarious contemporaries of the James gang were known for paying periodic nocturnal visits to Gallatin and dynamiting safes.

On its last excursion, the Reno gang made the fatal mistake of blowing open a safe belonging to the county. After they escaped with $23,000, Ballinger set out like a bloodhound to help track down the gang and eventually took part in capturing the leader, Jack Reno, who was subsequently tried and sentenced to the Missouri state penitentiary for twenty-five years.

Early in the morning, Frank James was escorted to the opera house by Sheriff Crozier. Owing to a sudden illness, Mr. Wallace was delayed for a quarter of an hour. After the prosecutor arrived, Judge Goodman brought the court to order and allowed each counsel one hour to present his case to the jury. Attorney Wallace stood first and delivered his statement.

Wallace said that, although it was customary to call attention to the magnitude of the crime committed and show the relative importance of the various pieces of evidence the state expected to introduce, he would merely state the facts without comment. Admitting that the accused had achieved considerable celebrity in his lifetime, the prosecutor asked the jury to dismiss the false notion that it was an honor "for such a poor and obscure person as McMillan to be shot down by an individual of such great fame," the defendant, Frank James. Wallace admonished the jury to remember their sworn duty, to render a verdict "free from all personal or sentimental bias."

Wallace then read the indictment against Frank James, charging him with the killing of Frank McMillan of Wilton, Iowa, on July 15, 1881, at or near Winston, Missouri. James's indictment actually consisted of three counts—murder in the first degree, committing a robbery, and being an accessory to murder with his brother Jesse and unspecified others. Wallace then discussed the motive for the murder, proclaiming it to be of the lowest kind—money.

The testimony the state intended to present would be circumstantial but so overwhelming, Wallace promised, that "no honest jury could refuse to convict after hearing it." The evidence would show that the Rock Island train was robbed on July 15, 1881, at Winston by five men. During the course of the robbery, Westfall, a conductor, and Frank McMillan, a passenger and stonemason by profession, were shot and killed. Testimony would show that both the robbery and the murders were committed by the James gang.

Wallace then proceeded to reconstruct the movements of the gang up to the time of the train holdup. He stated that Frank James, Jesse James, Dick Liddil, and Bill Ryan first got together at the gang's hideout in Tennessee. Testimony would show that Wood Hite was in constant communication with the gang. In Nashville, Jesse James used the alias of D. J. Howard, Frank James called himself B. J. Woodson, and Bill Ryan went by the name of Tom Hill. Ed Miller, James Cummins, and Bill Ryan—Wallace was careful to state—were not involved in the Winston affair.

In 1877 Jesse and Frank James, Wallace said, left Jackson County, Missouri, for Tennessee, where they remained until the spring of 1881. Their sudden departure was caused by an incident involving gang member Bill Ryan.

On March 26, 1881, Ryan, alias Tom Hill, was making his way to George Hite's on horseback. He dismounted at a country inn about eight miles out of Nashville, where he ate some oysters and drank whiskey. In a short time he became intoxicated and started a disturbance that brought the law to the scene.

At the sight of the lawman, Ryan reportedly leapt to this feet, placed his hands on his revolvers, and shouted, "Stand back! I'm a desperado and an outlaw! My name is Tom Hill!" Unfortunately for Ryan, he threatened the life of a justice of the peace, a Tennessean named W. L. Earthman, who threw himself upon the bandit and pinned his arms to his sides before he could draw his weapons.

Ryan was taken to jail in Nashville and searched. On his person was found a buckskin bag holding nearly thirteen hundred dollars in gold coins and other valuables and several pistols and cartridges jammed under his belt. Unable to adequately explain how he had come by the money or why he needed to carry such an arsenal of weapons, Ryan was promptly arrested and charged with assault with intent to kill.

From a description telegraphed to police chief Speers in Kansas City, the drunken tough who called himself Tom Hill was finally identified as Bill Ryan. It was an amazing stroke of luck. Purely by accident, the law had apprehended a lieutenant in the James gang. Hearing of Ryan's arrest, Liddil and Jesse James grew alarmed. They stole two horses and, accompanied by Frank James, lit out for Adairsville, Kentucky, where they were joined by Wood Hite. There the group laid low for a while.

It was in Kentucky that the four outlaws picked up a new member, Clarence Hite, a young man of twenty-one. These five men—Jesse James, Frank James, Dick Liddil, Wood Hite, and Clarence Hite—formed the robbing party that would subsequently lay siege to the train at Winston. The gang stayed in Kentucky for a while and then proceeded to Samuels'

Station, Nelson County, Missouri. They lived there for an unspecified length of time with a group of other men.

In May 1881, the party of robbers shipped their guns to John Ford in Lexington, Missouri, from which point they were forwarded to their final destination in Richmond, again in care of John Ford. John Ford was a brother of Bob and Charlie Ford. Included in this circuitous shipment of arms was a Winchester rifle that belonged to Frank James. (Wallace's purpose in tracing the guns was not to suggest that they were the weapons used in the Winston train robbery but to place the gang in the state of Missouri before the robbery.)

The wives of Frank and Jesse James had, by then, entered the state of Missouri, Jesse's wife going to Kansas City and Frank's to Page City with the intention of staying with the James's old friend General Shelby. Before leaving Tennessee, however, Frank's wife, Ann, purchased a sewing machine and had it shipped from Nashville to B. J. Woodson in Page City, from where it was forwarded to her mother, Mrs. Ralston, of Independence.

In Missouri the gang maintained two hideouts, one in Clay County at the home of Mattie Bolton, sister of the Ford brothers, and another at the farm of Mrs. Samuel, Frank's mother, near Kearney. Several witnesses would attest that just before and just after the Winston robbery, and again in October 1881, Frank James was at Mrs. Bolton's and that while there he went by the name of Hall.

But the crown jewel in the public prosecutor's case was the testimony of Dick Liddil which, according to the state's attorney, would be corroborated beyond question and would, among other things, place Frank James in the vicinity of Gallatin before the Winston robbery.

The most exciting part of Wallace's opening remarks was the full and detailed story of the Winston robbery. He told of how Clarence Hite and Dick Liddil had daringly commandeered the train's engine and of how Frank James had shot Frank McMillan in the head and killed him as the stonemason looked through the window of the smoking car.

Wallace also previewed upcoming testimony that would place the gang in Clay and Ray counties around the time of the robbery and Frank James in Winston on the night of the robbery. With these points, the prosecuting attorney concluded his statement and sat down. The defense then waived its right to address the jury in a seemingly glaring oversight. The court adjourned for lunch.

The excitement generated by the morning's compelling accounts of murder, robbery, and mayhem was topped during the noon hour when word got around that Harfield Davis and Alexander Irving had received another threatening letter. It had been mailed the day before from the West St. Louis post office and was sent in an envelope belonging to the Menger Hotel of San Antonio. It was addressed to both men and this time its message was cryptic:

Gents—
   Your evidence against Frank James will be watched by tried and true friends of the hero. No one but the writer and one other know how near Governor Crittenden came to biting the dust in April, 1882, on the Sunday afternoon that he rode in the chair car from Jefferson City to St. Louis. The pistol was cocked twice, and only policy prevented its use. Frank James has hundreds of friends who will never see him sacrificed, and will come to his aid at the proper time. If you are wise, you will be careful.

[signed] A. R. K.

The letter was written in red ink in bold handwriting. The text lacked punctuation and words were horribly misspelled, but this roughness was thought to be a ruse. Also, when the contents were shown to Governor Crittenden, he said he had no recollection of the trip to St. Louis. (The governor expressed no surprise at the letter, explaining that he had received many of similarly worded missives during the last year.) Attorneys for both sides perfunctorily denounced the letter and then got on with business.

The afternoon session marked the beginning of the state's case against Frank James. Out came the state's witnesses—Penn the stonemason, Wallcott the engineer, and Murray the express agent—who recounted in full detail the robbery of the train at Winston and what they saw of the shooting deaths of McMillan and Westfall.

Dr. D. M. Claggett of Winston, the county coroner, gave evidence that McMillan had died from a single wound inflicted by a bullet or a pointed object half an inch above the right eye. Dr. Homer E. Brooks, also of Winston, was called next. Just as the physician was taking the witness stand, however, the prosecution discovered to its embarrassment that Dr. Claggett had given his testimony without being sworn in. Claggett was recalled and under oath repeated his previous evidence. Dr. Brooks was then recalled and corroborated the statements of Dr. Claggett. Opening jitters were evident.

More witnesses were called. W. S. Earthman of Nashville, tax collector of Davidson County, Tennessee, was called to the stand. He identified Frank James as the man he had first known in 1879 as B. J. Woodson. Later he became better acquainted with the defendant at a horse race.

"Did you know Jesse James?" Earthman was asked. The defense objected that this was irrelevant; it was overruled by the court.

"Yes," the witness replied. Earthman had first met him using the name Howard at Frank's place and again at a horse race in 1879. He never suspected the men's true identity.

"Do you know one Tom Hill?" the prosecutor asked Earthman. Again the defense objected. The state explained that while Hill was not mentioned in the original indictment, it planned to show that Hill was Bill Ryan and that his arrest caused the James gang to leave Nashville, which was an important link in the chain of events leading up to the Winston robbery.

At this, defense counsel Johnson, in one of his innumerable objections seemingly aimed at disrupting the flow of the state's case, rose to argue that the prosecution was following an "incompetent course." The indictment was for murder, he stated, and the defendant was in Gallatin expressly to meet that charge and not an irrelevant one concerning the existence of a gang of robbers here and there in 1880. Furthermore, Johnson added, a specific allegation of conspiracy had not been included in the indictment.

The gauntlet had been flung down. Judge Goodman, sensing a long debate over the issue of conspiracy, ordered the jury to retire and then allowed attorneys for the state and defense to get things settled here and now.

Johnson was in fine speaking form and launched into his legal argument with eloquence. Conspiracy, he emphasized, was a specific crime and one punishable by specific statutes. It was also a substantive offense and would have to be proved. After due consideration and citing his own case references, Judge Goodman stated that Earthman's testimony was admissible and overruled the objection. Johnson, however, was not finished. He said that although a conspiracy would undoubtedly be proven, the state should be forced to produce proof of a conspiracy *before* introducing evidence that maligned the character of the defendant, or showed that he associated with men bearing a mulitiplicity of names.

It was clear now that Johnson was not only engaging in deliberate and classic courtroom pettifoggery but also losing credibility and testing the patience of the court. Goodman was kind when he replied that he understood the difficulties Johnson was having with the proceedings but that the court was not responsible for directing how the state ran its case. It was a mild rebuke and a warning at the same time.

The prosecution had no sooner resumed delving into Earthman's recollection of Tom Hill when Johnson once more protested the state's line of questioning, rising up and dropping back to his seat like a yo-yo with each objection. The verbal exchanges between state and defense counsels became more frequent and inflammatory, with Johnson objecting to his client being referred to as a "robber."

Wallace explained that he was permitted to call the accused a robber because the defendant was labeled as such in the indictment. Colonel Philips then entered the verbal fray for the defense, castigating Wallace for using the term and imploring the prosecution to prove the conspiracy and, in so many words, quit fooling around.

What started out as a polite disagreement over a minor legal issue had given way to a full-scale shouting match between opposing attorneys. Judge Goodman ordered the attorneys to halt their petty wrangling and get on with the trial.

The state completed its examination of Earthman without further incident. The county official also said that he was the one who arrested Tom Hill on March 25, 1881. The witness confirmed that Ryan, his belt packed with pistols and cartridges, was found to be carrying about thirteen hundred dollars in cash and that Ryan was deposited in the Nashville jail.

Earthman added that he had associated with B. J. Woodson (Frank James) for about two years while the latter worked on a farm and had always seen him in the best of company, and never with those parties mentioned in the indictment. Woodson was described by Earthman as a "peaceable and quiet man."

James Moffat, manager of the Louisville and Nashville railroad depot in Nashville, told the court that he knew Frank James as Woodson and that he saw him frequently in 1880. The manager also knew Jesse James as D. J. Howard, when he lived close to the railroad man on Fatherland Street. Howard was a grain buyer for Ray and Sons. He said he had seen Howard and Woodson together only once and never recalled them talking to one another. Moffat last saw Howard in March 1881.

John Trimble Jr., a real estate agent and fire insurance salesman in Nashville, testified that he rented a house on Fatherland Street in

February 1881 to B. J. Woodson for eight dollars a month, but he was not able to identify the defendant as the renter. Woodson occupied the house for about a month and a half, Trimble said.

Sarah Hite stated under oath that she first saw Frank James on March 20, 1881, when he came to her home early in the morning accompanied by Jesse James and Dick Liddil. Frank rode a horse, but the other two came on foot. None of them said where they had been. All were armed. Jesse had two pistols and a rifle, as did Liddil; Frank carried two pistols.

She said the men stayed a day or two, and then Clarence Hite and George Hite arrived. The group left on April 26, 1881, came back, and left again the next day. Mrs. Hite did not know where they went.

When they returned, they were still armed but had drawn a pursuit party. As three strangers on horseback approached the house, the outlaws became alarmed. With pistols drawn, they fanned out, Liddil covering the front door, Jesse the rear, and Frank taking up a position in the parlor. The pursuers, however, passed by the house without stopping and went on to Adairsville. Frank left the Hites's house the next day for parts unknown, and Mrs. Hite, after April 27, 1881, never saw him again. She was not cross-examined.

Silas Norris, father of Sarah Hite, testified that he first made the acquaintance of Jesse James at the Hites's house in March 1881 and that Jesse introduced him to Frank as his brother. Dick Liddil was with the James brothers. Frank, Jesse, and Liddil stayed for two days, left, came back for a week or ten days, and then left again, Norris said.

Nicholas D. Bishop, express agent in Lexington, Missouri, gave evidence that on May 13, 1881, a box arrived by express addressed to a J. T. Ford. The parcel weighed 140 pounds. It had been transferred to Bishop's firm in St. Louis from some other company. Bishop was ordered to forward the box to Richmond, Missouri, which he did on May 18, but he did not know who gave the order.

J. B. Bartley, agent for the Pacific Express company in Richmond, produced the books of the company to show that such a box had been received. The testimony brought an objection, which was overruled. The court then adjourned for the day.

★ ★ ★

Frank James (Courtesy State Historical Society of Missouri, Columbia. Reprinted with permission.)

In Missouri in the late 1800s, making opening statements in jury trials was an option, not a tradition or a requirement. It was quite unlike today, when evidence is showcased in forceful language to proclaim the innocence of the defendant in what is generally one of the most dramatic and memorable moments of the trial.

When James's attorneys waived their right to make an opening statement, they were in the jargon of the legal profession, "reserving" the opportunity. It was customary for clever and calculating defense specialists such as Colonel Johnson to wait until all the evidence had been presented by the prosecution and then spring their line of argument at the moment when it would have the greatest impact on the jury. It was all a matter of timing and, if orchestrated properly, the effect could be profound.

In the case of Frank James, the defense team deliberately chose not to make an opening statement. They knew that there were too many uncertainties about the testimony that could have an adverse effect on their trial strategy; under the circumstances, placing certain pretrial statements on record was too risky. As it turned out, delaying the opening statement worked to the advantage of the defense, but it was a situation aided inestimably by blind luck.

For the defense, the immediate and most crucial task was to prevent Dick Liddil from testifying. Without the informant's evidence, the state's case would be severely damaged, perhaps fatally so, and the demand for bolstering the defendant's weak alibi would not be as pressing. But if Liddil was allowed to testify, Johnson would be forced into a tight corner. In addition to refuting Liddil's testimony, he would have to come up with new and powerful evidence to save his case, and it was here that the identity of the fifth member of the robbing party became the pivotal issue.

At the outset, it was the unanimous opinion of all attorneys fighting the courtroom battle at Gallatin that five men held up the train at Winston. But the identity of the fifth man who accompanied Jesse James, Dick Liddil, and the two Hite brothers was at issue. Wallace contended that the man was unequivocally Frank James. To make their case, then, the defense would have to find a substitute for the defendant.

This Colonel Johnson did. He argued that the man seen about Winston before the robbery and the one in the smoking car on the train who fired the pistol that killed McMillan was not Frank James, but Jim Cummins, a petty crook and former James gang member whose footloose whereabouts around the time of the Winston holdup had never been clearly established, even by the state. This contention took full advantage of the fact that none of the train passengers had gotten a good look at the fifth man that night.

Cummins fit neatly into the defense's plan, but Johnson knew that, legally speaking, he was skating on thin ice. William Wallace was quite aware of the defense's plan to peddle Cummins as the fifth man and declared in his opening statement that Cummins was not involved in the train robbery or the double murder. This did not deter Johnson, though.

★ ★ ★

For those in the courtroom audience who wished to take a break from intense concentration on the trial or seek some relief from the oppressive atmosphere caused by a late summer heat wave, they only had to step out-side, for downtown Gallatin had been transformed into a carnival. Lining the main square, and siphoning off the pocket change of willing hordes of tourists and townspeople, were a motley mix of itinerant snake-oil sales-men and other sidewalk pitchmen peddling sundry items such as soap, jewelry, and toothpaste. They were joined by troupes of traveling show-men who offered puppet shows, shooting galleries, and other games of chance, as well as theatrical productions—all typical entertainments in late-nineteenth-century rural America.

Among the more lavish productions was an Indian show put on by a character who called himself "Wild Harry." It featured a "real" Indian princess who, in actuality, was Harry's wife, an out-of-work character ac-tress from Kansas City. Unable to draw as many patrons as a nearby Punch and Judy show, "Wild Harry," his courage fortified by whiskey, drove a wagon into the crowd. The ruckus brought Sheriff Crozier to the scene. He arrested Harry for disturbing the peace and escorted him to the county jail, where he shared company with another inmate of far greater note, Frank James.

Day 6   Liddil Creates a Disturbance

Bill Ryan, the liquored-up bandit whose big mouth landed him in jail in Nashville, Tennessee, went to trial in Independence in 1881 for his role in holding up a train two years previously—another James gang job. The event turned into an exciting little episode in state history because it showed how far the scales of justice could be tipped to put away a key mem-ber of the James gang.

The state's star witness against Ryan was Tucker Bassham, another former gang member who had been convicted of robbery and was presently serving time in prison. Since Bassham's testimony was disallowed in court because he was a felon, prosecutor Wallace argued that it was far better to rid society of Ryan, a great and dangerous menace, than the low-level raw recruit Bassham and convinced Governor Crittenden to pardon Bassham. The pardon papers arrived in the nick of time, being delivered to Bassham in court as he was about to testify. With the aid of Bassham's testimony, and to the astonishment of everyone present that day, the jury returned a verdict of guilty against Ryan.

Pardon power was thus invented, and it looked like a particularly useful tool for breaking up the James gang. Even though Ryan later refused to testify against Frank James, Wallace hoped that a governor's pardon for Liddil could work the same magic in court against Frank James as Bassham's had against Ryan.

* * *

With characteristic promptness, Judge Goodman called court at eight o'clock on Saturday, August 25, 1883. Another round of excitement was in store for the spectators and the press as Dick Liddil, erstwhile comrade-in-arms of the James brothers, was scheduled to testify. But as soon as Liddil had been sworn in and taken the stand, trouble broke out.

Defense attorney Philips immediately stood up and objected to Liddil on the grounds that he was an unpardoned felon and his testimony in court was therefore inadmissible. Judge Goodman, anticipating the objection and sensing another lengthy debate over the issue, stopped the proceedings long enough to excuse the jury. Then he sat back and allowed the attorneys to argue what constituted the force of a pardon in a legal sense. The debate lasted for two hours.

Philips started first. He offered as evidence the record of Liddil's conviction of grand larceny before the Vernon County circuit court and his sentencing to a three-and-one-half-year term in the state penitentiary in November 1877. (Liddil had been released from prison under the "three-quarter rule," a statute that allowed early release when three-quarters of the sentence had been served provided that the felon had exhibited good behavior and prison officials had formally recommended a pardon.)

Judge Goodman replied that the record would not constitute evidence unless the witness denied its statement on cross-examination. The defense attorney stated bluntly that Liddil's record was offered to bar the witness from testifying.

For the state, from a legal standpoint, there were only two ways of getting around Liddil's conviction and ability to testify: a pardon or a reversal of the conviction. Wallace admitted Liddil's past criminal record and, seeking to break the legal deadlock, sent for a copy of Liddil's pardon. While the court was waiting, the witness and the defendant, former friends and accomplices in crime, were left to stare at each other in silence. Finally, Wallace, having received a copy of the original pardon, complete with the seal of the secretary of state, triumphantly waved the paper in his hand and submitted it as evidence to the court, claiming that it legally restored Liddil's citizenship and his right to testify.

The defense was waiting for this moment like a crouched tiger. The Honorable John M. Glover immediately objected, challenging the authority of the pardon in Wallace's possession. He then delivered a long and exhaustive speech citing numerous authorities to show that felons were not allowed to vote, hold public office, or testify in courts. The attorney held that a pardon under the "three-quarter rule" did not restore the rights of citizenship, which had been forfeited by reason of commission and conviction of a crime. This, Glover maintained, could only be done by the governor granting a full and absolute pardon. In essence, counsel considered Liddil's document a commutation of a prison sentence, not a pardon.

Colonel Shanklin rebutted for the state. He disagreed, claiming that the governor, under the constitution of the state of Missouri, was empowered to either commute a prisoner's sentence, pardon him or conditionally pardon him. It was clear to Shanklin that the paper in question was not a commutation but a pardon.

Defense counsel Philips spoke next. He argued that the pardon under the "three-quarter rule" amounted to nothing more than remittance of punishment; it did not confer upon the subject the right to testify in court. No case in his long legal experience allowed the competency of a witness to be restored by a pardon such as this.

Back and forth, and around and around, the courtroom war of words went on. Finally, Judge Goodman, at eleven o'clock, ordered a recess for lunch and time to examine the points of law raised during the discussion. He retired to his chambers in the company of ex-judge and former congressman R. A. De Bolt of Trenton, an *amicus curiae* (impartial court advisor) whose opinion he wished to consult before ruling on the issue.

The text of Liddil's errant pardon read as follows:

The State of Missouri, to all whom these presents shall come: Greeting

Know ye that by virtue of authority in me vested by law, and upon recommendation of the inspectors of the penitentiary, I, Henry C. Brockmeyer, lieutenant acting governor of the state of Missouri, do hereby release, discharge and forever set free James A. Liddil, who was, at the November term, A.D. 1877, by a judgment of the circuit court of Vernon county, sentenced to imprisonment in the penitentiary of this state for the term of three and one-half years, for the offense of grand larceny, and do hereby entitle the said James A. Liddil to all the privileges and immunities which by law attach and result from the operation of these presents. Conditional, however, that the said James A. Liddil, immediately upon release, leave the county of Cole and never return thereto voluntarily and does not remain in the county of Callaway.

Witnessed June 30, 1877 . . .

Despite its official tone, two critical features are noteworthy: the word *pardon* does not appear in the document, and it was signed by the lieutenant governor, not the governor. When the court reconvened at 2:20, the judge announced his decision. After reviewing the authorities, he ruled that the defense had not sufficiently sustained its objection and was therefore overruled. Liddil was allowed to testify provided he could prove the genuineness of the pardon. The first blood had been drawn by the state.

At this juncture a sticky point was bared. Under questioning by the prosecution, Liddil made it known that he had been sent to the penitentiary in 1877 and had received a pardon, but tore it up the day he got it. His casual remark stunned the court. Further examination revealed that Liddil had not only destroyed the document, he hadn't even bothered to read it.

The judge interrupted at this point and asked the witness, "Who gave you the pardon?"

"I don't know," Liddil answered, "it was handed to me in the dining room. I think it was young Willis who gave it to me. I tore it up because I did not think it of any use."

Liddil further disclosed that he had not shown the pardon to anyone and destroyed it about ten minutes after receiving it while on the way to the train depot. The farcical interlude over the shredded pardon was mercifully brought to an end by Judge Goodman, who decided that the preliminary proof was sufficient and ordered the examination of Liddil to proceed.

Under Wallace's gentle lead, Dick Liddil, now officially legitimized before the court, proceeded to recount the details of his association with the James gang, embracing a period of time from 1870 through the robbing of the train at Winston in 1881. As summarized in the *Topeka Daily Capital,* August 26, 1883, it ran thus:

I am thirty-one years old and was reared in Jackson County. I became acquainted with Frank and Jesse James while working on a farm there. I saw them frequently between 1870 and 1875. There was a band known as the

James boys. I became a member four years ago last fall. This was in Jackson County.

Shortly afterwards, I left the state, going to Tennessee. In July, 1880, went to Nashville with Jesse James, found Frank James and family and Jesse's family there. I stayed nearly a year. Bill Ryan and Jim Cummings came there and Frank took the house in Nashville and lived there at 814 Fatherland Street.

Myself, Jesse James and Jim Cummings were there. In March, 1881, Frank, Jesse and myself left there. Bill Ryan got captured. We got a scare, lit out, went to Hite's place, stayed a few days, then went to a nephew of Hite's and afterward came back there. Arrangements to commit the robbery were made by Jesse and Frank James and Wood Hite was to come out to Missouri and take the express train somewhere up here. This was in May, 1881.

Frank went by the name of B. J. Woodson at Nashville, and Jesse by the name of Howard. Jesse and I came to Kearney in May, 1881, and rode to Mrs. Samuel's barn. Frank arrived a week later, found Clarence Wood there and Wood Hite came afterwards. About a week later, four of us started on horseback—Frank, Jesse, Wood, and myself. Clarence went on a train to Chillicothe [Mo.]. We met at Ford's farm near Richmond, arriving at three o'clock. In the morning, we started out from there, but afterwards went back.

Several days later, we started out again. Wood went on the train, the rest of us on horseback. We took horses near Richmond, were to meet Wood Hite at Gallatin. We rode most of the night, stopped the next day and night with a Dutch farmer. Proceeding, we came close to Gallatin. Jesse was taken sick with a toothache and we all went back, the party scattering.

Frank and I went to Ford's. A week later we started again, traveling apart. I got dinner near here and met others near Winston. We left our horses and went to town after dark, Wood and myself went together. Jesse, Frank, Wood, and myself were to capture the engineer, and the others were to take the baggage car. When we got out a little ways the train stopped and we heard shooting.

We shot a couple of times to scare the engineer. He stopped the train, and we made him move the train on. The engineer pulled the throttle and jumped off. We didn't know how to stop a train and Frank came through and stopped it. Wood and I got off the engine and went back and we all left the train.

Jesse and Frank said they thought they had killed a couple of men. Jesse said he was pretty sure he had killed one and Frank said a man had peeped in and he shot at the man and he fell off the train. We got $700 or $800 in all. The money was in packages and we rode hard all night after the robbery. We stopped in a pasture about daylight and divided the money. We went from there to Ford's where we stayed about a week.

This closed the direct examination of Dick Liddil. A reporter noticed that, from the moment Liddil took the witness stand until the close of his testimony, Frank James never took his eyes off the witness, yet he never displayed the slightest bit of emotion.

After a fifteen-minute recess, Liddil returned to the stand to reply to questions put forth by the defense that sought to clarify a small but important point. Liddil had allegedly told Governor Crittenden about a heated conversation that took place between Frank and Jesse James after the robbery. Frank apparently scolded his younger brother for the unnecessary bloodshed that had occurred during the holdup. The critical question was whether Frank was referring to Westfall or McMillan.

It was much better for the defense if Frank meant Westfall, since it had already been established through Liddil's testimony that Jesse, not Frank, had shot and killed the conductor. While testimony placing Frank James on the train that night under any circumstance was detrimental to the defense's argument, since it contradicted Frank's alibi, Crittenden did the next best thing by drawing attention to Westfall's death and away from Frank's possible role in killing McMillan. On this specific point, however, Liddil's memory was uncharacteristically dim:

> I went back to Jefferson City with Sheriff Timberlake in 1882. I was there shortly after that with Mr. Craig of Kansas City. I saw Governor Crittenden both times, first at the depot and the other time at his office.
>
> I don't remember telling the governor at either of those times that after the Winston robbery Frank James upbraided Jesse for killing anyone, or reminded him of the agreement before the robbery that no one should be hurt or killed.

At this point Governor Crittenden, with consent of counsels, was called to the stand out of turn to save him the trouble of staying over in Gallatin another day until his name was called. He appeared on behalf of the defense, and his testimony was necessary to bring out details of the conversation that he had had with Liddil. He said:

> Liddil did make such a statement to me as propounded just now. I think it was the second time he was at Jefferson City. This was before Frank James surrendered, which did not occur till October 5. It happened in the January or February previous to the surrender and prior to the killing of Jesse James in April, 1882.

I don't remember that there was any place fixed at which the conversation first quoted occurred, but it was after the robbery that the question was asked why Jesse had killed that innocent man engaged in his duties.

By that man I referred to conductor Westfall, and not to McMillan, whose killing is the basis of this action. There was no name called. I just said that innocent man on duty. I am very free to say I had reference to Westfall, the conductor. I did not mention any names.

He [Liddil] said that it was not the intention to do it; that the understanding was there was to be no killing; that Frank had said there was to be no bloodshed; and that after it was over, Frank said: "Jesse, why did you shoot that man? I thought the understanding was that no man was to be killed, and I would not have gone into it if I had known or thought there was to be anything of that sort done."

To which Jesse said: "By God, I thought that the boys were pulling from me, and I wanted to make them a common band of murderers to hold them up to me." The court adjourned at this point until Monday at eight o'clock.

★ ★ ★

Why conductor Westfall was killed by Jesse James during the Winston train robbery remains an enigma. While most of those who have studied the incident do not believe that it was done to bolster Jesse's leadership, they attach no particular significance to the murder, considering it just another random act of violence committed by a bloodthirsty killer whose past was full of such incidents. Others believe that Jesse shot the trainman out of spite [2]. According to this popular belief, Westfall was on the secret train in 1878 that carried the Pinkerton strike force to Kearney on the night of the bombing raid on the Samuel house, and Jesse was just getting even [3].

The revenge theory is supported by other circumstantial evidence. Since the smoking-car passengers were not robbed during the Winston train holdup, the armed intruders must have entered the car either to prevent the occupants from interfering with the robbery or to look for Westfall, or both. Jesse was apparently familiar enough with Westfall to recognize him on sight, and the decision to kill the conductor was probably an impulsive act on Jesse's part.

The hot argument in court over the validity of Liddil's pardon was a substantive one that would ultimately decide the fate of the state's legal pursuit of Frank James. Colonel Johnson and his team were bitterly disappointed that they had failed to prevent Liddil from testifying, but they felt that the court, ruling as it did against them, had virtually dealt James's defense a winning hand if the case were ever appealed to the state supreme court.

This day had been a successful one for the prosecution. Dick Liddil, gang member, confidante of Frank and Jesse James, and participant in the Winston holdup, had sworn under oath that Frank James, the defendant, not only helped conceive and plan the train robbery but also assisted in its perpetration and afterwards admitted to Liddil that he had shot McMillan during the course of the robbery. Liddil had testified, "Frank said a man peeped in and he shot at the man and he fell off the train." With these words, Jackson County prosecutor William Wallace hoped to hang Frank James.

Day 7   Liddil Is Raked Over the Coals

When you have no basis for an argument, abuse the plaintiff.
                                          Cicero

At eight o'clock Judge Goodman took his seat at the bench and the trial resumed. After Mrs. Samuel had been sworn in as a witness for the defense, Dick Liddil was recalled to the stand. Colonel Philips rose and stepped before the witness, ready to conduct an examination he had been relishing for some time. His goal was to remove the suffocating onus of guilt surrounding Frank James.

Having lost its challenge to legally quash the former gang member's evidence, the defense wasted no time trying to impeach it. The first item of business was to humiliate the witness. Liddil, under oath, was forced to admit that he had once been convicted of horse stealing and that he had also served a prison term.

With this humbling disclaimer on record, the defense went to work on Liddil's story to disclose inconsistencies and contradictions. Every avenue was assiduously explored, to bring out any bit of evidence that might discredit the witness. Such evidence was not hard to find; the rich criminal past of Dick Liddil afforded numerous examples.

Early in the cross-examination, Colonel Philips questioned Liddil about his involvement in the Glendale bank robbery in 1879. Wallace immediately objected, pointing out that the defense was trying to investigate a separate offense and that the witness had the right to decline to answer to avoid self-incrimination. The judge agreed.

Undaunted by this temporary setback, Philips pressed forward. He declared his full intention of investigating the Glendale robbery and said that the statute of limitations did not prevent it. Wallace objected again, declaring that the statute of limitations did not apply to acts of robbery. The court sustained the objection.

It was a mildly embarrassing moment for an attorney of Philips's stature. Temporarily flustered, his speech meandered and he finally asked if the Glendale affair might be a larceny, not a robbery, and hence subject to a statute of limitations. Tiring of Philips's digression, Wallace threatened to take up the Glendale robbery if the defense insisted on it. This remark sobered Phillips and he backed off. The last thing he wanted was to drag his client into another robbery, which the state knew, again with Liddil's help, was one in which Frank James had also participated.

The cross-examination of Liddil continued under a cloud of monstrous incivility, as months of pent-up indignation and hostility poured forth from the mouths of James's attorneys. As Wallace so aptly (and so acidly) noted in his closing remarks, the English language was ransacked for every term of vilification to slander the witness. In essence, the defense was putting Liddil on trial, rather than his testimony. It was a predictable and time-honored maneuver utilized by defense attorneys. Wallace had his hands full trying to legally protect Liddil.

The blistering cross-examination filled the morning and early part of the afternoon, a total of four hours. Liddil was questioned about his every move during the three years preceding the Winston train robbery. He was asked to remember meetings and conversations with various principals, notably General Shelby, which would have placed the defendant far from the scene of the crime. Liddil emphatically denied knowledge of them.

Emotions ran high. Philips's heavy-handed line of questioning led to angry exchanges with both the witness and prosecutor Wallace. Near the end of the cross-examination, during a pause, Liddil, much provoked, returned one of Philips's questions. The unexpected act caught the attorney off guard and also touched a raw nerve. Philips shot back, "It will be time for you to cross-examine me when that time comes!" Judge Goodman broke in and reprimanded Mr. Philips for his discourteous treatment of Liddil, explaining that the witness had every right to ask a question of counsel.

Despite his efforts, Philips failed to shake Liddil's story. Liddil remained firm as a rock throughout the intense grilling and exhibited a razor-sharp memory. As one Kansas newspaper editor remarked: "Dick Liddil was not as great a bandit as others of the gang, but as a witness he is unsurpassed. He has been cross-examined and re-cross-examined three or four times, but his story is always the same. . . . If Liddil is not telling the truth, he is certainly a very expert liar."

The day's proceedings did not prove particularly successful or satisfying for the defense. If anything, Liddil's divulging of more particulars about dates, persons, places, and general descriptions was even more complete and more detailed (and more damaging) than his testimony the day before. Many felt the cross-examination actually enhanced the prosecution's case.

It wasn't long, however, before Johnson, in an obviously preplanned move, made another attempt to strike Liddil's testimony on the grounds that officers of the law who had promised Liddil immunity had no right to do so, that Liddil was in reality an accomplice and practically a codefendant in this case, and, as long as a case against him had never been dismissed, Liddil was an incompetent witness. The maneuver was designed to force the pardon issue again, but it didn't work. The judge overruled the motion, stating that since Liddil's name was not mentioned in the original indictment, he was therefore not a codefendant.

The rest of the afternoon was relatively anticlimactic as the state paraded out more witnesses.

Mrs. Frank James's much traveled sewing machine once more occupied the courtroom spotlight. George Hall, station agent in Page City, testified to the receipt of the article in March 1881, and said it was consigned to a Mrs. Woodson. Daniel Ballard, agent for the Missouri Pacific railroad in Independence, stated under oath that he received the parcel at that location on April 28, 1881.

It might have seemed pointless and trivial for the state to focus so much attention on the machine, by methodically tracking its route from Nashville to Independence, but in doing so they placed Frank's wife in the state of Missouri just before the Winston affair. Wallace hoped that the jury might conclude that Frank James himself was not far away. Every shred of incriminating evidence, no matter how small or insignificant, was thrown into the state's case.

W. L. Earthman was recalled to the stand to attest, for identification purposes, that Frank James, when in Tennessee, wore a full beard.

John Ford, brother of Charles and Robert, testified that he met the defendant at Mrs. Bolton's place on July 18, 1881. Charles introduced the man as Hall, but the witness said he knew that Hall was Frank James and that the law was looking for him. During Ford's cross-examination, the witness proved to be somewhat confused about dates.

The testimony given by the next witness, Elias Ford, father of Robert and Charles, yielded no particular facts of interest until the defendant's counsel got into the shooting of Wood Hite at Mattie Bolton's house. Ford was asked if he had helped bury the body of Hite. Wallace immediately objected and the judge sustained the objection.

"Did Dick Liddil kill Wood Hite?" was the next question. Again the state made an objection and again it was sustained. Judge Goodman then instructed Ford that he need not answer such questions. This ruling provoked a sharp protest from the defense bench.

The defense held that Liddil, after killing Wood Hite, surrendered to the authorities and selfishly offered to sacrifice the rest of the James gang to avoid his own prosecution. The court headed off this ploy by proclaiming the line of questioning improper and stating that a witness's character could not be proven by special acts of wickedness or immorality. Liddil's credibility might be attacked, the judge explained, but not in this manner. While the defense was rebuffed in its attempt to put the star witness on trial, it did succeed in defaming Liddil to some degree.

The most important witness of the afternoon was Mattie Bolton, sister of the Ford boys. She swore that she first met Frank James at Charles Ford's house in May 1881, where he stayed a week and read Shakespeare and other books in his room. At that time, she said, Frank James wore side whiskers and a mustache and went by the name of Hall. Bolton saw the defendant again about two or three weeks later; again around the first of July, 1881, a week or so before the Winston robbery; once more at the end of July; and for the last time around October 1, 1881, in the company of Charles Ford, Clarence Hite, and Dick Liddil.

Bolton told of the law's raid on her house on January 6, 1882, when officers searched the premises for Hite's body. She also related how, after Liddil gave himself up on January 20, 1882, she traveled to Jefferson City on his behalf to make arrangements for his surrender.

Bolton also denied previous testimony given at Wood Hite's inquest that claimed she had not seen Frank James for the past two years.

Repeated attempts by defense counsels to force the witness to discuss the killing of Wood Hite, or her conduct on the day of his death, were peremptorily stopped by the judge, who instructed Mrs. Bolton to not answer the questions. After Mrs. Bolton stepped down, the court adjourned for the day.

★ ★ ★

Next to Dick Liddil, Mattie Bolton was the state's most important witness and also a thorn in the side of the defense. She stubbornly insisted that Frank James was present in the area just before and after the Winston robbery, which directly contradicted the defendant's staunch alibi that he had not set foot in the state of Missouri for the past four years.

Bolton had given the same testimony at Robert Ford's trial in St. Joseph, in October 1882, nearly a year earlier. At that time a newsman speculated that her evidence might assist in the prosecution of Frank James. That thought had already occurred to the attorneys representing James, who, with the gang leader scarcely a week in captivity, met with the Fords' lawyers in Lexington, Missouri, a few days after the trial ended. There the two teams struck an agreement: none of the James family would testify against Bob Ford if the Ford brothers promised to stay out of the way when Frank James went to trial. While Charles Ford attended the trial at Gallatin a year later, he did so as a spectator. He never took the stand for the state, making good his end of the bargain.

Day 8   The State Tightens the Noose

By the early 1880s, almost two decades after the Civil War had ended, army veterans of the North and the South were holding reunions, establishing a tradition that would grow in popularity and extend well into the twentieth century. The congregations were nostalgic affairs that allowed throngs of aging, gray-haired warriors to meet, spin familiar tales, and, if they chose, fight the battles all over again with crutch and cane. For ex-Confederates, the festivities tended to be marred by memories of a once-proud but defeated cause. Their Union counterparts, on the other hand, often felt a bitterness toward the former rebels for their treasonous behavior. For these reasons, the reunions in the beginning were strictly partisan affairs.

As the South became fully integrated into the nation, however, veterans on both sides began to meet and mingle. Among the first bipartisan reunions was one that began on Tuesday morning, August 28, in St. Louis. Nearly a thousand ex-Union and ex-Confederate soldiers poured into the city to enjoy three days of camaraderie and reminiscing. After marching through the streets in a morning parade, the former battlefield adversaries were officially welcomed by the mayor of the city. He was followed by General John S. Marmaduke and then the keynote speaker, General John B. Gordon of Tennessee.

Missourians' reactions to the reunion were quite polarized. While many people thought the idea a grand one, former Southern sympathizers felt strongly that it wasn't right for ex-Confederates to mix with "them Yankees" [4]. To these diehards, it seemed the war had never ended and that all attempts at national reconciliation had been in vain, at least in the state of Missouri.

On the same day, across the state at Gallatin, the state's case against Frank James was nearing completion. This particular day was to bring some unexpected developments and gruesome testimony, which would make it a particularly entertaining and satisfying one for sensation-minded spectators.

Another large crowd had gathered in the courtroom in the morning. Once again the female attendees caught the attention of the press. Every day since the trial had begun, a number of them occupied seats on the stage, dutifully arriving each morning before court opened and staying into the evening until court closed. The only time the ladies left their places was during the noon recess.

The judge ordered the proceedings open and excused the jury. This was done to accommodate Colonel Johnson, who wished to vehemently protest the court's refusal, the previous day, to let the defense examine Liddil, Ezra Ford, and the Boltons regarding the killing and burial of Wood Hite.

Colonel Johnson addressed the court and cited authorities supporting his view that the defense had every right to examine these witnesses under the circumstances. Wallace countered for the state. He reminded the court that Frank James was the one on trial at Gallatin for murder, not Dick Liddil, and claimed that the defense's sole purpose was to elicit the gory details of Hite's murder to impress the jury and thereby impeach the testimony of the state's key witnesses.

Johnson got in the last word. He stated that the witnesses were actually accomplices in the killing of Wood Hite and that he wished to bring this fact out.

The court then ruled that Mrs. Bolton might be recalled and reexamined, but not concerning the details of Liddil's connection with the shooting death of Hite or his whereabouts on the day of the shooting. She could only be questioned about the remarks she had made on Sunday, December 5, 1881, to neighbors who called on her. At that time the witness was calmly eating dinner while Wood Hite's body lay upstairs on the bedroom floor.

The jury returned and Johnson wasted no time in recalling Mrs. Bolton to the stand. The judge advised the witness she need not answer any questions that might subject her to a criminal prosecution.

As expected, Mattie Bolton proved to be a hostile witness. She admitted that Wood Hite had been shot and killed by Dick Liddil in her dining room during a private argument, but an extensive cross-examination by the defense failed to dislodge any useful information, such as when Hite's body had been taken upstairs or how and when it had been buried. Bolton either refused to answer the questions or claimed she could not remember. Like Liddil, Bolton was rudely treated on the stand by defense counsels.

After vigorously protesting the defense's treatment of the witness, state's attorney Wallace said that if Liddil's involvement in the Hite slaying was to be brought up, he threatened to bring Liddil back to the stand to answer that charge.

Elias "Cap" Ford was then recalled, and the judge warned the defense team that while they might show this witness's connection with the Hite murder, they could not attempt to show the same connection with any other witness. A few details concerning Hite's shooting and burial were elucidated by the witness. Ford testified that Hite was killed about nine in the morning and his dead body laid on the floor of the dining room for ten or fifteen minutes before it was dragged upstairs. Ford refused to say who buried the corpse for fear of incriminating himself (he had been a member of the impromptu burial party). He said that Hite's body was carried out that night and buried near the house.

"Dick Liddil was shot and wounded at this time and was a long time recovering from his wounds, wasn't he?" the defense suddenly asked the witness. "Yes" was the reply. The question was asked and answered so fast that the state could not lodge an objection before the jury heard the witness's answer. It was another minor score for the defense.

Ida Bolton, Mattie's thirteen-year-old daughter, wearing a blue dress and a straw summer hat, was the next witness. Although she had been at home the morning of Hite's shooting, she was not permitted by the court to speak about the incident. Instead, she testified about her familiarity with the defendant and the comings and goings of the various gang members at her mother's place during the spring and summer of 1881.

Willie Bolton, a sandy-haired lad of sixteen years and Ida's brother, was the best witness for the state, and the most entertaining for the audience. He positively identified Frank James as an associate of Liddil, Jesse James, and the two Hite brothers. Willie's description of Wood Hite's hasty and expeditious interment was both graphic and grisly.

The spectators, wide-eyed and hanging on every word, leaned forward as Willie added juicy details not covered in previous testimony. He described how Captain Ford, Robert Ford, and another family member, Wilder Ford, removed Hite's bloody coat, vest, and pants from the corpse, which had lain on the floor all day, dutifully saving the articles for future family use, and wrapped the body in an old horse blanket. Then at night, the four men carried Hite's body out to a pasture about a quarter of a mile from the house, where it was unceremoniously dumped into a three-foot-deep hole and covered over with dirt, rocks, and brush.

James Hughes, a resident of Richmond, was the last witness of the morning session. He swore that the man he met and talked to at the railroad station in Richmond in October 1881 was unquestionably the defendant. At this point, the court ordered a recess.

★ ★ ★

To the public, the legal sparring over the testimonies of the Ford family and particularly Mattie Bolton and her children seemed petty, but it actually involved an important point of law, namely, how evidence may be used to establish the credibility of witnesses. The day before, when the Fords and the Boltons testified, the court's refusal to allow their cross-examinations was based on the same evidentiary laws governing witness examinations that prevail today. Ordinarily in a court of law, prior acts of immoral or even criminal behavior cannot be brought into evidence to malign the credibility of a witness. In order to impeach a witness for "bad character," it must be shown that the witness's reputation for truth is bad, but specific instances of previous misconduct are not admissible.

On Tuesday, however, following defense attorney Johnson's strenuous arguments, the judge relented and allowed the cross-examinations to proceed, while advising the witnesses of their right to not incriminate themselves. Thus, the callous behavior of the Fords and the Boltons in connection with the death of Wood Hite and particularly the disposal of his body was finally allowed into evidence. Using it, the defense was able to paint the witnesses in a bad light and thereby discredit their testimonies.

Why the court backed down is a matter of conjecture. Possibly Judge Goodman was having second thoughts about his ruling that permitted Dick Liddil to testify and was trying to make up to the defense by allowing it to cross-examine the Fords and the Boltons. While the former decision was controversial, the latter was clearly in violation of standing courtroom regulations.

★ ★ ★

The afternoon session saw the trailing out of more witnesses for the state as Wallace sought to systematically nail down Frank James's presence at the crime scene.

James Mallory, a forty-two-year-old farmer living eight miles from Gallatin, testified that he was acquainted with Frank James. He saw the defendant on the Thursday before the train holdup in the company of another man at Potts's blacksmith shop, where the defendant was having his horse shod. Mallory talked with the stranger about the assassination of President Garfield and afterwards stated that the defendant said that he was going to Nodaway to officiate a horse race at the fair.

Blacksmith Jonas Potts was examined next by Mr. Hamilton for the state. Potts testified that he lived four miles northeast of Winston and first saw the defendant at his shop in late June 1881. Potts shod his horse, a good-sized sorrel with a blaze of white on its face. The two men talked for some time. In mid-July, according to the blacksmith, the defendant returned to Potts's place and had his horse shod again, this time a bay mare. On both visits, the defendant was accompanied by a companion, Liddil the first time and a man named Clarence the second.

Potts stated that he initially had reservations about identifying Frank James as the man whose horse he had shod. So, soon after the outlaw's surrender, Potts paid a visit to the Independence jail to get a good look at the prisoner. It was dark and Potts was still unsure, but after seeing James again in the Gallatin jail, he was dead certain he was the man.

On a subsequent cross-examination, Potts said that he had heard about a little bay mare in a livery stable in Liberty and made a special trip there to have a look. He recognized both the horse and the shoes on her front hooves, his handiwork, remarking, "I think I know my work when I see it."

The blacksmith's wife took the stand next and corroborated the evidence given by her husband.

Wash Wheaton, another Gallatin farmer, verified the testimonies of both Potts and Mallory. He was in the blacksmith's shop in July 1881 on the Monday before the Winston robbery and saw the defendant there, with another man, getting his horse shod. Another witness, Benjamin Mitchell, swore to the same thing.

Jamin Matchett, a minister and resident of Caldwell County, recalled that on the day before the train holdup two men stopped at his place and asked for dinner. One man rode a bay mare and the other a sorrel with two white hind legs. The one who called himself Willard said that he hailed from the Shenandoah Valley, in Virginia, but avoided answering questions about the area, as he did with other parts of Missouri he also claimed to be familiar with. Willard, in the course of idle conversation, stated that "no man ever lived like Shakespeare" and went on to quote a passage from one of the bard's poems. Matchett immediately pointed out Frank James as the man named Willard.

Ezra Soule, who lived near Winston, stepped to the stand and provided strong evidence for the prosecution. He stated that, on the afternoon of the day of the train robbery, he was out picking blackberries and ran across the defendant near the railroad line about two miles from Winston in a low, secluded place in the woods. The stranger said he was a stock buyer and was looking for a lost cow. The two men talked for an hour or so before the defendant was joined by his partner, who proved to be much more talkative and sociable.

Soule did not really believe the men's stories; the situation looked too suspicious. Before the witness happened upon James, Soule had run across a saddled and bridled horse on an old road that had not been used for the last twenty years. A short distance away, he found another horse similarly outfitted. He concluded that the two men were horse thieves. The next day Soule passed a railroad trestle north of Winston and discovered a spot where five horses had been tethered; he also found a piece of halter strap that had been cut or broken through. After seeing Frank James in the Gallatin courthouse in February 1883, Soule positively identified the defendant as the so-called stock man he had met that day.

At this juncture, unexpectedly, the court heard testimony from Frank R. O'Neil, a highly respected city editor and political columnist for the *Missouri Republican*. He was responsible for the first of two episodes of levity that broke up the otherwise serious mood of the trial. O'Neil was called to Gallatin as a witness because of a famous interview he had conducted with Frank James after his arrest.

In the fall of 1882, shortly before Frank James turned himself in, O'Neil was attending a political meeting in the northwest part of the state. A longtime acquaintance happened by and took the reporter aside. Although O'Neil never disclosed the true identity of his "friend," it was John Edwards, adviser to the James family. "How would you like to meet Frank James," Edwards asked bluntly. O'Neil's heart stopped for a moment at the heady prospect of pulling off the interview of the century.

Upon returning to St. Louis, the reporter made arrangements with Major Edwards to meet with James. There was, however, an important condition: O'Neil was forbidden to disclose where the meeting was held and who attended the meeting. The reporter agreed. His story of the interview was printed in the *Republican* on October 3, 1883, two days before James turned himself in.

The article ran five columns in length under the top header "He Came In." These three simple words were enough to inform readers that the last chapter of the James gang had officially closed. The story was telegraphed to every large newspaper in the nation. For O'Neil, it was the scoop of his long career.

Now, at Gallatin, O'Neil found himself on the witness stand being grilled about the interview by the state's prosecutors. He admitted to having talked to Frank James in Missouri and that he had published the text of the interview in the newspaper. He gave many details from the conversation, including where James lived while in Tennessee, what he was doing there, and why he left. But when Attorney Hamilton asked the witness where the interview was held, the newsman balked and refused to answer, asking permission of the court to say only that it was in the state of Missouri.

The question was temporarily withdrawn and O'Neil was next asked who was present at the meeting besides Frank James.

"Frank James's wife," he replied.

"Who else?"

The witness added to his growing predicament by refusing to disclose further information, stating that he felt no obligation to do so. Judge Goodman entered the examination at this point and reminded O'Neil that he was under oath and must answer the question. The reporter held his ground, explaining that he had made a promise of silence on the matter before the interview was held.

O'Neil seemed to think that he was protected by an unwritten code of the journalistic profession that superseded the written laws of the land. His silence, however, was protecting some of Frank James's closest friends (certainly Edwards and probably Jo Shelby as well), and in a court of law it was called contempt.

Johnson and Philips of the defense, rushing to the aid of the newsman, asked the court to excuse the witness from answering any more questions. The court refused and reiterated that O'Neil must answer if the prosecution insisted.

Mr. Hamilton insisted, and a seesaw battle went on between the attorney and the witness until the judge assumed control once more and directed O'Neil to answer. With a few minutes left in the afternoon session, Hamilton repeated the two key questions: Where was the interview held? and Were the other persons present at the meeting on the list of witnesses for this trial?

Threatened with contempt, which would bring a fine and possibly a day or two in jail, the bull-headed reporter held his ground, determined not to break his sacred vow of silence. O'Neil said that he would rather go to jail than answer the questions—a statement that much amused the audience but frustrated the judge and the state's attorneys. The matter would have to be resumed later, as the court recessed for the day.

Day 9   The State Rests Its Case

As the first week of the Frank James trial drew to a close, there were few places in the country where people had not followed the proceedings. Daily and weekly newspapers kept the population up to date on the latest developments—and shenanigans.

Some editors in Kansas and Missouri blasted the snail's pace of the trial. They viewed Frank James as a despicable, murderous villain and scourge

Major John Newman Edwards, ex-Confederate cavalryman and rabble-rousing political columnist whose devotion to the James brothers was legendary. (Courtesy State Historical Society of Missouri, Columbia. Reprinted with permission.)

of society in need of a swift dose of Western frontier justice. "Give him a fair trial, then hang him" was their blunt opinion.

Other editors, both close to and far from the scene of the trial, drew from the daily reports on the news wire a dire feeling of pessimism; a few even predicted that the infamous bandit would be acquitted. The threatening letters, in particular, helped to promote this feeling. Despite their crude and childish messages, they suggested that the James gang still had substantial influence in western Missouri and that their friends might, in the end, buy Frank's freedom. Halfway through the trial, and halfway across the country, the editor of the *Boise (Ida.) Statesman*, on August 28, sounded the following opinion:

Counsels for the defense pretend to believe that these letters are written by enemies of their client with a view of prejudicing his case, but it is clearly

Frank R. O'Neil, political editor of the *St. Louis Republican,* who accidentally caused a major rift in the legal defense of Frank James. (Cigarette advertising card, ca. 1890.)

more probable that they have their source in the lawless element of which the Jameses were such shining lights.

Frank James also benefited from the tremendous public sympathy and support in Missouri for those who had served on the Confederate side during the war—the same sympathy that had led to angry denunciations of reunions of former confederate and Union soldiers long after the war ended. The spirit of the stars and bars just wouldn't go away.

★ ★ ★

On Wednesday, August 29, the state rested its case against Frank James, and an early adjournment from court seemed likely. Wallace conducted the state's final round of examinations.

The first witness called to the stand was George McCraw, a Jackson County farmer, who said that Dick Liddil left an unclaimed wagon at his house for some time after the Winston robbery.

115

Miss Ella Kindig and her mother, who lived four miles from Winston, identified Liddil and Frank James as being together on the day of the holdup.

William Bray of Hamilton, Missouri, validated Liddil's story of the aborted robbery mission by stating that he took Jesse James in a buggy to Hamilton, where Jesse had a tooth pulled by a dentist. The farmer also positively identified Frank James and other gang members who visited his place that day.

R. E. Bray, son of the previous witness, and his wife confirmed the gang's visit to the Bray residence and identified the defendant as one of them.

Mrs. James Frank testified that two days before the Winston train robbery three men stopped and ate dinner at her house eight miles west of Gallatin. One of them strongly resembled the defendant.

Of all the state's witnesses who spoke on Wednesday, Frank Wolfenberger, a young farmer who lived eight miles southeast of Gallatin, gave the strongest testimony. It was at his house that the robbers stopped on the night of their return from the second trip to rob the train at Winston, when Jesse was taken sick, in late June 1881.

Wolfenberger accurately described the party of men. He referred to Clarence Hite as a "slouch" and recognized Liddil as one of the gang. The farmer described the conduct of the men, recounted conversations, and in general displayed a remarkable memory for details. The subject of horse races was brought up at the supper table, and one of the visitors, whom Wolfenberger identified without a moment's delay as the defendant, displayed an unusual familiarity with the celebrated race horses of the day. The farmer's account was verified by his wife, who testified next.

Dr. William E. Black, of Gallatin, told of an interview he had with Frank James in the jail in Independence in which the prisoner discussed the relative acting merits of Keene, McCullough, and Frederick Ward and quoted Shakespeare liberally.

Mr. Matthews, of Kearney, in Clay County, whose bay mare was stolen and allegedly ridden by Frank James, described the horse.

A few minutes remained until noon. Wallace announced that the state would conclude its case within ten minutes upon reopening. Court adjourned until one-thirty. When the court reconvened, Hamilton announced that the state was ready for Mr. O'Neil to respond to the questions put to him the day before. The journalist was recalled to the stand and asked by the court if he had received any legal advice concerning the matter for which he was being examined.

"I have not," O'Neil answered, adding that he had prepared a statement explaining more fully why he could not answer the state's questions and expressed hope that the court might at its discretion excuse him from answering them.

After the judge looked over the document, he handed it back to O'Neil and asked him to read it aloud. The reporter said that he was not attempting to obstruct the progress of justice, but, having given his pledge of confidence to the defendant before James's surrender, he felt, after James's surrender, that he had a moral obligation to act as an adviser to the defendant and should therefore be excused from responding to any further questions. The letter was filled with legal terms, making it obvious that one of the defense attorneys had helped O'Neil compose the statement over the noon hour.

It was now Wallace's turn to handle the examination. Hoping to coax something of testimonial value out of the uncooperative witness, the prosecutor asked that if O'Neil would just admit that he had never heard of any of the names connected with the James trial, the state would not insist on a reply. O'Neil once again refused to answer. After a pause, an exasperated Judge Goodman excused the embattled witness, stating that the court was taking the whole matter "under advisement"—the legal equivalent of giving up.

Frank O'Neil had remained unmoved under a steady and intense interrogation that made use of every form of persuasion known to courtroom lawyers—gentle wheedling, frank requests, stern commands, and dire threats—and had won the day for the defense. It was a brilliant performance. Frank O'Neil was not ordered to jail. Both the judge and the prosecution, by mutual consent, had thrown in the towel.

James R. Timberlake, sheriff of Clay County, then came to the stand and testified to having kept a bay mare for a Mr. Roberts for several days about the time of the Winston robbery. The lawman turned the horse over to a man named Graham, who came to claim it.

After the sheriff's brief statement, Wallace said, "Your honor, the state rests its case here," bringing to a close four and a half days of witness examination. The announcement startled the defense team. The state's case had not been as long or as thorough as they had expected. Attorney Johnson asked for an adjournment until the next morning to allow the defense team time to complete its statement and gather witnesses. The request was granted and the court closed for the day.

★ ★ ★

It was after the state had concluded its case that another of the many peculiar and unexpected turns of the trial took place. Henry Clay Dean of the defense team, in a fit of pique, quit the case. The event, though, was not wholly unexpected.

Dean had left Gallatin on Saturday, five days earlier, to address a state convention of coal miners in Colchester, Illinois, and was due back at Gallatin that Wednesday. While en route to Illinois on a train, he read the following comments published in the *St. Louis Post-Dispatch*:

> Henry Clay Dean sits at the far end of the table, waiting for the attorneys to consult him and looking like a poor boy at a frolic. The fact is the sage of Rebel Cove is only an attorney in this case by his own motion. The other counsel deny that he is associated with them.

Dean clipped out the article and enclosed it in a letter of resignation he wrote to General Shelby. In it, he explained that he was taking this drastic action to spare himself the embarrassment of being treated as a third-rate counsel. Dean categorically denied that he had deliberately barged in on the trial, claiming that Frank James had written him twice to urge him to come to Gallatin and help in James's defense. He also expressed hope for Frank's acquittal. Whatever his liabilities, by his bowing out, as one paper noted, Dean, the man who had once talked a client into pleading guilty to a criminal charge after extolling the virtues of prison life, robbed history of a memorable speech at summation time [5].

On the other side of the courtroom there reigned a mood of restrained jubilation. Prosecutor Wallace could look over his accomplishments so far in court and deservedly compliment himself on a job well done. He had carefully and thoroughly woven a net of incriminating circumstantial evidence around the accused, and people in general and the press in particular were impressed with his work.

While the case seemed airtight to Wallace, there were some holes. There was no hard eyewitness testimony to affirm that Frank James pulled the trigger of the gun that killed the stonemason. The closest testimony that could pin a murder rap on James was that given by Dick Liddil. He was there that night at Winston, and, although he didn't see Frank actually shoot McMillan, he bore witness to the next best thing: Frank's admission that he had. True, it was hearsay evidence from the mouth of a convicted criminal, or, as some people liked to say, the word of one robber against another. But Liddil's story, under constant attack by the defense through intimidation, innuendo, and slander, still stood as an imposing piece of evidence.

There seemed to be no doubt as to Frank James's participation in the Winston train holdup; a massive amount of circumstantial evidence supported it. Witness after witness, fifty-two in all, came forward and without a moment's hesitation or shred of doubt in their mind, pointed a finger at the defendant and placed him in the vicinity of Winston before and after the robbery, and always in the company of men later identified as the train robbers. Unlike Liddil, these witnesses were all of upstanding character, honest and hard-working pillars of the community. There was no impugning their word.

As for the defense, their turn in court was coming the next day. Frank James's attorneys met that evening. What nobody knew was that their plans for defending James had just been seriously breached and the meeting was an emergency work session.

Day 10   The Tide Turns

Hi, boys! Make a noise!
The Yankees are afraid.
The river's up, hell's to pay,
Shelby's on a raid!

Chorus from "Shelby's Mule," an old Confederate troopers' song

The morning of August 30 dawned cool and breezy, but by eight o'clock, when the trial officially reconvened, the air had become quiet and still, and the temperature, and humidity, were rising steadily. By the time people arrived at the opera house, their faces glistened with sweat and their clothes clung to their bodies. It was going to be a summer scorcher, one of those days Missourians referred to as "hotter'n the hubs of a sulfur wagon in hell." It was a day when cotton bandannas and hand-held fans were essential in the stifling atmosphere of the courtroom.

Personal discomfort would be forgotten this day, though, because soon to take place was the most dramatic and event-filled day of the trial. Today the defense, suddenly changing its tactics, would gain the initiative and throw the state's team into disarray.

The court opened to a scant audience. Besides the jury, the defendant, and court officials, only four men were in the auditorium and sixteen ladies and two reporters were seated on the stage. Attendance swelled rapidly, though, as the proceedings got underway. Things started innocently with William Rush making some preliminary remarks for the defense. He gave thanks for the continued good health of all parties involved in the trial and pronounced it the greatest Gallatin had ever seen.

Rush then eased into his main argument, capsulizing the state's case and chronicling Frank James's efforts to break away from the gang. Again he insisted that the defendant was not present at the Winston train robbery. "The only witness who placed him there was James A. Liddil," he explained. He went on to defame Liddil and stressed that the state's star witness could not be believed.

Rush, however, was only beginning to name liars among the state's witnesses. He also named the entire Ford and Bolton families. Indeed, all of the state's witnesses, the attorney claimed, were in league with local officers of the law in a massive conspiracy to hang his client, which was motivated purely by revenge.

As Rush continued to speak, he stressed that Frank James and brother Jesse had been forced into a life of crime by circumstances beyond their control. "For fifteen years he [Frank James] had been hunted through a country grid-ironed with railroads and with a web of wires overhead to ascertain his whereabouts," Rush began. After the war, raiders like James were despised and warned not to come home. Those that tried, like poor Bill Poole, were shot down from behind. The community had sanctioned the Pinkerton bombing raid on the family residence in Kearney, which blew off part of Mrs. Samuel's arm and killed Frank's infant half-brother in cold blood—a dastardly act that caused the defendant not to trust anyone. In essence, the unwelcome son of the Confederacy, Frank James, was refused a home.

After thirty minutes of highly emotional and aggrandizing pleading for his client, Rush said that he would introduce evidence showing that only *four men,* not five, had held up the train at Winston and that Frank James was not one of them. This new theory was based on the fact that only two robbers—Jesse James and Wood Hite—had entered the smoking car. The former shot and killed conductor Westfall, Rush pronounced, and the latter, McMillan.

An eerie quiet enveloped the courtroom. The press and the audience were thunderstruck, but not William Wallace. The trap he had set the day before had been sprung. In despair the defense had been forced to distance itself from the "five-man theory" of the robbery, just as fast as the words could get out of Rush's mouth.

The defense counsels had been driven to this extreme by a remark made by a witness who had gone far out of his way to aid the defense's case, Frank O'Neil. In a moment of digression, O'Neil recalled how Frank James described Jim Cummins as "an illiterate, indolent fellow" and mocked his long drawl. Wallace deliberately made O'Neil reproduce the slow, stuttering speech of Cummins.

O'Neil's casual remark was loaded with implications that froze the hearts of Johnson and his colleagues. It blew apart the defense's carefully laid but poorly supported plan of accusing Cummins as the murderer in absentia. It was absurd now to try to pass off the uncultured backwoods ruffians as the ardent student of English literature who regaled rural residents of Daviess County with flowing recitations of Shakespearean prose. To make matters worse for Johnson, not one shred of evidence had been brought forth in court yet to place Cummins even in the state of Missouri after the fall of 1880, nearly a year before the Winston train robbery.

Lacking a suspect to take the place of the defendant, Colonel Johnson had no choice but to change horses in midstream. One can only imagine the frantic scene in the defense chambers the evening before as the panicked attorneys hastily concocted a fresh plan of attack to save face with the court and the jury and to save the fate of their client.

Johnson's move, however, proved to be an adroit courtroom gambit. While Wallace had forced the defense to abandon the Jim Cummins theory, he was not expecting Johnson to go so far as to propose a four-man scenario for the robbery. The abrupt turnaround caught the prosecution completely off guard. By removing the third man in the smoking car from the scene of the crime, the defense had deftly placed the state on the defensive and made it harder to implicate Frank James as the murderer of the stonemason McMillan.

Johnson was only able to get away with this act because he never made an opening statement. If he had formally taken the position at the start of the trial that five men had held up the train, switching to a four-man theory later would have made a total mockery of the defense. This fact lends support to the theory that the defense was too unsure of its plans to risk announcing them in opening remarks. No one could have predicted that O'Neil's offhand remark would instantly sabotage an entire defense scheme. However, what appears to have been brilliant courtroom foresight on Johnson's part was probably more a case of incredible luck.

Meanwhile, waiting patiently at Gallatin to be called as a witness was none other than Jim Cummins, the infamous "fifth man." He had been subpoenaed by the state but was never asked to testify. Why remains a mystery to this day. Perhaps Wallace was keeping him in reserve until the last moment if the defense persisted in claiming Cummins as the fifth bandit.

Johnson's unusual move served another critically important purpose, that of patching up a large hole in Frank James's alibi. Everything was covered now. Even if reasonable proof came forward that Frank was around Winston before or after the robbery (something the defense never admitted and planned to strenuously deny), it made no difference because Frank was never on the train itself, the one place that really counted.

Rush's explosive little speech served as a belated opening statement. Whether it was planned as such is a moot point, but it served the attorney's purpose: to jettison the Cummins theory with speed and dispatch and at the same time avoid damaging his credibility with the jury.

The first witness called for the defense was Samuel C. Brosius, an attorney in Gallatin who was riding in the smoking car the night of the robbery and double murder. He told how two men entered the car with drawn pistols and cried out, "Holdup!" The larger man covered the conductor, while the smaller one attended to the passengers. Suddenly all hell broke loose when the larger man opened fire on the conductor. Brosius, his hands held high, stared deeply into the eyes of the shorter man, who was also firing his revolver in the car. Asked if either robber was the defendant, the witness looked directly at Frank James and answered, "I don't think the defendant is the man I saw in the car."

On cross-examination, attorney Brosius was not able to describe the clothing either man wore, but, more importantly, he resolutely maintained that only two men came into the smoking car during the robbery, not three. Brosius, as a witness, was a maddening nuisance for the prosecution. On further cross-examination, he admitted to being badly scared, and while he could not describe either robber who was there, he continued to swear who was *not* there, Frank James. Further hard questioning did not change the attorney's story.

Outside the courtroom in Gallatin, the lawyer's recall of the robbery was becoming a town joke. Almost a dozen citizens came forward and impeached Brosius's account. Brosius had confided to friends that he was so scared that "the men looked fifteen feet high, and their pistols four feet long with muzzles as big as your hat." Some people even said, among other defamatory accusations aimed at Brosius, that he admitted being under a seat the whole time and had really seen nothing. Brosius vehemently denied this on the stand.

Next came Fletcher Horn, a police detective from Nashville. He testified that he knew the defendant as B. J. Woodson from the summer of 1877 until March 1881, during which time Woodson lived in what was known as White's Creek settlement and was involved in farming and hauling logs for the Indiana Lumber Company. Horn said that he saw Woodson at least once a week and described him as being a gentleman and a hard worker. The witness was acquainted with Woodson's friends, remembering Liddil as Smith and Jesse James as J. B. Howard. All of Woodson's friends, Horn said, were peaceable and caused no trouble.

Raymond B. Sloan, of Nashville, an attorney who once represented the defendant in a legal matter, then took the stand. He had casually known the defendant since the spring of 1877, swore that he wore a full beard and a mustache, and described details of Frank James's life in Nashville.

Mrs. Elizabeth Montgomery, who lived a mile and a half from Winston, testified that two men took supper at her home on the night of the robbery. The older man had dark whiskers and a mustache; the younger one was taller with a light complexion and burnside whiskers. The witness didn't think either man was the defendant, but she couldn't be sure. Her daughter, Missouri Montgomery, the next witness, offered essentially the same testimony.

A farmer, John L. Dean, claimed to have been at Jonas Potts's blacksmith shop on November 20, 1881, when two men came up in a wagon and wanted a neck yoke fixed. After they left, Potts, agitated, declared to the witness: "Those are the two men I shod horses for before the Winston robbery."

Dean had taken a good look at the two men. The larger one, he said, was heavyset, dark complexioned, and sported a heavy growth of whiskers; the other was fair and had no beard at all. Potts, well known locally for his general lack of sobriety, told Dean that the defendant was definitely not one of them. On another occasion, after the blacksmith had returned from a trip to Independence to have a look at the famous prisoner, Dean asked Potts if he had seen Frank James. "Yes," replied Potts, "for the first time in my life."

Marion Duncan, another farmer, testified that Potts told him that he, Potts, had recognized Jesse James from a picture in the newspaper after the assassination as the man whose horse he had shod. Gus Chapman, the next witness, supported this claim.

As the last event before noon recess, the defense formally lodged its protest of Liddil's testimony by offering into evidence a record of his trial and conviction for horse stealing in Vernon County in 1874. The purpose was to impeach Liddil's evidence on the grounds that he was guilty of grand larceny and a convicted felon. Despite the state's objection, the court allowed the statement to be read to the jury. The court adjourned until one-thirty.

★ ★ ★

During the noon hour, the town gossip centered around a group of cattlemen who had just arrived in town: Dave Poole, an old Quantrill guerrilla and now a wealthy stockman in Texas; Allen Parmer, Frank James's brother-in-law; and several other riders. Rumors swirled that these men would help provide an alibi for the defendant.

★ ★ ★

The first witness called after recess was General Joseph Orville Shelby, former Confederate cavalry commander and leader of the famed Iron Brigade. He liked friends to call him Jo, using the initials of his forenames after the fashion of another popular Southern general, Jeb Stewart. The confident, slender-framed man of fifty-two, with a brown beard now streaked with gray, entered the courtroom "with the stride of a dragoon, and with a savage glare in his eyes which promised trouble," a reporter noted.

The air was tense. Shelby had a palpable aura of intensity and excitability about him that, like a pistol cocked in the firing position, made the old soldier seem ready to explode at the slightest provocation. It was clear that something was wrong with the general when he had trouble finding the witness chair and had to be helped to it. As he sat there casting a cold, steely gaze over the assembled mass, nobody could have guessed what comic events were about to unfold.

Shelby demanded to see the judge. After Judge Goodman was pointed out to him, the old soldier greeted him warmly. Another awkward moment passed and then the general inquired where the jury was. When he finally caught sight of the jury box, he bowed and sat down again quietly to answer questions.

The illustrious general was first examined by John Philips. A strange feeling must have come over Philips as he stared into Shelby's eyes. The two had met before, several times, but never as friends.

The first occasion was twenty-one years ago. The place was Georgetown, in Pettis County, in the spring of 1861. It was a time of great tension and danger. The country had just been plunged into war, and President Lincoln had ordered the governor of Missouri to raise a militia, specifically ten regiments of cavalry, to serve in the Union army. It was the governor's subsequent calling for volunteers that finally precipitated North–South hostilities in the border state. Philips, at the age of twenty-seven, had just started his law practice in Georgetown. He vividly remembered the day General Shelby rode into town at the head of a squad of men displaying the first Confederate flag Philips had ever seen.

Shelby was a splendid horseman and cut a dashing figure in his colorful uniform. The two men met and talked, but, as Philips was a Union man with pronounced views and Shelby a rebel zealot spoiling for a fight, the conversation was quite strained. Philips breathed a sigh of relief when the general and his band of undisciplined riders finally left town.

Philips, despite his Kentuckian parentage and the ardent pleading of his best friend and later law partner, George Vest, to "go south" and enlist with him in the Confederate army (as Vest in joining General Price's staff), cast his lot with the North and was commissioned a colonel in the Missouri cavalry. He recruited men for a regiment, the Seventh, which he commanded. On Philips's staff was another colonel, Thomas T. Crittenden, who assisted in raising volunteers.

After the war commenced in Missouri, Philips crossed paths on the battlefield with Shelby two times, as mortal enemies now but at a respectful distance. From his experiences, he developed an utmost esteem for the wily, lion-hearted rebel cavalry leader.

In 1862, Philips's regiment was with General John Schofield in Arkansas trying to keep the elusive Shelby, then attached to General Hindman's army, from reentering Missouri. Philips was ordered to cut off Hindman's retreat while Schofield made a frontal assault on the Confederate lines.

After a long day's march and a cold night in the mountains near White River, north of Fayetteville, Philips's men the next morning stumbled into the camp of Hindman's main army, which had moved unexpectedly during the night. Their arrival surprised the graycoats and they quickly scattered. But Shelby covered Hindman's retreat and covered it well, luring Philips's cavalry into a swamp and escaping with few casualties. All Philips and his men captured were a few skillets and some hoecakes, the enemy's breakfast.

In October 1864, the two adversaries met again, but this time the occasion was marked by a series of deadly skirmishes. The scene was Westport, south of Kansas City, in Jackson County, Missouri, where Philips earned his battle stripes.

Philips was now in command of a brigade of cavalry under General Pleasanton, and Shelby was with Price's main army. Intense fighting developed over the next several days and many men fell. At a crucial point in the battle, Confederate troops, outflanking the Union army, successfully crossed the Blue River at a point called Byram's Ford and scattered the blue-coated troops before them. The Union commander panicked during the attack and was relieved on the spot. Philips assumed command and led a mounted attack into the face of the enemy, routing the rebels. This courageous action earned Philips the nickname "Hero of Byram's Ford."

Shelby was also involved in the fighting at Westport, where his intuitively brilliant maneuvering saved the last Confederate army in the West from total destruction. Despite being cornered on two occasions, Shelby, like a slippery eel, managed to get away and lead his men to safety.

In the courtroom in Gallatin, the two former foes were now aligned on the same side of battle. They were fighting for the freedom of an ex-Confederate raider.

Opening statements by Shelby recounted various meetings with Jesse James and Dick Liddil in 1880 and 1881. The witness said that he never saw Frank James during this period of time; in fact, he had not seen him since 1872. Then Shelby, who was facing the defendant and had been asked to point out Frank James, turned to the judge and asked, "With the permission of the court, having recognized an old Confederate comrade, can I be tolerated to shake his hand?"

"No, sir, not now," came the judge's amused reply.

This innocent and friendly but totally inappropriate gesture in a formal court of law caused a few smiles to break out in the audience—and perhaps a few eyebrows to raise as well.

Under the gentle guidance of Philips, General Shelby continued his testimony. Then his mood grew dark and he began to take verbal swipes at Dick Liddil (there was bitter hatred between them). The witness recounted a meeting he had with Ann James, who asked him to intercede with the governor on her husband's behalf because "Liddil and others are committing depredations in the South, and they are holding my husband amenable for it."

From this point on, Shelby's composure and testimony rapidly deteriorated. He rambled on and on, and it became apparent to all present that Shelby was not quite himself. It didn't take long to figure out why: the old man had fortified himself with strong spirits before his appointment in court and was drunk.

While the inebriated old soldier proved a harmless and humorous courtroom diversion under the solicitous lead of Philips, it was a totally different matter when the state stepped in to cross-examine the witness. The fueled-up Shelby led the state's counsel, Attorney Wallace, around and around in a maddening and fruitless chase for evidence. Every question he put to Shelby was met with a rude, evasive, and argumentative answer. To add to the prosecutor's exasperation, the general lapsed frequently into meaningless chitchat, slandered Liddil at every opportunity, and, despite warnings from the bench that he might be cited for contempt, continued to give Wallace a very hard time.

At two different points, the defense attorneys rose and stated that the witness was in no condition to testify, but the judge refused to stop the examination. There was little doubt in Wallace's mind that Shelby, drunk or not, had been heavily coached for his performance and was deliberately shading the truth. Although the prosecutor phrased his next few questions with extreme tact, it wasn't long before Shelby, even in his dazed condition, recognized the obvious implications of the questions and indignantly fired back, "Do you, sir, accuse me of lying?"

The judge calmed the witness down. Then Wallace asked Shelby if he was protecting Frank James's wife.

"I protect nobody," the witness answered fiercely, "but I will do what I can, sir, to feed a comrade, or succor a woman, even if it was Jennison's wife!" (Union colonel Jennison from Kansas was leader of the hated Red Legs and considered an enemy by many Missourians.) Shelby's remark drew a blistering reprimand from the bench. Wallace smiled scornfully. The general caught his gaze and fixed the attorney instantly with a cold glare. "Mr. Wallace," Shelby said with deadly earnestness, "if you want to make this a personal matter, you can do so."

The implication of the general's remark was clear to everyone in the courtroom; it was an invitation to a duel. Wallace was a highly religious and peace-loving man and was not frightened by Shelby's blustery challenge. He informed the general that he would have to answer questions like everyone else. Even so, Wallace wrapped up the remainder of Shelby's cross-examination in short order.

The general's temper had settled down for good as he concluded his testimony. Shelby said that in the fall of 1881, upon returning to his house, he found Jesse James, Jim Cummins, Bill Ryan, and Dick Liddil there.

Shelby added that at about the same time, Jesse, Wood Hite, Cummins, and Liddil paid the old man another visit. According to Shelby, Jesse said that Frank had been south for years and that Liddil had not seen Frank for the past two years.

The witness stated that he knew Jim Cummins from the war and that Cummins had been in Shelby's house many times. Shelby also swore that Frank James's wife visited him in 1881 with her little boy. The examination of Shelby had barely finished when once again the old rebel leader asked permission of the court to shake hands with the defendant. "You can call on him some other time," the judge replied, coldly this time. As he stepped down from the witness stand, Shelby turned to James and said, "God bless you, old fellow."

During the rest of the afternoon, the defense called out a procession of witnesses in an effort to repudiate evidence given by the state.

Frank Tutt, coal-oil inspector, was called to the stand. He recalled meeting Dick Liddil around October 1882. The gang member, when questioned by Tutt, said that he did not know the whereabouts of Frank, and he added that Frank and Jesse were not getting along too well and had not seen each other for years.

Joseph B. Chiles of Kansas City next swore that Dick Liddil, in a conversation about six months previous and prior to his leaving for Alabama, told him that Frank James was not involved in the last three train robberies (which included the one at Winston). Chiles also stated under oath that, in his opinion, the defendant bore a striking resemblance to Wood Hite.

Thomas M. Mimms, cousin of Frank James, testified that he was at Mrs. Samuel's house twice in June 1881, where he saw Jesse, the Hite brothers, and Dick Liddil but not the defendant. No one there knew where Frank was.

William Nicholson, son-in-law of Mrs. Samuel and a resident near Kearney, said that the four men just mentioned were at his place in the summer of 1881 and that Frank James was not with them.

By now, the midday heat in the courtroom had reached the point of suffocation. Beads of sweat were streaming down the attentive faces, and the rapid fluttering of fans sounded like a flock of ducks about to hit the water. To allow everybody a chance to step outside and cool off, the court ordered a short recess of fifteen minutes.

After the break, the defense paraded out ten witnesses with the sole purpose of impugning the testimony of the Ford and Bolton families. Each witness made a brief statement declaring that the reputation of the Fords and the Boltons for truthfulness was "bad." These witnesses were Mayor Williams, M. Duval, Mr. Norwalk, G. W. Trigg, James L. Farris, Arthur B. Elliott, John Millstead, James Duval, John Warrenstaff, and Thomas D. Woodson. The court then adjourned for the day.

Day 11 A Day of Wonders

Although the court officially opened at eight-thirty, proceedings were delayed for a short while as the attorneys trickled in to take their places. The crowd in the courtroom on August 31 was the largest since the trial began.

The first witness for the defense was James M. DeMasters, justice of the peace at Richmond. He testified that at Wood Hite's inquest Mrs. Bolton said that she had not seen Frank James for two years, and that she last saw him at her father's house, not hers.

Before the next witness was called, there was a commotion at the front door of the opera house. Colonel Philips rose and interrupted the session. He had just learned that General Shelby was at the door and wished to make a statement. Permission was granted.

Into the courtroom strode a sober and sedate Jo Shelby. He approached the bench and stopped. In front of a hushed house, Shelby, hat in hand, saluted the court with a low, sweeping bow. Then in a clear voice that could be heard across town, he announced, "If anything that I may have said or done yesterday offended the dignity of the court, I regret it exceedingly." After a pause, he turned to the team of prosecutors and added, "As to other parties, I have no regrets."

Judge Goodman, his patience exhausted, lit into the old man. "General Shelby, I must say your conduct yesterday in appearing before the court in an unfit condition and showing an insubordinate spirit was reprehensible in the extreme, as it was not only defiance of the dignity of the court, but calculated to prejudice the interest of the defendant.

"You are a man of national reputation and enjoy the respect and confidence of a large number of people of Missouri. I can only say that I was much astonished at your very reprehensible actions. It is in testimony that you have drawn a pistol right in the verge of the court which is in itself a contempt of court." (The judge was referring to an incident that took place in a hotel dining room two nights before. Shelby, in an alcoholic haze, mistook a traveling salesman from Chicago for his archenemy, Dick Liddil, and threatened him with a drawn revolver.)

General Shelby interrupted the judge. "That, sir, is false!" he roared in anger.

"The marshal of Lexington testified to it under oath," the judge replied in equal volume.

"Then he lied!" shouted the general.

Goodman ignored the comment and continued to speak. "The court is amply satisfied with your apology to it, but your attitude towards the attorneys for the state yesterday in answering in a threatening and offensive manner and talk of calling them to personal account cannot be overlooked."

After the severe public scolding, Goodman declared Shelby in contempt of court and laid a ten-dollar fine on the old man. It was a light slap on the wrist, but it had its effect. The general paid his fine and thanked the court with the look of a man who had just been granted a huge favor. He turned on his heels and walked silently away.

After the general's departure, the trial resumed with the defense continuing to hammer away at the state's case.

James Cullason, a longtime Ray County native, stated under oath that Mattie Bolton once told him that she thought Frank James was not involved in the Blue Cut or Winston robberies, and in fact wasn't even in the state of Missouri during the whole time.

James Duval was recalled. He said that after Wood Hite's inquest Mattie Bolton declared to him that she had not seen the defendant for the past two years.

John T. Samuel, half-brother of Frank James and a permanent resident of the Samuel household at Kearney, said that he had seen Frank only one time since 1877, at home. In May 1881, the witness saw Jesse with Dick Liddil at Mrs. Samuel's residence. John heard them both say that they had left Frank in Kentucky, that he was in bad health, and that he was considering going south. The young man also said that he thought Wood Hite looked a lot like the defendant.

When cross-examined, the young Samuel boy admitted that he knew that the men who came to visit at Mrs. Samuel's were all outlaws and said were always heavily armed. He had read in the newspapers that they robbed banks and trains.

Mrs. Zerelda Samuel, the portly matriarch of the James family, her hair white as snow, took the stand next. She testified that she had lived in Clay County near Kearney for the past forty years and was the mother of the defendant. Asked about the date of Jesse's death, the old lady broke down and cried. In a choked voice she replied, "Jesse was at my house in May 1881. He was accompanied by Dick Liddil. I asked Jesse where Frank was, and he told me that he had left him in Kentucky in bad health."

"I commenced crying and said, 'Son, you know he is dead and you might as well tell me.'

"He said, 'No, he's alive and in Kentucky,' and then Dick Liddil spoke up and said the same thing.

"Jesse was in and out of the house with Dick Liddil and the Hites until after the Winston robbery. The last time I saw my son Frank before I met him at Independence was seven years ago this fall when Sheriff Brown came to my house and shot at him."

Cross-examined, Mrs. Samuel said that she did not see Frank James during the summer of 1881 and did not know where he was, but thought him dead. The witness recalled the departure of the wagon in August and admitted that she furnished a dress, bonnet, and apron to the men.

"And why did you do that," Wallace asked.

"Because they wanted to pass one of the gentlemen for a lady so you folks could not catch them," came the answer, the old lady smiling proudly.

Next Allen H. Parmer, brother-in-law of the defendant and a stock rancher of Wichita, Texas, stated that in August 1881, when he returned from a trip to Fort Worth, he found Frank at his home. Parmer testified that he never asked the defendant where he had been or where he was going. The witness did not see Frank James again until the day before in jail. Parmer was carefully cross-examined by the state, but stuck to his story.

The afternoon session began with Mr. Rush of the defense asking the judge to exempt General Shelby from the rule requiring witnesses to leave the courtroom after testifying. (The record is not explicit about what happened, but apparently Shelby accompanied the defense team back into court.) Permission was granted by the court.

Mrs. Susan Parmer, sister of Frank James, was the next witness. She testified that the defendant arrived at her home in Texas for a visit on June 1, 1881, left around the first of July for two or three weeks, and then returned. She did not know where he went.

Bud Harbison, a neighbor of Mrs. Bolton's, testified to seeing strange persons moving about his place in May 1881, but said the defendant was not one of them. He also said that he had seen Frank James there several times in the past, that Dick Liddil was introduced to him in 1882 at Mattie Bolton's as Mr. Anderson, and that he had recognized Liddil when the state's witness came to Gallatin.

At the request of the defense the court ordered a brief recess. The pause was unexpected, but its import was sensed immediately by everyone in the courtroom. Fifteen minutes later, when the court reopened, a feeling of intense expectation and excitement seized the audience. It was the moment they had been waiting for, the culmination of a week and a half of courtroom drama.

A silence fell over the room, punctuated only by the rapid clicking of hand-held fans. All eyes turned to watch the familiar figure materialize in the doorway, as Frank James, the last witness for the defense, made his dramatic entrance into the courtroom. This time he would have to abandon the sphinx-like demeanor he had maintained at the defense table and assume a speaking role. His limp was slight but still noticeable, the result of an old bullet wound suffered many years ago during the Northfield bank robbery. The defendant strode confidently to the witness stand and took his seat. At last the gallery of spectators gathered at Gallatin, and indeed the world, would hear the accused tell his side of the story.

In terms of courtroom strategy and pure emotional effect the defendant's appearance on the witness stand was perfectly timed and well executed. Colonel Johnson knew that he was taking a drastic step, but it was something Frank James had insisted on. The defendant's alibi was on shaky ground and it required Frank's personal touch to restore its strength. While putting the accused on the stand always carried grave risks, in the case of Frank James they were minimal. The man possessed an iron constitution, and his ability to remain calm and collected under fire was legendary. A rigorous cross-examination, sure to follow, would be child's play to this professional, and, if he didn't stumble, the advantages falling to the defendant could be enormous.

The famed outlaw was sworn in. Frank James exuded the same quiet self-assurance that he had displayed since the day he turned himself in. James looked directly at the jury and, in a voice described by the press as "clear, distinct and well modulated," gave his testimony, as condensed here:

"I am the defendant in this case. In the winter of 1876, I went from Missouri to Tennessee, came to Nashville in July 1877, and rented a farm in the White River neighborhood. In 1880, I was logging for the Indiana Lumber Company. It was hard work and my health became impaired.

"I moved into Nashville to go into other business. I first met Jesse the year after I went to Nashville. It was in a store that he stepped up and spoke to me, but we used no names. He said he was living in Hampburn County, Tennessee, and buying grain.

"I saw Bill Ryan in 1879 but did not see Dick Liddil. Ryan and Jesse were together very often. I left Nashville firstly to look for livelihood for my family, secondly to get away from these parties.

"We went to George Hite's in Kentucky. When the officers appeared near Hite's, three men approached, and Jesse said, 'They are after us.' I said, 'No, they can't be after us,' when Dick Liddil said, 'Jesse and I borrowed a couple of horses at Nashville and they are after us.'

"The officers passed and did not come back. Wood Hite followed them a short distance. It was said that there was a strong resemblance between Wood Hite and myself. We went from Hite's to Logan County, Kentucky, and Jesse and Dick went away. I don't know where.

"No arrangements were made between them and me to rob the express at Kansas City. On the contrary, I tried to dissuade them from going to Missouri, as it was unsafe. I advised Dick to go to work.

"Between the 10th and 15th of May, 1881, I went to Louisville and thence to Clay County, Texas. I went to Mrs. Parmer's in June, and stayed five or six weeks. I went from there to the Indian nation, 120 miles distant. I returned to Mrs. Parmer's when I heard of the Winston robbery because I supposed I would be looked for as having a hand in that transaction.

"While away on that trip, I heard of the Blue Cut robbery. When I left Tennessee, I instructed my wife to go to General Shelby and see if anything could be done for me, as I wanted to surrender if I could have a fair and impartial trial.

"I told her nothing could be done and to go to her brother's in California, which she did. I did not stay for my health was bad. From there I returned to Tennessee. I met my wife in Kentucky and we traveled through Tennessee and Virginia and North Carolina, looking for a secluded place of residence and finally returned to Lynchburg, Virginia.

"In April, I heard of Jesse's assassination. I saw an interview with Governor Crittenden in which the governor stated when the question was asked, What about Frank James?, that as none of Frank's friends had ever said anything to him about it, he would not say what he would do. This gave me hope that I might be permitted to give myself up and have a fair trial.

"I had nothing to do with shipping arms into Missouri. I was not in the state from the time I went to Tennessee in 1876 to when I passed through from Texas in 1881."

On cross-examination, Frank James added the following comment:

"I went to Tennessee in a wagon. Jesse and I separated in southeast Missouri. I don't know where he went then.

"I have known Liddil several years.

"I remember I had an interview with Frank O'Neil. I do not remember whether I made the statement ascribed. If I did, it was a statement made to a newspaper reporter, but now I am stating facts on oath."

When pressed by Wallace to describe the route from Denison, Texas, to the house of his sister, Mrs. Parmer, the defendant could not provide details of the trip, or even the names of people whom he had visited in Clay County, Texas, with the sole exception of a cowboy named Haynes.

With the cross-examination completed, the defense rested its case and the court recessed for the day. The state planned to introduce witnesses in rebuttal the next day, after which instructions to the jury would be given. On Monday, final arguments would begin.

★ ★ ★

As in ancient Greek plays when a god was lowered to the stage in a mechanical contraption to speak mortal words and decide the final outcome, so Frank James might have seemed to the jurors and members of the audience when he left the defense's bench and took his seat in the witness box to say his piece. The brief alibi and declaration of innocence offered by the defendant, however, was little more than a casual story of his wanderings throughout the South with his wife and boy, which covered thousands of miles and consumed months of time. At the time of the Winston affair, according to James, he was visiting his sister in Texas, hundreds of miles from Winston. Yet no one but his sister and brother-in-law could back up his alibi. It was the flimsiest of stories.

★ ★ ★

The heated confrontation between Wallace and General Shelby in court the day before led to a tense but amusing incident later that day. It seems that word was sent to Wallace that Shelby was looking for him and that he had made threats to shoot the attorney. When Wallace ran into Shelby that evening, the two men stared at each other from opposite ends of a wooden plank laying across a muddy stretch of the street. The tension unexpectedly eased when Shelby stepped courteously to the side and, bowing, said, "After you, Mr. Wallace."

★ ★ ★

Before the day ended, the last and most intimidating in the string of anonymous threatening letters was received by Alexander Irving and Harfield Davis, two of the state's witnesses. The handwriting was similar to the others, but this letter had been mailed from New Mexico.

> All evidence against Frank James will be watched by solid true and sworn friends of the hero. You may think as stated in the papers that these letters are written to injure Frank, but you and all others who will get up and testify against him . . . will see ere it is too late that these letters mean business. Every damned son of a bitch will be in hell before another year rolls over your damned prejudiced heads. Dick Liddil, the damned son of a bitch of a traitor will never live to see another year after that trial is over, and the damned Ford boys' days are numbered—and don't you forget it! Frank James has got hundreds of friends in New Mexico, and some of them are in Gallatin to-day and will be there until all is over, and every witness will be spotted. Frank James was not in any of the robberies or murders that he is now being tried for. His brother Jesse was there and done all the killing. Jesse had lots of men yet to kill when he died, and he would have killed them to-day, and by God, I will fight for Frank as long as there is a drop of blood in my body, and if Frank should be convicted, which he can not be without perjury, there will be a life for every hair in Frank's head and you will see it if

your life is spared long enough. You had better save this letter and keep it where you can get it in the future, and you or your friends can look at it sometime and say if we had only taken more notice of this letter and been careful and not taken it for a blow, many of our friends would live to-day, and hundreds of lives would have been saved. These threats will be carried out to the end, so help me God!

[signed] A Friend

The letter once again was not taken seriously. "It seems that the fools or cowards still have access to pen, ink and paper," a reporter wrote, summing up the situation.

★ ★ ★

Of all the men who rode into town for the trial, none, after Frank James, drew more stares from the public than Joseph Orville Shelby, former cavalry leader of the Confederacy, who hailed from Waverley, Missouri. The charismatic and eccentric Shelby, beloved war hero of Missouri, was a household name throughout the state long after the thunders of war had been stilled. The mere mention of his name was enough to make Confederate veterans remove their hats and bow their heads in reverence.

Beyond Missouri's borders the veneration stopped, however, and Shelby was often the butt of jokes, especially in the North. The *Chicago News*, for example, following the general's highly publicized debacle in court at Gallatin, lashed out at the old soldier: "This Shelby was during the war the leader of an unorganized band of horse thieves, a gang of night-prowling bandits who never knew what legitimate warfare was, and whose most gallant charges were made against unguarded chicken coops." Shelby's popularity in Missouri, however, was never hurt by such remarks. In fact, had his ambitions ever turned political, he would have been a shoo-in for governor of the state, but the old man never had use of politics and refused to let his reputation be sullied by such an association.

Shelby's unqualified allegiance to the men who had once born arms under him was proverbial; he supported and protected them no matter how small or insignificant the circumstances. While Frank and Jesse James had only served briefly in Shelby's brigade during one of his raids into Missouri, the general always considered them "my boys." After the war, Shelby opened his heart and his home to Frank and Jesse, their families, and even members of the gang whenever the need arose. Jesse even made an extended recuperation at Shelby's following a bank robbery in which he received a bullet wound in the chest.

Those who knew the old man would have said that there was nothing Shelby loved more than a good cause and a good fight. But he never understood when he had lost.

Born in Lexington, Missouri, in 1831, Shelby spent his early manhood farming and made a quite comfortable living growing hemp and making rope. When he left civilian life to fight in the Civil War, he showed himself to be a natural-born leader. He entered the rebel forces as a colonel in Kirby Smith's army, and although he had never had a lick of military training in his life, he soon demonstrated a remarkable prowess on the battlefield.

Shelby was one of a long list of successful horse-mounted raiders for the Confederacy that included men such as Mosby, Forrest, Morgan, Ashby, and Wheeler. All of them specialized in hit-and-run sorties behind Union lines aimed at disrupting lines of communication and supply, inflicting heavy losses in men and materiel, and damaging Yankee morale. The South seemed uncommonly blessed with such unconventional warriors, a factor that helped even the battle odds. While the rebel forces were lacking in numbers of men and weapons, these guerrilla leaders fostered an indomitable fighting spirit and a sense of pride and purpose in their soldiers.

Jo Shelby, in his mid-thirties, reed-thin, and youthful-looking, became a major general in command of a full division of Missouri cavalry. He made a striking figure astride his horse with his sharply angled face and sunken cheeks set off by a long, flowing chestnut beard. Shelby wore a black-felt campaign hat, with one side pinned up with a golden buckle and a long, sweeping, black ostrich feather planted firmly in the crown. The plume was his personal signature and a rallying point for his men amid the fire and smoke of battle.

Four years of cavalry command during the Civil War in Missouri and Arkansas transformed Shelby into a polished, professional soldier and a formidable foe. He never knew the meaning of the word defeat. His courage, gallantry, and uncanny intuition in battle earned him the unswerving love and devotion of his troops, as well as high praise and respect from the enemy. "The best cavalry general of the South," Union General Alfred Pleasanton once said of Jo Shelby. To the detriment of the Confederacy, however, the talents of Shelby and his cavalrymen were largely wasted.

They spent much of the war fighting rear-guard actions to protect forces retreating under less than able battlefield commanders.

For all the campaigns Shelby fought in as a Confederate soldier, he is best known not for what he did during the war, but for what he did after it. The story, chronicled by Shelby's official staff adjutant, Major John Edwards, is one of romance and pathos about one man's grandiose and preposterous dream.

In June 1865, the order to lay down arms reached Shelby in Eagle Pass, Texas, where he had gone to escape Sheridan's armies in hot pursuit. He was still in command of his men, the last unsurrendered contingent of Confederate troops in the field. It was ragtag lot, six hundred or so young, lean, and battle-hardened men, each armed with two or more revolvers, a heavy saber, and a new Sharps carbine. The procession moved along to the south slowly, kicking up a tall cloud of dust that could be seen for miles.

Jo Shelby, however, had no intention of surrendering; his thirst for blood had not yet been slaked. He didn't follow the normal rules of warfare, but did things his own way. A full two months after the formal surrender at Appomattox, he directed his lost division to proceed across the Rio Grande into Mexico, which was fighting a war against France. There, he said, he planned to fight on.

Shelby and his men were not alone in this bizarre expedition. His military ranks were swelled by an assortment of suddenly unemployed Confederate politicians—Senator Trusten Polk of Missouri and Governors Allen of Louisiana, Morehead of Kentucky, Reynolds of Missouri, and Murrah of Texas—who had nothing left to govern, and a handful of army generals—Sterling Price, Kirby Smith, John B. Magruder, John B. Clark, Oscar Watkins, and Simon Bolivar Buckner—who no longer had armies to lead. They all followed blindly in the footsteps of the cavalry commander, who led them onward into the great unknown, to a new war and a new glory perhaps, known only to Jo Shelby.

As he was about to leave the United States and cross over onto foreign soil, Shelby ordered a halt. In a brief ceremony, Shelby bid a personal farewell to the lost cause of the Confederacy. He folded up the battle-scarred banner of his cavalry division, slipping into its folds the black ostrich feather from his hat, and sank the sacred bundle in the muddy-brown waters of the Rio Grande. Much later in time the site would be mockingly referred to as the "graveyard of the Confederacy."

It was outside Piedras Negras on the Mexican side that Shelby encamped. There he held a meeting with a Mexican governor who said he ruled the states of Tamaulipas, Coahuila, and Nuevo Leon for the deposed president, Benito Juarez, who had been thrown out of office by the French and was hiding somewhere in Texas. Shelby proposed an outrageous scheme: he would take his army of disbanded Confederate soldiers and fight his way through to the capitol, Mexico City, force out the Austrian archduke, Emperor Maximilian, and return the country to Juarez. The plan was accepted.

History might have been rewritten had Shelby not taken the next step. He assembled his men, outlined the plan, and asked their opinion. To his surprise, they voted against it, unanimously. They suggested that they offer their services to the pretender, Maximilian, instead. Shelby assented and led his army of tattered troops to Mexico City, where, in an act of supreme irony and humiliation, Maximilian turned him down. With their hopes gone and dreams shattered, the loyal legion of Shelby's followers, roving soldiers of fortune, finally broke up and scattered to the winds.

Some went home. Others stayed on for a year or two at a colony established southwest of Mexico City near Cordoba on a large tract of land. The property, previously expropriated from the church by Juarez before his fall, had been bequeathed to Shelby and his men in a gesture of friendship by Maximilian. Carlotta, the Southerners called it, after the Austrian empress. Here the expatriates raised cotton and coffee and made a gallant effort to recreate the glory of the Dixie they had once known, complete with balls, receptions, and other elegant social events staged in faded, threadbare finery.

Shelby organized a freight service and ran supplies from the colony to the coast, General Price ran a plantation near Veracruz, and Major Edwards edited a newspaper. Supporters of Juarez, however, rose up in revolt, gained strength, and began driving out the French invaders. With the death of Maximilian and the overthrow of the protective puppet government, the death knell was sounded for the colony at Carlotta, and Shelby, along with the other Southern émigrés, was forced to leave the country.

And so they all came home, including the disillusioned Shelby, the vanquished knight errant of the Confederacy. He returned to find his home and fortunes gone. He had gambled and lost in his vainglorious and futile attempt to resurrect a new order of the South in Mexico [6–8].

Day 12   Closing Arguments

The object of oratory is not truth, but persuasion.
Thomas Babington Macaulay

September 1 was a Saturday and a short business day. The defense had concluded its case, and it was time for the state to make its final rebuttals before closing arguments began. Wallace and his colleagues had their hands full trying to recoup some of the momentum they had lost over the preceding two days.

Attorney Brosius was recalled to the witness stand and his memory picked as to exactly who and how many men entered the smoking car the night of the robbery. Then numerous witnesses, fellow passengers on the train, took the stand and impeached Brosius's evidence.

Mrs. Sarah Hite came forward to state that there was no physical resemblance at all between her dead brother-in-law, Wood Hite, and Frank James.

Silas Norris concurred, testifying that Wood Hite was not as tall as Frank and bore little likeness to the defendant. When Norris stepped down, the state and defense announced their cases concluded. The court adjourned until Monday.

★ ★ ★

The first week of the trial had come to an end, but signs of strain and fatigue were visible among the principals, especially the attorneys were failing to show up on time in court each morning. The audience, too, seemed tired after listening to the seemingly endless flow of witnesses, the exhaustive cross-examinations and reexaminations, and the constant verbal sniping engaged in by opposing attorneys.

Reporting the trial was particularly grueling. It was not unusual for a journalist to end up with one- to two-hundred pages of handwritten notes after a busy day in court. To those who happened to know it, shorthand was a godsend. When the gavel fell at day's end, the reporters' work was far from finished. Retiring to a quiet place, they deciphered and edited their hastily scribbled jottings and composed a synopsis of the day's activities, which then had to be transmitted by wire to their editorial offices.

This last act was made difficult by the fact that there was only one telegraph office in the entire town of Gallatin. One can imagine the frantic scene in the small office every night as a stream of tired newsmen converged on it to send off their official reports before retiring for the night.

The second week of the trial brought forth the attorneys' closing arguments, or "addresses to the jury," as they were called then. The Frank James trial had, by this time, drawn considerable attention across the country, a fact that had not escaped the notice of the trial attorneys. Knowing that they were players on a national stage, they stood on the brink of a once-in-a-lifetime opportunity, one that all trial lawyers dream of, namely, the chance to leave their mark on history. The temptation to grandstand was overwhelming.

It would take four days for the state and defense to deliver their final messages to the jury. The time was unusually long because each of the thirteen attorneys involved in the trial, six for the state and seven for the defense, were entitled to speak, as was the procedure of the day. The surplus of lawyers in the first place was due to the sensational nature of the trial.

Thus came that peculiar moment in a trial when its direction is taken over by the power of speech, when silver-tongued persuasion is used to transcend the facts and overturn evidence, and even deny common sense, in order to swing a jury's vote. It was time for the case to be judged by the weight of legal argument rather than the weight of testimony. It was time for the lawyers to become good actors, and the better actors they became, the better lawyers they were. Thus, on a few insufferably hot days in the autumn of 1883 the audience in the rickety opera house in Gallatin, Missouri, was treated to speaking performances worthy of the great stages of America. The wooden walls would soon reverberate with the sounds of history.

The two sides generally alternated, with William Wallace, the state's main spokesperson, scheduled to speak last. In all, nine speeches were given. Hamilton, Hicklin, Shanklin, and Wallace made addresses for the state; Glover, Garner, Slover, Philips, and Johnson did likewise for the defense.

Slated first were the less experienced or less glib attorneys who, for the most part, had remained silent at their duty posts during the long hours of the trial. Their important work was done in the privacy of their offices before and after the day's proceedings, rather than before the eyes and ears of the public. The primary purpose of these legal minions at summation time was not to make flowery speeches but to present the evidence in a straightforward way and establish basic lines of argument. Then their more articulate colleagues, the closers, would take over and restate the facts in far more persuasive language.

The big speaking guns were Philips for the defense and Wallace for the state. Each was unaccustomed to losing. The two men had uncommon flair, guile, and might and stood ready to expound, plead, cajole, demand, and beg in order to win the opinion of the jury.

Records of the Gallatin trial are incomplete. What some of the attorneys said at this stage of the trial remains unknown. Their speeches were unrecorded, and only summaries were reported in newspapers. The complete texts of the arguments given by Philips and Wallace, on the other hand, have been preserved. Over a hundred years later, they still make a profound impression. Their appeal is enhanced by the wonderfully expressive, if old-fashioned, language the orators used. The speeches are generously embellished with metaphors, aphorisms, similes, and quotations from the Bible and the classics. Added to both orations were liberal doses of sarcasm. It proved a weighty means of persuasion in the hands of both Philips and Wallace who, as masters of courtroom soliloquy, applied it with consummate skill and adroitness to tear down the opposition's painstakingly constructed arguments.

The forceful speeches entered the jurors' minds like the flow of a mighty tide, sweeping aside preconceived notions and staunch convictions. They could not help but vacillate back and forth. To hear Philips speak was to vote for acquittal; to hear Wallace was to vote for guilt—so well did the two courtroom titans argue.

Day 13   Testimony Revisited

The trial got a late start on Monday, September 3, 1883. The day was hot and muggy, as the heat spell, which had been building over the past few days, reached its peak and settled in for an uncomfortable stay. It wasn't until twenty minutes to ten that Judge Goodman finally entered the courtroom, having spent the early morning hours going over jury instructions. Court commenced and the instructions were handed to the attorneys.

Frank James, his face pale and wearing a conventional black suit, made his entrance with Sheriff Crozier. He exchanged a few words with Johnson, Glover, and Philips at the defense table. It was the first time during the trial that the defendant was seen speaking to his attorneys in court.

Ann Ralston James, Frank's wife (ca. 1870s). A devoted wife and mother, she was mostly responsible for getting her husband to abandon his life of crime. (Courtesy Jesse James Farm & Museum, Kearney, Missouri. Reprinted with permission.)

Mrs. Frank James, smartly dressed and leading her five-year-old son by the hand, followed shortly and took a seat to the left of her husband. She wore a high-necked gray dress and a short cape casually draped over her shoulders. Her long blond hair was rolled up and covered by a black hat sporting an ostrich plume of the same color. Generally one to adorn herself with a lot of jewelry, the defendant's wife wisely chose to tone down her appearance by wearing a solitary coral brooch pinned at the throat. Ann James "cannot be said to be handsome, but she has an intelligent face, and large, expressive gray eyes," one journalist noted. Another newsman, though, wrote that she carried a "weary, broken look" and a complexion "inclined to be sallow." Frank's son, described as "a bright looking, handsome little fellow of five years," received a good deal of attention from visitors and friends of the family.

The judge announced that each side would be given ten hours to present their closing arguments and then gave the order of the nine speeches. The state would speak first, fourth, seventh, and last, leaving the defense two opportunities to give back-to-back speeches. The case would then go the jury on Wednesday.

Mr. Hamilton read the state's instructions to the jury. Frank James was charged with three indictments, but only the first was presented to the jury. It stated in three counts that the defendant shot and killed passenger McMillan; that, as a member of the group of train robbers, the defendant was responsible for the death of McMillan, and that the defendant robbed the train at Winston.

When Hamilton finished, Colonel Philips rose and objected to the order of speeches, declaring them to be unfair. The court noted his objection and directed Philips to proceed, whereupon counsel read the defense's instructions to the jury.

When Philips finished, state's counsel Shanklin, in a rare display of courtroom courtesy, moved that the court extend the time allotted for the defense from ten to twelve hours since it had more lawyers. Judge Goodman, undoubtedly shocked by the fleeting thaw in icy relations, immediately granted the motion.

First to speak for the state was William Hamilton, prosecuting attorney of Daviess County. This was the public prosecutor's first murder trial and he was clearly nervous at the outset, but he soon became more at ease. Hamilton declared the trial the most remarkable in Missouri's history, made so primarily by the magnitude of the crimes committed by the defendant.

After paying a few compliments to the jury, Hamilton described in detail the train robbery at Winston and the shooting of McMillan.

The state bore no malice toward Frank James, Hamilton said, but the evidence showed positively that he was guilty. Then he prodded the jury with a challenge. Whether they considered the testimony of Dick Liddil or that given by the state's witnesses, he said, in either case they would find an abundance of evidence to convict the defendant. Taken together, the proof was overwhelming.

This was one of the cornerstones of the state's case, as laid out by William Wallace. He wanted the jury and the world to know that even without Liddil's testimony there was enough circumstantial evidence left to hang Frank James. Hamilton continued to pound away at this point, reviewing the substantiating testimonies in minute detail and mocking the defendant's lame alibi as "the last hope and refuge of thieves."

The prosecutor closed his arguments at eleven-thirty. Of all the speeches made to the jury, Hamilton's was the shortest, a little over an hour. The court recessed until one-thirty in the afternoon. After lunch, John Milton Glover stood before the jury to make the opening statement for the defense. The young man with the boyish face was the son of Samuel T. Glover, an eminent attorney whose firm, Glover and Shepley, enjoyed a fine reputation in St. Louis.

Counsel Glover started by summarily dismissing the testimonies of the Fords and Boltons. While he considered them to be honest people who believed they were telling the truth, he said they were mistaken. The remainder of Glover's speech, as expected, focused entirely on the four-man theory of the robbery. He reviewed the evidence given by the state, particularly that of Liddil and others who were on the train that night, and proclaimed categorically that none of it proved there were more than four men who took part in the holdup. Counsel added that the witness who claimed that Frank James was in the party in the smoking car mistook the defendant for Wood Hite. The attorney brought his arguments to an emphatic close at four o'clock. He had spoken for two hours and forty minutes.

Why Glover, relatively inexperienced in trials of this magnitude, was allowed to open the case for the defense puzzled some observers. It was a formidable undertaking, requiring experience and an analytical legal mind to evaluate all the evidence, isolate and attack weak points in the state's evidence, and marshal the strengths of the defense's evidence into a solid case. While Glover performed his role well, he constantly referred to or read aloud from hand-held notes. Yet despite some awkward pauses and an overall herky-jerky style delivery, the youthful lawyer presented an argument that the press judged to be "strong and impressive."

The last speaker of the day was defense counsel Christopher Trigg Garner. The elderly ex-colonel, the pride of Ray County and a well-respected patriarch of the court, added more prestige than substance to the proceedings. Garner's main function in the trial up to this point had been to keep the state's attorneys off balance by continually registering objections for the defense. This activity prompted one journalist to comment that the old man seemed to have a set of springs built into the seat of his pants.

Garner addressed the general lack of evidence on the state's part and was particularly harsh in his treatment of Liddil, the Fords, and the Boltons. He made an attempt to pick up the lines of argument established by Mr. Glover but in so doing traveled over much of the same testimonial ground as his colleague. It was far from a spellbinding oration. After talking for over two and a half hours, Garner had failed to make much of an impression on the jury. Around seven o'clock, he concluded his remarks.

The court adjourned until nine o'clock the next day. The defense attorneys continued to express their extreme displeasure at the speaking order established by Judge Goodman. They explained to the court that it was not right to sandwich Colonel Johnson between Shanklin and Wallace, thereby permitting the state to have, in effect, two speeches in closing instead of one. A more equitable arrangement, they felt, would be to have both Philips and Johnson speak after Shanklin. The judge, however, remained inflexible on the issue and refused to rescind his decision.

Day 14   Bombast and Brickbats

On September 4 the court reconvened to a standing-room-only crowd. The audience was swelled by many out-of-town lawyers (especially prosecuting attorneys from nearby counties), who had poured into Gallatin on the morning trains or those of the night before to hear their more esteemed colleagues address the jury.

As soon as court was in session, Joshua Hicklin began his address for the prosecution. His mission was to shore up the testimonies of Dick Liddil, the Fords, and the Boltons, which were catching the brunt of the defense's attack. Over the next two hours, Hicklin, in a blunt and driving manner, detailed the testimony given by state's witnesses, compared it to that given for the defense, weighed both for probability and logic, sifted out the false from the true, and, in the end, connected the state's evidence together into a solid argument against the defendant.

On the heels of Hicklin came defense attorney James H. Slover, partner in the law firm of Cummingo and Slover in Independence. (Slover had actually helped William Wallace win the Cathey case in 1877, which brought Wallace so much public acclaim, but now the two men were arguing on opposite sides.) Since it was close to noon now, the judge asked Slover if he wished to start, knowing that he might be interrupted by the midday recess. He replied that he could "stop his mental machinery at any time" but preferred to get on with his speech.

Slover was tall, thin, and handsome—a fact that did not go unnoticed by the ladies in the courtroom. "Just too cute for anything" was how one young woman described Slover as he made his debut in court on the day Liddil gave his testimony. Slover, however, was no ladies' man. The shy gentleman attorney would have blushed at such gushing remarks. This shyness made him an atypical lawyer. Unlike most of his colleagues, Slover, who guarded his privacy fiercely, deliberately avoided the public limelight. In fact, he almost never gave speeches in public and even refused to sit for photographs [9]. Shortly after eleven, Slover began his oration, speaking in a soft, quiet voice.

Slover spent most of his time elaborating on the four-man theory propounded the day before by defense counsel Glover, drawing support from the testimony given by Liddil and Daviess County witnesses for the defense. Speaking for slightly more than two hours, Slover declared that the state waged its case against the defendant for the benefit of those in high authority, namely, the "power and wealth of the great railroad corporations," and was aided in this effort by the perjury of Dick Liddil, the Fords, and the Boltons.

When Mr. Slover sat down, the court announced a brief recess of ten minutes. Few persons left their seats, though, for fear of losing them.

The rest of the afternoon belonged to John F. Philips, the smooth-talking trial lawyer from Kansas City, who spoke on behalf of Frank James. Although as leader of the defense team, Colonel Johnson had the traditional honor of speaking last for his side, it was acknowledged by many (including William Wallace) that Philips, far more renowned for his courtroom eloquence than Johnson, was the greater threat to the state's case.

Philips was fifty years old and at the peak of his career when he came to Gallatin. In name and prestige, he stood head and shoulders above William Wallace. For the past twenty-five years, Philips had faithfully served Missouri as lawyer, statesman, soldier, legislator, congressman, and supreme court commissioner, and later he served as a federal judge.

John Finis Philips was born in 1834 on a farm near Richland, Missouri. Regarding his unusual middle name, he liked to say, "I was born on the last day of the month in the last month of the year, the last child of a large family, and Finis is very appropriately my middle name." He attended the best schools in the area and later graduated from Centre College in Danville, Kentucky, where Thomas Crittenden was a classmate. Philips became interested in law and served an apprenticeship under John B. Clark of Fayette, Missouri. He was admitted to the Missouri bar in 1857 and immediately began his practice in Georgetown, where he first displayed his natural skills at courtroom pleading.

Philips was a devout Presbyterian and a strict and uncompromising constitutionalist. A Union man, he found his loyalty put to the supreme test in 1861 when, with war imminent, Missouri teetered on the brink of secession. The attorney's loud and outspoken stand on the need to preserve the nation soon led him, temporarily, on a path to politics. He was chosen as the Union delegate from his senatorial district to the state convention in 1861, which was holding discussions on the momentous question of secession. His forceful and moving speeches there helped bind the people of state to the Union, while the government of the state seceded.

He attracted the attention of Lincoln's newly appointed governor, Hamilton R. Gamble, who, when war was finally declared, commissioned Philips as a colonel in the Missouri militia and authorized him to raise a regiment of cavalry. At the war's end, Philips was breveted out as a brigadier general [10].

Philips's decision to defend Frank James was not based solely on sentiment. The attorney was strenuously opposed to capital punishment and refused to prosecute a man who faced a death sentence. He preferred to defend him. Philips looked upon himself and his profession as an important instrument in the protection of human rights. As for fees, it surprised no one in his legal circle that Philips took the James case without pay. He had never been a big-money lawyer. In fact, he liked to chide colleagues who took cases, not for the legal issues involved, but for the size of the fees.

Philips took satisfaction in defending the common man when he felt the cause was just.

If John Philips had a failing, it was perhaps that he talked too much. He sometimes got so carried away by his own words that he forgot (intentionally, some said) to address pertinent issues. Like many lawyers, he argued cases not so much from evidence and carefully constructed points of law but by using the sheer, crushing weight of words, especially when the evidence on his side was thin. In Philips's day this approach was sometimes referred to, with a wink, as "speaking by ear," and those who favored the style were called, with considerable disdain, "country lawyers." Today the term "country lawyer" is used more or less respectfully to refer to someone who exhibits certain pleasantly old-fashioned professional qualities. A century ago, the term did not have this positive connotation. John Philips was a product of a loose and freewheeling time in Missouri's history, the 1850s and 1860s, when the legal profession had lax entrance standards and did not enjoy a particularly savory reputation. Applicants to the bar were either self-educated at home or learned law through apprenticeship (as Wallace and Philips did), and many were examined and admitted under less than proper, and sometimes totally specious, circumstances. They tended to be judged less on knowledge of the written law than raw speaking talent and, more importantly, the influential people they knew. "Country lawyers" were good at making speeches at Fourth of July parades, schoolhouse dedications, and temperance meetings, but in a court of law they usually did not fare so well. Their indictments were usually quashed, and as a result few convictions stood to their credit.

To some people in the legal profession (Wallace included), Colonel Philips was the quintessential country lawyer. He was just a pontificating and self-righteous old windbag who liked to spout a lot of hot air in his narrow pursuit of justice, or to quote Shakespeare, "he draweth out the thread of his verbosity finer than the staple of his argument."

Attorney Philips stood and faced the jury. With his well-trimmed mustache, full cheeks, and gray-streaked hair, the attorney, some said, bore a striking resemblance to Otto von Bismarck, Germany's chancellor. For four solid hours, he filled the courtroom with long-winded and well-oiled oratory. To the members of the audience (and jury) who were sympathetic to the defendant, Philips's fell upon their ears like sweet chords of music. The rest heard only sentimental claptrap.

There was no real mystery about what Philips was going to say. The defense's strategy, for the most part, had been made clear since the second day of the trial: to denounce Dick Liddil and his testimony, refute evidence given by the Boltons, Fords, and other witnesses for the state, and make Frank James invisible during the robbery by pushing the four-men theory. In a speech peppered with folksy homilies, quotations from the Bible, analogies from Greek mythology, and incorporating cajolery, supplication, ridicule, and sarcasm, Philips led the opera house congregation down the golden path of truth as he saw it.

He opened with a few remarks to set the mood and soften up the audience. Philips recalled the bitter years of the war when "Frank James and I stood in mortal antagonism" and then blamed the brutalities and privations of that war for the formation of the James gang. He also remembered his heart "beating a little warmly" when he read of the prisoner's plan to "throw himself upon the justice of the law" and called Frank James "a brave man" for doing so. In just a few sentences, he reminded the jury of the defendant's faithful service to the Confederacy during the war and reinforced the popular notion that, by voluntarily surrendering, Frank James had performed a humanitarian deed. His aim was to show the jury that the defendant, despite his reputation, possessed a conscientious and caring side.

Philips next pronounced that "common fame has invested this defendant with unmerited notoriety." Calling public rumor a "false and a foul thing," the attorney went on to explain that Frank James had been blamed for every vicious crime committed "between the mountains of West Virginia and the Ozarks of Arkansas and Missouri within the last six years," skirting the fact that he was known to have had a hand in some of these crimes. According to Philips, Frank had already left the gang at the time of the Winston robbery and was living peaceably in Tennessee with his wife and child.

Then, moving into high gear, Philips turned to "that pink of a witness, Dick Liddil," the man who "should never have been permitted to pollute the Bible by taking the oath." For well over an hour, Philips attacked Liddil without mercy. He recounted details of the gang's activities in the few years preceding the affair at Winston as testified to by Liddil and then launched into a tirade on Liddil's character.

The name-calling and personal insults heaped on Liddil by the defense team and General Shelby earlier in the trial paled in comparison to Philips's all-out verbal onslaught. The attorney painted the state's witness variously as "a slimy serpent of evil," "prince of scoundrels and liars," "penitentiary graduate," and one "so morally dead that like Lazarus he stinketh in the nostrils of every honest man." Thrown in for added effect were more common epithets such as "perjurer," "wretch," "rogue," and "panderer." In effect, he argued that anyone as bad as Liddil, a convicted horse thief, was incapable of telling the truth. (Naturally, he avoided drawing a similar conclusion about his own client, Frank James.)

Philips made a big issue of Liddil turning state's evidence over the shooting of Wood Hite. In the counsel's mind, this was an unspeakable, cowardly, and unmanly thing to do—arguing the point not from truth but from morality. "Yes, he turned patriot—the last refuge of a scoundrel," Philips thundered triumphantly. The despicable act, he said, added to Liddil's "crown of infamies, the words: informer and perjurer." It was a trump card, the accusation of a traitor, which was sure to strike home with the jury. Whether there was a single word of truth in Liddil's statements seemed to matter not. The witness was simply "unworthy of belief," according to defense counsel.

Finally tearing himself away from Liddil, Philips paused to poke fun at the prosecution's unrelenting pursuit of Ann James's sewing machine, remarking, "Wallace has run that machine down with the whole detective force of two railroads and all the express companies between Kentucky and Kansas." Referring sarcastically to the mundane article as a "remarkable piece of evidence," Philips conjectured further that the state had planned to use the testimony about the sewing machine as a substitute for Liddil's story, if the former gang member were barred from telling it.

The next order of business on Philips's list was to neutralize the testimony given by the Fords, the Boltons, and the rest of the state's witnesses, whose evidence placed Frank James in the vicinity of Winston before and after the robbery. Again, Philips ignored the evidence and concentrated on personalities.

Mattie Bolton was "a bad woman," Philips proclaimed, and, in fact, "her whole family are wicked and degraded." The attorney went on to ridicule Mrs. Bolton for her behavior on the day Wood Hite was shot and killed in her dining room, when she had entertained guests in the parlor all afternoon while Hite's bloody corpse lay upstairs. Based on her actions and insistence that she did not see Hite's body that day at all, Philips drew the conclusion that she was lying, and continued to lie in her other testimony.

Using this ridiculous premise, Philips went on to impugn Mattie's children as "chips off the old block" who "reflect the teachings of the dragon that bred them." They were liars too, according to Philips.

The Fords and the rest of the local townspeople who claimed to have seen Frank in the area of the robbery and murder were also untrustworthy. "How unreliable is the judgment, how fallible the human mind, in a matter of identity," Philips propounded, stressing how much Wood Hite and Frank James looked alike. These good citizens (whose honesty was not at question) had made a mistake.

Philips then moved ahead and belabored a crucially important point: that Liddil's testimony had to be substantiated beyond a reasonable doubt. He spoke at length on the various instructions given to the jury by the court. In particular, he focused on the need for corroboration of Liddil's testimony and the conditions for convicting a defendant using evidence given by an accomplice in crime:

"You, gentlemen of the jury, must not forget in your deliberations that this corroboration . . . must be material, independent, facts showing the actual presence of the prisoner . . . at the time and place of the homicide. . . . Who corroborates Dick Liddil that Frank James was present at the homicide? . . . No one saw him; no one pretends to have recognized him there. Who shot the deceased, McMillan, or how the person did it, no one knows, so far as we can judge from this testimony. . . . Outside of Liddil's testimony, there is not a man on this jury who can place his hand on his heart and say that the prisoner was within ten miles of the tragedy. To sacrifice the life of Frank James at the behest of popular prejudice and clamor is to wound and cut down the spirit of justice, and murder liberty at the altar. . . . Let your verdict be his vindication."

Philips continued to drum into the heads of the jurors that only four men were involved in the robbery. More than enough reasonable doubt existed over the identification of Frank James to find the defendant innocent of charges.

Philips's arguments sounded plausible, but only on an emotional level. A flaw of logic prevented them from constituting reasonable rebuttal of state's evidence. By declaring all testimony incriminating Frank James to be a pack of lies, how could Liddil's testimony—or that from any of the state's witnesses, for that matter—possibly be verified?

Certainly no corroboration could be expected from the men involved in the robbery. Of the five who purportedly held up the train, three were already dead: Jesse James, Clarence Hite and Wood Hite. According to the defense, the fourth man, Frank James, didn't count because he was on trial. The fifth man, Dick Liddil, didn't count either, because, as Philips and his staff maintained, he had lied on the stand. The defense had made it impossible for anyone to substantiate Liddil's testimony under these conditions. Although the high-powered and effusive speech made by Colonel Philips, was pure humbug, it provided a crutch to jurors who were inclined to excuse the defendant's past.

But Philips was not quite through yet. There still remained pressing need to beef up Frank James's alibi.

The defendant had been forced to move around the South, Mr. Philips said, because the "miseries and ghosts of the war hung around his footsteps in Missouri." The former rebel raider found a new home and a new life on a farm in Nashville. James couldn't have committed any crimes in Missouri from the spring of 1876 to the spring of 1881 because he never was there. He was either in Nashville or in Texas, as he had testified.

To cover the glaring paucity of testimony substantiating Frank's presence in Texas at the time of the Winston robbery, Philips conjured up another argument. Traveling alone and staying with relatives, Frank James had no occasion to use hotels, Philips explained. Furthermore, the defendant had to exercise extreme caution in moving about and making acquaintances for fear of being found out. As a result, only his relatives could vouch for the defendant's travels to and from Texas.

At the end of his speech, Colonel Philips made a final plea for justice: "To convict this man because some town politician or public clamor demands it, would not only be cowardice but judicial murder. The men who cry out for the life of the so-called outlaw, no matter what the proof or the law, are themselves outlaws and demons. No, gentlemen, this court house is the temple of justice. The voice of clamor, the breath of prejudice, must not enter here. . . . Do your duty. Stand and stand forever on your oaths. . . . Let you verdict be a loyal response to the evidence and the spirit of the law." The court adjourned for the noon hour as Philips sat down, exhausted.

★ ★ ★

On the day of defense's first closing statements, a letter from Dick Liddil to General Shelby was published in the *Kansas City Evening Star* on

September 4. Liddil had judiciously skipped town and returned to Kansas City as soon as his testimony was over. In so many words, Liddil called Shelby a liar, saying he felt compelled to set the record straight. The letter also expressed indignation at the slurs Shelby had made against Liddil during the trial.

> Since coming back from Gallatin where I went as a witness in the Frank James trial, I notice that the papers quoted General Shelby as having used the most abusive language against me in connection with my testimony against Frank James. I think General Shelby has gone outside the trial to abuse me, well knowing that what he might say would go to the public.
>
> His story before the jury at Gallatin is not supported by the evidence, and was badly broken by Mr. Wallace. His statement that he met me after the Winston robbery with Cummings in Lafayette county is not so. I never saw General Shelby but twice in my life before going to Gallatin, and that was in the fall of 1880 near his house, after the Glendale robbery.
>
> I went there with Jim Cummings by appointment with Jesse James and Bill Ryan, both of whom arrived the same evening. At that time, General Shelby claims to have seen me (the year of the Winston robbery). Jim Cummings and Jesse James were not on good terms, and it was well known by all of us that Jesse and Frank were looking for Jim to kill him, and had been since he left them at Nashville. Under these circumstances, I could not have been in General Shelby's locality at the time he mentioned.
>
> Since my surrender to the state through Sheriff Timberland and Captain Craig, I have acted in good faith, doing everything that I promised to do, and neither General Shelby nor anyone else can frighten me into doing otherwise. I surrendered for reasons known to the officers and myself, and propose to remain as I am until my services are no longer needed, and am not to be driven away. This is for the eyes of General Shelby, for the friends of Frank James, and the public at large.

[signed] James A. Liddil

The adversarial roles played by Shelby and Liddil had a profound bearing on the outcome of the trial, specifically in connection with Frank James's alibi. There were many others in Gallatin at the time of the trial who, like Shelby, regarded Frank James as a hero and Dick Liddil as a treacherous liar and a thief. But if excuses were to be made for either, most would have chosen Liddil. Liddil was an ignorant man, born and raised in rough, uncultured surroundings, while James was the son of a Baptist clergyman brought up in a God-fearing household. There was no reason why Frank James should have become a robber and a murderer; he became such because the man was by nature cold and vicious. Dick Liddil, on the other hand, was probably made what he was, not by choice, but by his environment.

Day 15   Point and Counterpoint

The trial was drawing to a close and attendance on September 5 was large but not excessive. Among the visitors were U.S. Senators Kenna of West Virginia and Ingalls of Kansas. The entire morning was taken up with a speech by John H. Shanklin of the state's team. Shanklin was an ex-colonel in the Union army, one of the area's most distinguished attorneys, and immediate past president of the Missouri Bar Association. In his professional past, he had had a close association with the railroads, which caused the state considerable grief because it had to constantly refute vicious pretrial rumors that the Frank James trial was a "railroad prosecution."

The colonel, a tall, thin, and gangly man, wore a long, black alpaca coat that hung loosely over his frame like a horse blanket draped over a sawhorse. He was partially bald, with gray, bushy eyebrows and white chin whiskers tinged with a little dash of yellow, the telltale sign of a man who enjoys a chew of tobacco. His face and neck were bright red, almost purple, and were perpetually bathed in sweat.

The lawyer from Trenton was not a particularly graceful or polished public speaker; he used plain words, sometimes a bit crude or corny, and even plainer logic. He was clearly not in the same league as the more able speakers in the courtroom at Gallatin such as Philips or Wallace. What the Colonel lacked in oratorial skills, however, was more than made up for by his dignified, imposing looks, and rich and resounding bass voice. When Shanklin spoke, people listened.

Precisely at nine o'clock the state's counsel started his speech. His first remarks were meant to set the record straight; he flatly denied he was at Gallatin as attorney for the Chicago and Rock Island Railroad, adding that he had severed all professional ties to the railroad over twenty months ago. If that railroad company had utilized the means at its disposal to bring Frank James to justice, by contributing to Crittenden's reward, counsel concluded, it had only done its duty.

Next Shanklin exposed the fallacy of Mr. Philips's argument of the day before, specifically that the defendant's criminal past could be blamed on his having been on the losing side of the war. Drawing parallels between Frank James and General Cockrell, Senator Vest, and Attorney General McIntyre (all close friends of Philips, not so coincidentally), Shanklin pointed out that the latter three also fought for the Confederacy but had no trouble forgetting the past and building new lives for themselves in post-war Missouri. The defendant, too, might have become a law-abiding citizen, Shanklin explained, but he chose not to, becoming an outlaw instead. It was a matter of personal choice, not social circumstances.

The rest of Shanklin's speech was devoted to going over all the testimony corroborating that given by Liddil, as he hammered away at the defendant like a blacksmith at the anvil. True to form the plain-speaking Shanklin referred to the outlaw brothers as the "Jeems boys," described the train passengers as "skeered and excited," and, like all the other lawyers involved in the case, constantly spoke of "the great state of Missourah." He clung to his line of argument with a death-like grip, piling up the evidence. He doggedly retraced Frank James's movements from Nashville to Winston, like a bloodhound on his trail, to puncture his alibi and show that James was indeed in Winston at the time of the murder and robbery. This so-called argument of locality was the foundation of the state's case against Frank James. He reminded the jury that the eleven men who swore to seeing the defendant in the vicinity of Winston around the time of the robbery were residents of Daviess County and were all known to be truthful men.

Shanklin never made a misstatement, never repeated himself, never glossed over any point of evidence, and never used a word that the dullest of juries could not understand. The only time emotion rose during his speech was when he came to the tragic shooting of McMillan. There was a touch of manly grief in Shanklin's voice when he spoke of the poor stone-mason who was brutally murdered in a setting of presumed security.

The attorney's speech could not match the rich imagery, glowing rhetoric, and captivating eloquence of the one made by Colonel Philips, but he had presented a remarkably powerful argument, built on logic, that welded together all the pieces of evidence against the defendant, link by link.

★ ★ ★

At the noon recess, the jury marched out with the bailiff and the audience followed. They filed down the steps of the old opera house into the warm sunshine. Many of the male element headed without delay to the local saloon. (Because of an exorbitant liquor license fee of eight hundred dollars, and the prevailing strength of local temperance laws, the entire population of Daviess County and the town of Gallatin was served by a single saloon.) Seated in a large, unadorned room, the thirsty male crowd discussed details of the trial over a cool drink. When the slaking rite was over, they returned to the opera house.

★ ★ ★

The afternoon session was due to open at one-thirty, but so great was the public's enthusiasm to hear the closing arguments of Mr. Johnson and Mr. Wallace that they began arriving at the opera house a full hour ahead of time. By one o'clock, not a single person more could fit inside the packed hall. A large contingent of women were seated on the stage in back of the judge's table, and all the distinguished visiting senators and lawyers sat near the trial attorneys within the bar.

The defense's last chance to address the jury came when ex-lieutenant governor Charles P. Johnson rose to speak. One of the best-known criminal trial attorneys in the state of Missouri, he had come to Gallatin in the twilight of his career to lend his skillful hand and influential voice on behalf of Missouri's greatest criminal. It would be Johnson's last big case.

Johnson was a quiet man well known for his temperate habits and puritanical outlook on life. A Kansas City newspaper referred to him as "the author of the law that makes gambling a felony, and who wishes to make an indulgence in beer and other beverages, save water, the same thing." Slender and clean-shaven, Johnson was clad in a black coat, the standard courtroom uniform of the day.

Johnson's first words to the jury were spoken in such a low voice that they could not be heard by the audience. But within moments, his melodious voice reached everyone in the opera house, including those standing in the farthest corners of the room with their backs pressed against the wall. The colonel spoke first of duty, first to his client and then as an officer of the court. He then directed his attention to the jury and stated that, under the terms of the indictment and the judge's instructions, they must either convict the defendant or let him go free.

Johnson then began to delve into the evidence given by the state's witnesses. He echoed the points made the day before by Colonel Philips: Dick Liddil was a murderer, a liar, and a traitor and should not be believed. The same went for the other witnesses, whose testimonies were presented as "confirmations strong as proofs of holy writ," and were no different from Liddil's. Johnson also brought out one of the defense's main themes by spouting forth in highly sentimental rhetoric on the subject of Frank James's loving concern for his wife, his child, his mother, and his sister.

The defense attorney's argument, based on the fallacy of circumstantial evidence, stressed that the eleven witnesses who claimed they had seen Frank James in Daviess and Ray counties around the time of the robbery had made a mistake. At no point did he construct a defense for the defendant; that is, he never posed, or answered, the simple question, "Where was Frank James on the night of the Winston robbery?" Instead, the attorney droned on for three hours with sanctimonious pleading, until the jury, judge, and spectators grew weary. One man, though, was listening intently. Frank James glanced back and forth between Philips and the jury, the press reported, with a beseeching look on his face.

The lead counsel for the defense closed his remarks with yet another sentimental story, this one of questionable authenticity. Johnson told how once in St. Louis he had watched a five-story building on fire. In one of the upper windows he spotted a man trapped in the flames with no means of escape. His wife stood below in the street with a look of helpless anguish on her face. Her prayers were answered when, miraculously, a fireman snatched the doomed victim from the inferno and carried him to her loving arms.

The analogy between the St. Louis couple and Frank and Ann James, with the fireman being the jury, was quite obvious. While to some it may have been a heartwarming story, to the state it was a predictable end to a pitiful speech, and another example of the sentimental rubbish Johnson was trying to foist off on a gullible audience. Nonetheless, Johnson's speech was considered by many in the audience to be a magnificent piece of oratory, and when he sat down at four-thirty, there was a spontaneous burst of applause from the gallery.

By now, the late afternoon sun was casting long shadows on the courtroom floor. Some hoped that there would still be time for Mr. Wallace to deliver his closing remarks, but the judge declared that the jury, having listened to arguments for six hours, was tired. Court was therefore adjourned until the following morning.

★ ★ ★

Later that evening Johnson received six bouquets of flowers from lady admirers in appreciation of his fine speaking effort in court. Johnson, along with Phillips, planned to stay in Gallatin until a verdict was reached. Their colleagues—Garner, Slover, and Glover—had already returned home.

At no time since the beginning had there been as much talk in town about the trial. The closing arguments of Shanklin, for the prosecution, and Johnson, for the defense, were both considered quite convincing. Speculation soared as to what effect William Wallace's speech would have on the direction of the trial and what the verdict would be. Gallatin and the expectant world would have the answer within twenty-four hours.

Day 16   Judgment Day

> Furl that banner for 'tis weary,
> Round its staff 'tis drooping dreary;
> Furl it, fold it, let it rest.
> —From Wallace's closing arguments

As the court opened on the last day of the Frank James trial, September 6, the opera house was packed with spectators who had come to see and to hear the special prosecutor sum up the state's case. Johnson's grand speech of the day before was still ringing in the ears of the townspeople. As one newspaper reported, friends of the defendant felt confident of victory, believing that no one could overcome the forcefulness and logic of Johnson's speech.

It was up to William H. Wallace, the fighting attorney from Jackson County, to convince the jury of Frank James's guilt. For the last three days, the defense attorneys, in over twelve hours of argument on behalf of the defendant, twice as much as that used by the prosecution, had worked to sway the jury. Wallace knew as well as any other level-headed observer that what the defense had offered was largely heart-tugging drivel designed to draw sympathy for Frank James. It would difficult for Wallace to bring the jurymen back to reality and make them pass judgment on hard evidence.

Wallace was certainly not inferior to the likes of Johnson and Philips in his speaking abilities. Like a modern-day Cicero, he could turn a phrase, recite grandiloquent verse from Homer or Horace or other ancient poets and philosophers, and punctuate his speech with pithy quotes from the Bible.

In short, he could magnetize a jury as well as, if not better than, Johnson and Philips. The difference was that Wallace confined his comments to facts.

Wallace had already deemed the jury to be prejudiced and knew it would be an uphill battle to win them over. He also knew that if he lost the case, the best that could be mustered against Frank James, all hope of sending him to the gallows, let alone prison, would vanish forever. Everything was riding on the attorney's performance that morning.

Judging from what he was about to say, Wallace had no intention of beating the defense at their own game. He saw no advantage in using emotionally charged oratory or diversionary tactics. Instead, Wallace discharged his duties in a thoroughly professional way; he presented the incriminating evidence in hand in the hope that it would influence the jury.

In the courtroom that morning, the dark-haired and rather handsome attorney, with his short, neatly trimmed mustache and sideburn whiskers, looked relaxed and collected, seemingly oblivious to the grave task that lay before him. His calm demeanor belied the fact that he had faced threats on his life during the course of the trial.

Twice he had been challenged to duels (not counting Shelby's veiled threat on the witness stand), and twice he stood up to the callers. Both backed down. Wallace said with dry humor that it took more courage to decline or ignore an invitation to the "field of honor" than to accept one. A more serious threat came one evening, as Wallace prepared to take a horseback ride out into the country, his way of relaxing after each day's session, when he was warned that a noted gunslinger planned to shoot him on sight. Undaunted, Wallace took his ride anyway, and continued to do so every night for the remainder of the trial.

The attorney exuded a strong sense of confidence, one that came from knowing he was master of the situation and intimately familiar with every detail of the trial that had transpired over the last two weeks. The time came for Wallace to speak. When the room became quiet, the judge turned to the prosecutor and said, "Mr. Wallace, proceed with your argument." It was twenty minutes before nine when the youthful William Wallace rose to his feet and trained his sharp blue eyes on the men in the jury. Few likely noticed that the public prosecutor, as he began speaking, did so extemporaneously, drawing entirely upon his memory.

Attorney Wallace got down to business by attacking several points made by the defense. They were smokescreens as far as the prosecutor was concerned, thinly disguised attempts to generate sympathy for the defendant and excuse his wrongdoings.

The first concerned the influence of the war, and specifically its lingering emotional impact on various principals involved in the trial. The defense had used the trial as a public forum to reenact the war and stir up old feelings. General Shelby was the most flagrant example, swaggering into court and unfurling the faded colors of the Confederacy, and treating the ex-Quantrill raider like a hero.

Philips and Johnson had milked this theme of a Confederate hero gone bad. They blamed the war and the immediate post-war period for emotionally scarring Frank James and turning him against civilized society. Wallace attempted to expose this preposterous claim by recounting his own painful experiences of the war.

Northwest Missouri was originally settled by Tennesseans and Kentuckians, and at the outbreak of the Civil War these people naturally became sympathetic to the South's cause. Wallace's father, a minister of the Presbyterian church, was a Kentuckian by birth who owned slaves and was a staunch Confederate supporter. All of these factors spelled trouble for the clergyman and his family.

Prosecutor Wallace recalled how, as a teenage boy too young to fight, he, too, had faced the dangers and suffered the privations of the great war, but he held no malice against those who participated in it, even Union General Ewing. He was the man who promulgated and enforced Order No. 11 of August 23, 1863, which punished Confederate sympathizers in Jackson, Cass, Bates, and Vernon Counties in western Missouri and practically depopulated Cass and Bates Counties in the process. William Wallace vividly recalled how his father's land was burned and the family was forced out of their home in Lees Summit to "wander as outcasts and refugees in this world" before eventually finding a haven in nearby Fulton. Arguing that the war was long over and best forgotten, Wallace scolded the defense for dredging it up and using it as a convenient apology and rallying cry for Frank James.

The state's attorney also could not resist the temptation to take a few shots at the esteemed panel of lawyers lined up against him at Gallatin, who had gone out of their way to ridicule the Jackson County prosecutor for horning in on a case outside his jurisdiction. He lauded their credentials in half-mocking language, one by one. For Colonel Garner, Wallace had special "praise." He referred to the aged attorney as a "grim old lion whose deep voice has been heard reverberating in all the courts up and down the

Missouri Valley for thirty years or more, and beneath whose thunders I trembled when he turned on me, for it is said he has been accustomed . . . to eat a young lawyer raw for breakfast whenever his appetite calls for so delicate a dish."

Wallace's aim was not to draw laughs. To the contrary, he was earnestly imploring the jury not to be seduced by the defense's soaring flights of rhetoric. "Such, gentlemen, are the giants whom the prisoner has called forth to fight his battle with the law," Wallace concluded. Then he ridiculed their futile efforts to "stay back the resistless tide of evidence."

With sincere apologies, Wallace went on to pay his respects to the forgotten man whose name had scarcely been mentioned since the day the trial began, Frank McMillan, the fallen victim of the Winston train robbery and the reason for the prosecution of Frank James at Gallatin.

The public attorney surprised many by briefly expressing profound respect and sympathy for Frank James's wife, who, according to Wallace, remained blind to the faults of her husband but nonetheless possessed the love, courage, and devotion to stand faithfully by his side through all the rough times.

Wallace last turned his attention to Frank James, calling the accused a cold-blooded killer, and not the saintlike model depicted by the defense team. Certainly he was not "one of the most remarkable men of the age," as defense attorney Rush had called him. Wallace reminded the jury of God's laws, "Thou shalt not kill," and the penalty for committing murder: "He that sheddeth man's blood, by man shall his blood be shed." Frank James, the prosecutor charged, "has willfully and deliberately broken that law." Then Wallace beseeched the jury, "You can not on your sacred oaths do otherwise than inflict the penalty he so richly deserves."

Wallace concluded this segment of his speech by posing the question, "Which is stronger in Missouri, the arm of the bandit or the arm of the law?" After the trial, this query would become the catchphrase for Wallace's oration.

Wallace also took time to insist that the James trial was not a "railroad prosecution." This false rumor had been circulated by the defense even before the trial started, he said. Based on Colonel Shanklin's close relationship with the state's major railroads, it was meant to impugn the state's motives, but it also tapped the deep hatred harbored by average Missourians toward the rich and powerful railroad barons. Wallace knew this was another ploy to gather public support for the defendant that needed to be addressed.

The prosecutor announced that his own hands were clean of any connection to the railroad companies. Furthermore, he was proud to say, he had paid his own way to Gallatin from Kansas City on the Rock Island train, and fully expected to pay his own way back, too.

The next matter was a critical one dealing with the jury instructions. Wallace, putting himself in the place of an average jurist, saw in the formality a number of pitfalls. The defense, he realized, was trying to force the jury into an acquittal verdict by creating the false impression that if no eye witness could come forward and swear conclusively that Frank James was the one who actually pulled the trigger of the gun that killed McMillan, the defendant was innocent of the charge of murder. What the defense neglected to mention was that if Frank James was "present, aiding, abetting, or counseling" someone who did shoot and kill the stonemason, then the defendant was equally guilty of first-degree murder.

The defense was doing what Wallace called "technical gimlet-boring," that is, creating holes in the evidence that would enable the jury to let the defendant off the hook. At issue specifically was how many robbers were on the train at Winston and whether Frank James was one of them.

The public prosecutor attempted to replace an argument based on "gimlet-holes" with one based on common sense. "Five men rob a train," he explained. "All five of them have navy pistols strapped to their persons, loaded and charged with powder and ball; a man is killed in that robbery, and the human mind exclaims instinctively—they are guilty, every last single one of them. They came prepared to kill. They did kill. It is murder!" Wallace appealed to the jury: "I will tell you, gentlemen, it was murder in them all, damned and foul, and you can make nothing else out of it!"

There remained yet another problem that demanded Wallace's urgent attention. The members of the jury were farmers, many of whom had had little or no formal education. To them the technical terminology in the long and involved legal instructions must have sounded like a foreign language. Using a tone of voice that was neither demeaning nor condescending, Wallace, like a country schoolmaster guiding his students through a difficult lesson, read through each set of instructions, explaining them word for word. He defined key words such as "willfully," "deliberately," "premeditatively," and "malice aforethought." He carefully differentiated between murder in the first degree and murder in the second degree.

Some instructions, in Wallace's view, required special clarification and emphasis. One of them concerned testimony given by a defendant in his or her defense and how it was left for the jury to decide how much was credible and how much was not. Just as the defense had cast doubt on Dick Liddil's credibility, it was now Wallace's turn to do the same with Frank James. "His life is at stake, and he sits in the witness chair with the fearful picture of the gallows constantly before his eyes. If ever a man would swear falsely, it is then," the prosecutor exclaimed confidently.

Wallace also stressed another instruction understandably avoided by the defense team: "The jury may convict on the testimony of an accomplice without any corroboration of his statements," assuming, of course, that the facts offered to the court by other witnesses were at least partially supportive. It was far too late to undo all the damage that been done, but Wallace derived some small measure of satisfaction from proving that the defense had made a calculated bluff in demanding what amounted to full corroboration of Liddil's testimony.

Wallace also went over the most important instruction of all, not to convict the defendant if there remained any "reasonable doubt" in their minds. Presenting the hypothetical situation of two farmers arguing over how to grow a good crop, the state's counsel was able to demonstrate what constitutes "real and substantial" doubt, and what does not. The simple bucolic yarn was perfectly tailored for the jury.

Lastly, Wallace informed the jury members that if they found the defendant guilty as charged, they were not required to set the punishment, be it prison or the gallows. That, counsel assured them, was the responsibility of the court.

Those who had been impressed with the logic and comprehensiveness of Shanklin's speech the day before were in for an even greater performance from Wallace. Riding a wave of oratorical momentum, he drove home the state's case by reviewing the evidence.

From the assorted travels of Ann James's sewing machine to the type of boots worn by Jesse James, from the piece of broken bridle picked up near the railroad tracks after the robbery to the identification of the little bay mare in a stable in Liberty, Wallace took all the bits of information and methodically molded them into a virtually airtight case of circumstantial evidence against Frank James.

Wallace reconstructed the story of the gang's formation in Nashville, its eventual migration into Missouri, and the perpetration of the train robbery and double murder at Winston. It was based entirely on testimony provided by various state's witnesses. One by one the prosecutor identified each witness for the jury and recounted their incriminating evidence with unerring and deadly accuracy.

Among the points of evidence, Wallace argued, the weightiest concerned the number of men who participated in the Winston robbery. Was it four or five? The answer to this question was vital to Wallace's argument. The prosecutor knew that the four-man hypothesis was a desperate measure on the defense's part to draw attention away from Frank James's tenuous alibi—a courtroom dodge that Wallace described to the jury as "an insult to your intelligence."

The issue essentially boiled down to whether two or three robbers entered the nightmarish scene in the smoking car that night on the train. The defense contended there were only two—a supposition supported only by the confused and easily impeached testimony of attorney Brosius. Going further on a limb, the defense purported that the man who cut the bell rope was not one of the robbers at all, but some mysterious person, presumably a train official, whose identity they boldly claimed was deliberately being withheld by the railroad company and the state's team of lawyers.

Wallace buried this preposterous argument with an avalanche of contradictory evidence. Beginning with Major McGee's sworn statement that "three men entered the car, I am certain," Wallace enumerated and thoroughly described each of the five named robbers seen around Winston before and after the robbery. He listed their distinguishing physical characteristics (even the type of mustache and beard) based on sworn testimony and, for the sake of completeness, did the same for each of the horses the five men rode.

Up until this point, prosecutor Wallace had never once mentioned the name of Dick Liddil, or relied on Liddil's testimony to draw any conclusions. All the evidence covered so far was provided by other witnesses. Wallace's aim was to show how strong the state's case was without Liddil (and, of course, not to flaunt Liddil's name before the jury).

Attorney Wallace then turned his attention to shoring up the testimony of his main witness, not an easy task after the constant bashing Liddil had been subjected to during the trial. "Let us now examine Liddil's testimony, not him, but his testimony." With painstaking care, Wallace went over the majority of Liddil's evidence and showed that, by his own count, fifty-six material instances were corroborated by other witnesses. "With all these details, he is not contradicted in a single instance," the attorney declared.

Wallace summarized Liddil's testimony as follows: "No man could manufacture such a story, carrying it along with hundreds of details over a distance of sixteen hundred miles, without contradicting himself, much less have scores of witnesses come in and corroborate him at every point."

While enumerating the defense's efforts to contradict Liddil's story, he referred specifically to the testimony provided by General Shelby, declaring that Shelby had lied on the stand. The accusation prompted an angry interruption from Colonel Philips: "Mr. Wallace, do you mean to say that I, as an attorney, would write out a false question and put it to a witness?" The prosecutor rephrased his comment by placing the blame on Shelby, who, he declared to the jury, had asked defense counsels to write out the questions he would be asked and then let the defense team coach his replies.

Of the state's witnesses then discussed in turn by the prosecutor, one stood out in particular: Reverend Matchett. The preacher who, in Wallace's words, "notices minutiae like a woman," told on the stand how he quizzed his uninvited and mysterious dinner guests and found one of them to be quite familiar with Shakespeare, even to the point of reciting passages from the poet's plays. He was referring, of course to the man Wallace claimed was Frank James. With a note of triumph in his voice, Mr. Wallace remarked: "A man, gentlemen, may change the exterior of his person, but he can not change the complexion of the mind within. This is a most remarkable mental characteristic for a western bandit. To say that it is nothing uncommon for a train robber to go through the land spouting Shakespeare is preposterous."

William Wallace made light of Frank James's feeble alibi, or, as the prosecutor preferred to call it, "attempted alibi." Wallace found it almost amusing to reiterate the defendant's stock answer, "can't remember," to a number of the state's questions concerning his trip to Texas. It led Wallace to comment, "He [James] is one of those alibi witnesses seen quite often in our courts who bobs up and swears to one single fact, and then falls back forever into the oblivion of forgetfulness."

The prosecutor was nearing the end of his speech. He made it clear that under no circumstance should Frank James be acquitted because he "surrendered" and called the idea a fanciful and self-serving notion. The truth was that the defendant's days were numbered as the gang crumbled around him, "when, as the last one of the band, he was left helpless and alone, and the messengers of the law were hot upon his tracks." That was why James surrendered, Wallace explained.

In the same vein, Wallace urged the jury not to acquit the accused because the defendant "was a soldier in the lost cause." It was on the subject of the war that Wallace had started his speech, and it was also where he ended it. "Why unfurl the old Confederate banner here?" asked Wallace, begging the jury not to confuse any aspect of the rebel cause in Frank James's case with "pillage, plunder, train robbery and murder." The ghosts of Robert E. Lee, Stonewall Jackson, Sterling Price, and "all the gallant host of southern chiefs" would say no to this perverted thought, counsel proclaimed. It was not respect for the Confederacy that led the James gang to Winston to rob a train and shoot down two passengers, Wallace said; it was "money, money, money."

The prosecutor closed his remarkable oration by pointing out to the jury that if it acquitted the defendant in the face of the overwhelming evidence against him, it would be a greater stain upon the state than all the robberies committed in the state since the war. Wallace's final words were quoted from the scriptures: "Gentlemen, my task is ended. May 'God who ruleth in the armies of Heaven and doeth his pleasure amongst all inhabitants of the earth,' 'who holdeth the hearts of all men in his hands, and turneth them as the rivers of water are turned'; may the 'God of the widow and the fatherless'—of McMillan's wife and child—come into your hearts and guide you to a righteous verdict in this case. I thank you for your kind attention."

Wallace finished shortly after noon, having spoken for three and one-half hours. A crackle of applause erupted as the lead prosecutor sat down.

It had now come time for the jurors to perform their duty and bring the trial to a close. The court handed the instructions to the jury foreman and administered the usual oath to the sheriff and his deputies, who had charge of the jurors. The jury then retired and the court took a recess until four o'clock that afternoon.

When the court reconvened, the opera house was full of anxious, expectant spectators. As the judge prepared to take up other legal matters before the court, he was advised by Sheriff Crozier that the jury had reached a decision. Surprised at the brief deliberation, a little less than four hours, Goodman ordered, "Bring in the jury and the defendant, Mr. Sheriff."

In a few minutes Frank James and his wife entered the room and took their seats. Through the jailhouse pallor the defendant's face still bore the same impassive expression that had been present throughout the trial. Frank's wife, on the other hand, could not hide the effects of two weeks of constant emotional strain. As one journalist described her, she "wore an expression of suffering that made it painful to look upon."

The jurors filed into courtroom and, under Frank's piercing stare, sat down. After the roll was called, the judge inquired, "Gentlemen of the jury, have you arrived at a verdict?"

"We have," answered the foreman.

"Hand up your verdict," directed the judge.

The foreman, William Richardson, passed the official pronouncement to the judge, who read it aloud:

State of Missouri v. Frank James——murder: We, the jury in the above entitled cause, find the defendant not guilty as charged in the indictment."

At the announcement, an enthusiastic ripple of applause broke out in the courtroom that was abruptly silenced by an order from the court. Frank James remained stonily unmoved by the news, not registering the slightest reaction. His wife, though, seemed instantly relieved and could not hide her joy. Rising from her seat, she smiled broadly and bowed in acknowledgment to the jury.

A young man standing on the stage made a sudden move as if to throw his hat into the air. He was immediately hauled before the judge, who demanded an explanation. After a profuse apology for what he claimed was an uncontrollable act, he asked forgiveness. The judge excused the overly enthusiastic demonstrator, who was later discovered to be a cousin of Frank James.

The other two cases lined up against the defendant—one for being an accessory to the murder of conductor Westfall and the other for the murder of Captain Sheets—were carried over to the October term of the Daviess County circuit court. The jury was discharged and the defendant was led back to jail. As a precaution against a public disturbance, Gallatin's only saloon was ordered closed.

4 REDEMPTION AND RECRIMINATION

A Public in Shock

News of Frank James's acquittal stunned the nation. At the scene of the trial, most people were taken by surprise and denounced the verdict as an outrage against law and order. The people of Gallatin may have been prepared for a hung jury but never acquittal, a reprieve from the gallows. Yet it had taken the jury only two rounds of votes, in less than four hours of deliberation, to arrive at its decision. The result of the first ballot was eleven to one for acquittal, before the second ballot made it unanimous.

Within moments of rendering their verdict in the Frank James trial, members of the jury, along with the many James sympathizers in town, vanished into thin air. They paid their hotel bills and left for home, melting quickly and unobtrusively into the mainstream of life. One former juryman was sarcastically invited to return for the next Frank James trial.

Law-abiding citizens everywhere could not understand how Frank James had been found innocent. Rumors of a fixed jury, popular before the trial started, were revived in a rush. "There are at least twelve greater scoundrels in Missouri than Frank James, [namely,]the infamous jurymen who acquitted the train robber, thief and murderer," exclaimed a Kansas newspaper editor [1].

Word of Frank James's acquittal spread quickly around the state. In Kansas City, the verdict was the main topic of conversation among all classes of people. Some declared the decision just. There was not enough evidence to convict Frank James, and the statements of the prosecution's witnesses were simply not believable, they said. The great majority of people, however, declared the jury's decision a black eye for the state of Missouri. One dissatisfied and highly opinionated old gentleman declared that, of the various means available to the public, lynching remained the only satisfactory means of delivering justice [2]. Another man, a commercial traveler, was astounded at the news. He had attended the trial for several days but then left town before it concluded because the evidence against the defendant seemed so strong that he felt there was no chance of Frank James escaping the hangman's noose.

News reached Jefferson City between four and five o'clock and immediately spread through town. Governor Crittenden, asked for a comment, gave none. "It is the verdict of a jury," he stated, "and it would be improper for me to comment on it."

Word also reached Robert Ford in Indianapolis, where he was acting in a play at the Zoo Theater called "The Brothers' Oath." He was surprised. "I never believed that it was possible for the jury to acquit," he said, "knowing as I did, that he was guilty. Even this afternoon I had offered to wager one thousand dollars on his conviction" [3].

The press decried the outcome of the trial. From Maine came the blunt comment, "James is a border ruffian of the daring and picturesque type, and his acquittal will encourage the young amateurs of murder . . . to go to Missouri where popular appreciation renders the broad methods of the art of homicide possible." On September 27, the *New York Tribune* ruefully noted, "The acquittal of Frank James could not have caused surprise anywhere. The announcement that the jury was composed entirely of Democrats was probably enough to determine in advance the verdict that would be passed." Just about every newspaper in America following the James trial broadcast the outcome, noting with particular emphasis that the audience cheered the verdict. "A most unfortunate advertisement," bemoaned another Kansas editor.

The Gold Watch

Wallace considered his loss at Gallatin only a temporary setback and had no intention of quitting his legal pursuit of Frank James. Other cases were pending against the outlaw, and Wallace said that if convictions could be obtained, he would be ready to go back to trial. "I am sure of one thing," he stated. "I won't dismiss the cases against him in the county. Bill Ryan was sent up for twenty-five years on one-third the testimony we have against Frank James."

Despite the verdict, many of Gallatin's leading citizens wanted to express the community's deep gratitude to Wallace for conducting such a valiant battle in court. They met soon after the trial ended and raised a fund, chiefly through the efforts of bankers T. B. Yates of the Farmers' Exchange and George Tuggle of the Daviess County Savings Association. The ceremony was held one night at Judge McDougal's law office and was attended by almost all of Gallatin's property owners and business merchants.

170

Harfield Davis made a short speech of appreciation and presented Wallace with a gold watch.

Touched by the town's warm display of generosity, Wallace thanked the group profusely but respectfully declined the gift because, as an elected official, it was inappropriate for him to accept it. The prosecutor assured his friends that, although he appreciated the value of the fine gold watch, he treasured more the sentiments behind it. Someone then suggested that the group apply the money toward the printing of Wallace's closing arguments, calling it a moving monologue that would be remembered by friends of justice in Gallatin for many years to come.

The group, though, had a problem obtaining a copy of the speech. Wallace did not possess one because he had given the speech extemporaneously. The only existing transcript was in the hands of the stenographer, John Robinson of St. Louis, who had since returned home after the trial. It was later learned by the prosecuting team that the defense had privately hired Robinson for the express purpose of publishing a complete account of the trial, ostensibly to defray expenses. The Gallatin group telegrammed Robinson, asking how much it would cost to obtain a copy of Wallace's speech. Fifty dollars, Robinson replied.

The gold watch was returned to the jeweler for a refund, but by the time the deal was consummated, the price of the manuscript had risen to one hundred dollars. Robinson explained that he had been instructed by his employers to raise the price. Wallace paid the bill with money forwarded by the Gallatin businessmen, making out the check to his erstwhile opponent Charles P. Johnson.

It was because of this transaction that the only known records of the Frank James trial came to be preserved for posterity [4]. (The defense's book was never published.) For the money, Wallace ended up not only with a copy of his speech but the mostly complete written records of the trial. Wallace's closing speech was printed up and circulated in local schools, where it was held up as one of the finest pieces of courtroom oratory extant. Senator Ingalls of Kansas called it "one of the finest productions in the English tongue."

Following the famous trial in Gallatin, three more cases were lined up against Frank James: accessory to the murder of William Westfall by Jesse James, the killing of John Sheets in the Gallatin bank robbery, and larceny at the Winston train holdup. There were also indictments for the robbery in Muscle Shoals, Alabama, involvement in the Blue Cut train robbery and

Independence bank robbery, and the murder of cashier Heywood during the Northfield, Minnesota, bank raid. While Missouri's notorious bandit still had a formidable legal gauntlet to run, he knew that he had won the most important battle of his life in the little town of Gallatin. From here on, Frank James knew things would be easier.

A Bitter Pill

As an addendum to the Frank James trial, the confession of Clarence Hite was made public. It had never been kept a secret before, but its publication only made prosecutor Wallace wince. Clarence Hite, the youngest member of the James gang who was in on the Winston train robbery, was captured in Logan County, Kentucky, on February 13, 1882, shortly after Liddil's surrender. Convicted for complicity in the Winston and Blue Cut train holdups, Hite was sentenced to twenty-five years in prison.

Commissioner Craig of Kansas City, within a week of the closure of the Frank James trial, had the text of Hite's confession published on September 12. Hite had told everything to Governor Crittenden, Craig, and Sheriff Timberlake soon after his incarceration in the state penitentiary in February 1882, two months before the death of Jesse James. Hite was eventually pardoned due to his rapidly failing health and died a few days after receiving the pardon. Just before his death, he made another statement to a reporter, which was published at the time and substantially matched that given to Craig.

In both disclosures, Hite described various movements of the gang during his association with it, confirming every detail of Liddil's testimony at Frank James's trial and implicating James in the Winston robbery. Hite's story also agreed with Liddil's assertion that Frank participated in the Blue Cut train robbery, as well.

Hite's confession was significant on several counts: It was made before Liddil testified, and there was no known arrangement or collusion between Hite and Liddil. James's counsel maintained that Liddil, because of his hostility toward Frank James, caused him to contrive a story at the Gallatin trial. No such motive compelled Clarence Hite to tell the same story. Besides, Hite was Frank James's cousin.

Hite's information completely removed the shine and glory from James's storied past. Frank's life, according to Hite, had been one of skulking, hiding, and continuous fear of being discovered. Clarence Hite's confession may have served to relieve a dying man's conscience, but it really wasn't needed to seal Frank James's guilt; that was already evident [5].

The War Argument Considered

William Wallace, interviewed by the press in Kansas City soon after the trial ended, while disappointed with the state's defeat, remained upbeat and optimistic. He confessed to being less surprised by the jury's verdict than most people because of his premonitions about the jury. "The jury was in sympathy with Frank James," Wallace explained. "It was not a sympathy that was aroused during the trial, but they came to Gallatin with sympathy for him." In his summary analysis, Wallace attributed Frank James's victory to the "old war spirit." It was a theme that the defendant's lawyers had leaned on in their closing arguments and throughout the trial, both in and out of court.

To our ears today, the war argument, presented with such polish by John Philips, seems overdramatized and contrived, almost absurd; it is easy to dismiss it as the last-ditch effort of a desperate attorney fighting for the life of a guilty client. Did it have any validity?

To answer this question, it is necessary to go back in time and examine the impact of the war on the national conscience and specifically attitudes toward ex-Confederates during the period before the trial commenced at Gallatin.

★ ★ ★

The Civil War was a critical test of survival, a stormy and bloody rite of passage, for a young nation barely a hundred years old. It tore the country apart, pitting friend against friend, brother against brother. But after four years of bitter and bloody fighting, the nation was able to mend itself.

The North's hatred for the rebels gave way to compassion as soon as the generals met at the peace table at Appomattox. When General Grant entered the McLean farmhouse and first met the South's commander, Robert E. Lee, seated in the parlor, the Union commander's first reaction was sadness, not jubilation. As Grant wrote later, "I felt like anything rather than rejoicing at the downfall of a foe who had fought so long and valiantly, and had suffered so much for a cause."

The terms of the Southern army's surrender, penned on the spot by a deeply humbled Grant, were generous ones, even allowing Confederate cavalrymen and artillerymen to keep their horses, and Lee and the other officers their sidearms. After the signing of the documents, Grant and his staff removed their hats and stood respectfully at attention as Lee and his aides rode away.

After the fighting had stopped, clemency was the keynote struck by President Lincoln, who was anxious to put the war behind the country as soon as possible. "The nightmare is over," he had said when he received the news of the South's imminent surrender. Lincoln made it clear that he was eager "to get the men composing the Confederate armies back to their homes, at work on their farms or in their shops."

Despite the North's leniency toward the former Confederacy, many in the South continued to feel bitterness toward the Union. They remembered not only the soldiers who were slain but also the civilians who suffered and died at Northern hands. The Missouri Union militia's attack on Dr. Samuel and Jesse at the Samuel's farm was not an unusual event. Many innocent bystanders were caught up in the conflagration and became war casualties.

As a "border state," Missouri was too distant from the heart of Dixie to be unanimous in its support of the South. Public sentiment was divided, creating a potentially explosive situation. In parts of western Missouri, the minority population of Southern sympathizers were periodically singled out for harsh treatment by Union soldiers, as was the case under General Ewing's Order No. 11.

Frank and Jesse James's experiences in war were anomalous. As members of a specialized hit-and-run battle unit, the brothers were expected to follow the examples set by their fanatic and bloodthirsty commanders, and they did so quite readily. Before the Civil War closed, Quantrill and especially Bill Anderson and George Todd became obsessed with killing. They did not distinguish between enemy civilians and enemy soldiers.

Their blood lust spread through the ranks. At a certain point, no doubt, killing became an emotionless act. Certainly the massacres at Lawrence and Centralia amply demonstrate the raiders' barbarous behavior.

After the trial, some observers believed that Frank and Jesse James had been dehumanized by Quantrill. Lacking any vestige of civility or morality, the brothers had chosen to follow a criminal life once the war ended. At the same time, they thought that the boys should be lauded for imperiling their lives during the war in defense of a principle, even though their side lost. It was also alleged that the James brothers had suffered after the war—that, like many other Confederate veterans in western Missouri, they faced hostility and violent prejudice from those who had sided with the Union. But more than this, as rebel raiders, Frank and Jesse were viewed as predatory and murderous cutthroats, and former neighbors and friends were eager to settle old accounts with them.

Public sympathy for the James brothers was evident in the response to the announcement of Governor Crittenden's reward for bringing in any James gang members in 1882. When men of high social and political rank attacked the governor for his highhanded action, the outlaw brothers acquired a veneer of respectability.

Persuasive arguments on behalf of the James brothers also appeared in the press. The following elegantly worded editorial written by John Edwards was published in the *Sedalia Weekly Democrat* soon after Frank surrendered. It attempted to pay tribute to the Confederate guerrillas and the protective role they played during the war.

> It is an unsettled question whether, when the white-winged messenger of peace settled down upon the country, the Jameses could not have returned to peaceful pursuits. They have always claimed that the barbarity of remembered wrongs forced them back into the saddle, and they became hunted animals. With their history as defenders of the faith, how natural it was for a generous people to extenuate the crimes that for seventeen perilous years have been charged to these men. If the Confederate women crowned the Jameses with unfading laurels, there were also plain, practical, unsentimental men who could not forget the hands which sometimes stood fearful guard over their household treasures. But there should be no mistake about this feeling toward the outlaws. The gratitude and remembrance were for Frank James, the Confederate defender—not for Frank James, the bandit. Therefore we repeat, that his surrender necessarily destroys the last vestige of the disturbing recollections of the war, and will tend to remove at once the unhallowed divisions that would otherwise have perished with the return of peace.

A large segment of the population vehemently disagreed with this assessment, however. They rightfully asked: Were the sufferings experienced by Frank and Jesse James before, during, and after the war enough to justify their robbing and killing? Or were their criminal careers just an extension of an unrestrained and murderous lifestyle learned in war?

175

The majority of people were not blinded by sentimentality and did not swallow the self-serving theories offered by men such as Philips and Edwards. The skeptics' line of reasoning ran as follows: The close of the Civil War released into society a number of fearless young men, tested and hardened by the terrible rigors of war, who were either too adventuresome, too restless, or too lazy to earn an honest living. The lure of easy money attracted these misfits, and it wasn't long before they pounced upon unsuspecting victims and enforced their demands at the end of a revolver. The life of a bandit satisfied the need for excitement and reckless adventure that these men had become accustomed to.

While the violence inflicted on the James family by the Union militia was deplorable, hundreds of other households in the border territories experienced similar acts of lawlessness and brutality.

Furthermore, the "accomplishments" of Frank and Jesse James were hardly admirable. The two brothers were free and willing participants in the bloodbath at Centralia, as Frank was at Lawrence, and both deserved the public scorn and shame directed at those who took part in these senseless atrocities [6].

The romanticizing of men like William Quantrill and the other raider leaders covered up the fact that these men were ruthless killers engaged in unconventional warfare under the guise of professional soldiering. Some idea of their callousness is suggested by a comment made an annual reunion of Quantrill's old command at Independence in September 1905. One of the former raiders, referring to the Lawrence raid of 1863, was quoted in the press as saying, "I am sorry now we did not wipe the __ __ town out!"

This insensitive comment stirred up a hornet's nest among residents in Lawrence, whose memories of the raid had not dimmed, even forty-two years later. Infuriated, the townspeople petitioned Kansas Governor Hoch to extradite from Missouri and prosecute any of the twenty-three raiders still living who had originally been indicted for murder two months after the attack. The list included the names of William Quantrill, Bill Anderson, and George Todd (all three long since dead) but not the James brothers. Nothing came of the petition.

The claim the James brothers were prevented from returning to a normal, peaceful life because of the hostility toward them in Clay and Ray counties also does not hold up. Other veterans of the war, many of whom had soldiered with Quantrill, William Poole, and Bill Anderson, had no trouble reassimilating themselves into their communities as useful citizens.

Moreover, when the James boys returned home after the war, they were not persecuted in the manner painted by Frank's lawyers at Gallatin. To the contrary, Frank and Jesse were feted as lions of the day. People assumed that they had served the Confederate cause honorably—an impression the James brothers took great care to promote by never discussing the details of their bloody escapades during the war.

The truth was that the James boys never lowered their flag at war's end because they did not want peace. War, especially the looting part, suited them admirably. They found robbing trains much more profitable than farming. Entering a bank with guns drawn, in addition to being more exciting, was easier work than plowing up a stump-filled section of land.

The newspapers in Missouri and Kansas came out strongly in support of these contentions. Following the trial at Gallatin, for example, the *Kansas City Evening Star* declared as utter nonsense the feeble excuses offered in defense of Frank James's life of crime:

> The fact that the older members of this band of outlawry during the war affected to be in sympathy with the Confederate side, has been ingenuously used to build up in the rural districts of this and adjoining counties a feeling more or less of sympathy for the "boys," as they were affectionately termed.
>
> This sympathy, though wholly unmerited, is the sole agency which, in the way of popular repute, has raised these men, or any of them, above their real level of vulgar outlaws. The truth is there never has been the slightest justification of their crimes in the allegation that they were driven by the war into the career of outlawry, now ended.
>
> This was the shallowest of pretexts. There are today hundreds of men, now good, honorable and trustworthy citizens in the border counties of the state, who had just as good, if not better, cause to continue a predatory warfare against society at the close of the war than any James boy.
>
> No, the James gang deliberately chose the career of thieving lawlessness, the closing chapter of which effectually strips them, one and all, of the slightest claim to sympathy from either honest men or law-abiding citizens, and clearly displays them in their true light of vulgar, self-elected thieves and cutthroats.

Likewise, on September 8, 1883 the *Atchison Daily Champion* summed up the trial's outcome this way:

> The acquittal of Frank James is another backset for Missouri. Just as the country was beginning to hope that Missouri was to be rid of the last and worst of bandits, comes this outburst of sympathy for this villain, James,

beginning before the the trial, continued through it, and culminating in his acquittal.

Frank James is a murderer and robber of the lowest and most fiendish type; a man who has made a trade of murder and robbery for nearly twenty years; a robber and murderer, like John A. Murrell in the South, or the California bandit, Joaquin Murrieta, a murderous thief, who killed men and wrenched money from their chilling, stiffening fingers; a man who killed the helpless and unresisting; men who he had never seen before, and, in many cases, with no motive except the mere pleasure of shedding blood.

Everybody in Missouri knew this. Every man on the jury who tried him knew it. Since 1869, for fourteen years, it had been believed in Gallatin and Daviess county, that he and his brother killed Capt. Sheets, in Gallatin. Yet he comes back to the county and aids and abets in killing two men, and after his third murder in the county, a train of circumstances lands him a prisoner in the Gallatin jail.

One would suppose that here, if anywhere, he would be regarded with detestation. But, instead, he is feted, petted, worshipped as if he were a public benefactor instead of a scourge and pest among men, as a wolf is among sheep.

His trial comes on, and women admire his thief's face in the court room. A jury is empanneled, and men say, from the first, that he will be acquitted, or that the jury will fail to agree. He has no defense. His attempt to prove an alibi is a pitiful failure. He dare not himself fix a location for himself on the night of the robbery. That he was at Winston is proved as clearly as that the Rock Island train was there on that fatal evening; and, after all, he is acquitted, and nobody is greatly surprised at the verdict.

The reason Frank James is acquitted is because there is in Missouri a feeling that to have been a rebel bushwhacker in the war was commendable; that to have participated in the hellish atrocities committed by Quantrell, Pool, and others was heroic and praiseworthy. That is the reason this red-handed professional murderer was acquitted, and there was no other reason.

★ ★ ★

The war argument, however, and lingering public sympathy for the Confederate cause also benefited other members of the James gang. In Minnesota, the forgotten Younger brothers, were leading model lives as prisoners in the penitentiary at Stillwater. For years following their incarceration in 1876 with life sentences, letters poured into the office of the Minnesota governor, imploring that he pardon the Younger brothers. The arguments were familiar: the Youngers had been driven into a life of crime

178

because of their experiences during the war and the persecution of their families.

Most of the letters were written by ex-Confederate officers such as General Shelby, Major John Edwards, and Colonel Vard Edwards (Cole Younger's former commanding officer), who all worked tirelessly on behalf of the Youngers. As time went on, the list of petitioners became a long and impressive one. In 1885, among the thousands of letters that passed across the desk of Minnesota governor Hubbard were those of George Vest and Francis Cockrell, former law partners of Missouri governor Crittenden and John Philips and now U.S. Senators, who sought to use their influence to obtain pardons for the three men.

Ex-Confederates weren't the only ones to jump on the Younger bandwagon; nonpartisan citizens of Missouri and Minnesota as well as former Minnesota governor Marshall also lent their support. As time softened unpleasant memories of the war, many people had a change of heart toward the former gang members. The biggest surprise came in 1897 when William Wallace, the chief prosecutor at Gallatin, added his name to the list of those lobbying for the Youngers.

This turnabout in Minnesota was remarkable. For many years after the outlaws were imprisoned, every candidate for the office of governor of Minnesota had been required to sign a document stating that under no circumstances would he, if elected, grant a pardon to the Younger brothers. But, beginning in 1895, hostility toward the former outlaws was showing signs of weakening. Attempts were made in each session of the Minnesota state legislature to enact a law permitting the parole of the state's notorious prisoners.

Finally, in the winter of 1900, the Minnesota Board of Pardons was given power to set the prisoners free. The following July, Cole and Jim Younger were paroled after spending twenty-five years in confinement and two years later received a full pardon. The action came too late for Robert Younger, however, who never saw the light of freedom again. In failing health for a number of years, he died in prison of tuberculosis in 1899.

Innocent or Guilty?

Acquittal of the guilty damns the judge.
Horace

Certain fundamental questions arise from this important trial. Did Frank James get away with murder? Yes. The incriminating evidence against him was overpowering. Was there reasonable doubt about his guilt? No. But the most frequent question posed by defenders of Frank James's innocence at Gallatin is, Did Dick Liddil lie on the stand? This question immediately begs another: Do all bank robbers, by definition, habitually lie? If the answer is yes, and Liddil lied, then, following the same logic, so did Frank James.

However, the popular argument says that Liddil had nothing to lose and everything to gain by lying, that he would not say or do anything to jeopardize the precious personal liberty granted by his pardon. But what of Frank James? What he put on the line and risked losing was his life, not merely his freedom.

While it is theoretically possible that Liddil lied, it is very unlikely. He might have been an intuitively clever and quick-thinking fellow, but it would require a very remarkable person to fabricate such a long and involved story (even a prepared one), memorize it, and then regurgitate it upon demand in minute detail. It is also pushing long odds to think that Liddil possessed the concentration, presence of mind, and mental endurance to withstand four hours of intense and exhaustive grilling on the witness stand without once making a mistake, especially given that he was examined by a team of seasoned defense attorneys highly skilled at tripping up witnesses.

The reason why the defense failed to find holes in Liddil's story is that there were simply no holes to be found; Liddil was speaking the truth. Added to this was the inordinate amount of corroborating evidence given by other witnesses. Although it was never placed in evidence by the prosecution, the confession of Clarence Hite speaks for itself and also bolsters this argument. It is one thing to cast doubt on the word of one man because of his character and background, but it is untenable to believe that every witness for the state who gave hard evidence was mistaken in his or her testimony and lied under oath. Thus, the conspiracy theory is a flimsy one.

If Frank James was guilty, how and why did the justice system fail? Clearly, the jury was the source of the problem. The jurors arrived at a not-guilty verdict in spite of overpowering incriminating evidence. The explanation offered by the prosecution, the press, courtroom observers, and historians ever since the trial ended is that they were sympathetic to the defendant.

It is likely that a few of the jurors went into the trial fully intending to free Frank James, no matter what evidence was brought to bear against him. Indeed, on the eve of the trial, one juror was quoted in a newspaper as saying exactly that. But what was the reason for this sympathy? What was it about Frank James, Missouri's public enemy number one, that so appealed to the jurors that they would ignore the facts, risk public censure, and let him go free?

The decision to acquit may have been partly due to the common tendency of human beings to forget and forgive with the passage of time. Socrates once referred to time as "a kindly god." Indeed, time acts as a kind of strainer, sifting out a man's bad deeds and leaving the good, by which he is often ultimately measured.

Though we do not know if any of the jurors at the Gallatin trial knew the defendant personally, the chances are almost certain that none did. It is almost certain as well that the jurors, given the long-standing and widespread reputation of the James brothers in western Missouri, had already formed definite personal opinions of Frank James—good, bad, or indifferent. While most newspapers in Kansas and Missouri fostered public opinion against the Jameses in the years after the war, there were still large numbers of James sympathizers residing in Clay, Ray, Jackson, and other nearby counties, including Daviess County, from which the jurors were drawn.

It is also fairly certain that no member of the jury (or his family) was ever personally harmed or even threatened by the defendant and therefore held no grudge against him. In addition, many people on the frontier at the time had a rather permissive attitude toward the crime of robbery, as long as innocent bystanders were not hurt and outlaws confined their robbing to banks and railroads (specifically, express companies). Since the monetary losses had to be absorbed by the companies themselves, few people really cared; most people believed that these same companies were stealing from the public anyway. Thus, the big losers were mostly carpetbaggers who had come south after the war and assumed control of the banks and railroads, and the average person in Missouri had little sympathy for them.

Like the local residents who had once provided Frank, Jesse, and other gang members with shelter while they were on the run, the jurors at Gallatin protected Frank James from the clutches of the law. To them the defendant was not just a name but a legend, and they accepted the exaggerated depiction of James by the press as a modern-day Robin Hood. And, when all was said, Frank James was still a son of the Missouri soil, country bred and country raised, just like them.

Like many other people in Missouri at the time, the jurors may have felt a deep, secret pride in the daring accomplishments of the James boys, who made such fools of the law, the press, and other symbols of authority in the state. The human tendency to root for the underdog, even one who breaks the law, is strong, especially when that underdog has the boldness and flair of a Frank or Jesse James.

Perhaps the jurors even considered James's prosecution pointless. The James gang was no more and Frank James could no longer cause any further trouble. Why not then be lenient and excuse him for his misdeeds perpetrated so long ago?

Besides, Frank James seemed to be an honest-to-goodness family man, sitting in the courtroom day after day with his innocent-looking wife and sometimes his child. Furthermore, everybody who met James for the first time, including politicians, bank presidents, and other businessmen of importance, were captivated by his engaging and friendly personality. One Gallatin resident J. P. Matthews had this to say after the trial: "The verdict is all right. The James boys have atoned for their crimes, and Frank should be allowed to settle down and live quietly as he would. Worse men than he are being used as witnesses against him." Such sentiments were widespread.

Another question that arose about Frank James's trial was whether the Gallatin jury was rigged against the state, as William Wallace charged. And if so, did it happen by chance or by design?

Here there is much fertile ground for speculation and argument, but few real answers emerge because the available information is either contradictory or inconclusive. On the one hand we have William Wallace's emphatic charge of collusion between defense attorney Rush and Sheriff Crozier, who, he said, conspired to load the venire with "desirable" candidates. This was clearly a breach of the law. The only proof of this, however, comes from Wallace himself, in his memoirs, which were written long after the fact and published in 1914. Although Wallace was a scrupulously honest man, corroborative proof of his claim is virtually nonexistent.

There are just a few bits of information that might support the notion of jury rigging. The *Kansas City Times,* for example, published the following posttrial opinion which many people believed to be true at the time: "If counsel acquitted Frank James, it is more due to [Mr. Rush] than any one employed in the case. He has been an indefatigable worker." Another hint can be found in the contents of a letter from Frank James to Rush, residing in the archives of the Jesse James Farm and Museum near Kearney, Missouri. The letter, dated March 4, 1884, was written six months after the Gallatin trial ended and acknowledges the fact that the industrious attorney performed "all the work" at Gallatin. What is meant by "all the work" is left to the reader's imagination.

Wild rumors concerning the jury were rife throughout the trial. According to one, unknown men on horseback rode through various parts of the county several weeks before the proceedings began, urging known James sympathizers to make themselves available for jury duty. According to another, five of the final forty jury candidates were hand-picked by the defense from a list attorney Rush gave Sheriff Crozier.

The latter story mushroomed into a more elaborate one that ran as follows: William Wallace, angered when he found out about the list, was given the choice of either scratching the five jurors in question or summoning the jury all over again, this time in the hands of someone other than the sheriff. By now, though, it had become quite clear to the capable prosecutor that landing a fair jury was a hopeless task, and neither choice offered an advantage. So Wallace, with grave misgivings, elected to remove the five jurors.

The record, as it is currently known, does not confirm that illegalities were committed by Sheriff Crozier during the impaneling of the jurors or defense attorney Rush during the final jury selection. It was widely believed, however, that Mr. Rush's behind-the-scenes manipulations during the twenty-four period when the jury panel was reduced from forty to twelve men were extremely helpful to the defense's cause. Neither Crozier nor Rush ever made public statements that would implicate them in this alleged conspiracy.

An interesting, if puzzling, fragment is the photograph of the jury entered according to Act of Congress in 1883, by Jas. S. Thomason in the Office of the Library of Congress, Washington, D.C. Titled "The Jury that Cleared Frank James," the reason for its remarkable existence is unclear. Was it an ironic battle trophy intended by and for the jurors? An

Titled "The Jury that Cleared Frank James," this photograph was entered according to Act of Congress, in the 1883, by Jas. S. Thomason in the Office of the Library of Congress, at Washington, D.C. Left to (back row) J. Snyder, B. F. Feurt, C. R. Nance, Jos. B. Smith, B. H. Shellman, Wm. R. Merritt, Jason Winburn, Oscar Chamberlain; (front row) W. F. Richardson, L. W. Gilreath, R. E. Hale, and J. W. Boggs. (Courtesy State Historical Society of Missouri, Columbia. Reprinted with permission.)

intentional slap in the face of proponents of law and order? The copyrighting of the photograph suggests its purpose was commercial, but if it was intended for publication, along with trial records, perhaps to recoup fees, it was never used by James's attorneys.

Another irregularity of the Frank James trial was the behavior of the presiding judge, Charles Goodman, which was not always above reproach. In a grievous judicial error, he failed to investigate legitimate claims of illegal subterfuge taking place during jury selection. This error may have been compounded by his response to news of the state's plan to file for a mistrial. If he had bullied prosecutors Wallace and Hamilton into not taking action—an unconscionable subversion of power—as some alleged, the judge bore some responsibility for allowing Frank James to escape Gallatin with his life.

Here, as with the issue of jury selection, one unanswered question leads to another. The principals involved in this dramatic backroom squabble—Goodman, Wallace, Hamilton, and possibly others—deliberately hushed up the incident. News of it never made the press, and the secrecy is mystifying. Wallace had everything to gain by making the private affair a public one. The protest from the defense, sure to follow, would likely have forced Goodman to change his mind and declare a mistrial.

Why did Wallace cave in? Why did the determined Jackson County prosecutor allow the issue of jury selection to be swept under the rug by the judge, who, from all outward appearances, was clearly running scared and overstepping his authority?

Explanations are not easy to come by. It is hard to believe that the threat of violence in the streets of Gallatin was so great as to interfere with the better judgment of either Goodman or Wallace. To further muddy the water, a juicy press item was published late in the trial claiming that Judge Goodman had been "so disgusted with the jury that had he been in possession of all the facts in connection of its selection when first impaneled, he would have discharged the jury and turned the venire over to the coroner of the county." Goodman himself, on the night the trial ended, confided to state's counsel Henry Clay McDougal, "Well, it's all over and I suppose I am the only man living that has no right to swear about that acquittal." This was an astonishing and damning confession, coming from a presiding judge.

It seems likely that Wallace simply became so fed up with the sham of a jury that he gave up, realizing that an impartial jury could never be seated in Gallatin, even in a new trial. Why else would he react with such anger and threaten to quit? As a highly competent professional, he would not be expected to tolerate any act of judicial misconduct in a case of this importance, and yet he did not take proper legal recourse. Not to do so would jeopardize his professional reputation and political future, and betray his sense of duty and honor.

Did any witnesses lie under oath?

It is fair to say that witnesses for both sides were extremely well coached for their performances on the stand at the Gallatin trial. In the case of the defense, however, there were instances of lying, or as Colonel Johnson might have preferred to see it, judicious bending of the facts. The most glaring example was General Shelby. In his mind the end justified the means; if lying was necessary to help acquit his longtime friend, the old cavalry commander stood ready to do it. He was called on this issue twice by prosecutor Wallace.

But testimony from other defense witnesses is suspect, too. From the various testimonies given, a subtle but discernible pattern emerges, leaving the distinct impression that some of them were instructed to give false evidence. A case in point concerns the supposed physical similarity between the defendant and fellow gang member Wood Hite, an essential factor in establishing Frank James's alibi. Wood Hite was dead at the time of the Frank James trial, making it impossible for jurors to directly compare the two men. But, suddenly and inexplicably, in the middle of other testimony, several defense witnesses declared that Hite and James looked alike. It was too much of a coincidence, especially in light of contrary evidence offered by state's witnesses who, being much more familiar with both parties, were better qualified to say.

There was one tiny but potent piece of testimony by a state's witness that stood out and helped solidify the case against Frank James. It was the story told by Reverend Matchett about the stranger at his house who recited Shakespearean poetry. That the uninvited house guest could not have been anyone else but Frank James was a point driven home with dramatic emphasis by prosecutor Wallace in his closing arguments, to wit: "That it is nothing uncommon for a train robber to go through the land spouting Shakespeare is preposterous." The defense's sudden abandonment of Jim Cummins as the so-called fifth man in the robbery backs up this contention.

The Bolton children were also potent witnesses for the prosecution. With all the sweet innocence and honesty of youth, they calmly identified Frank James as the man who was at their home.

The exact role that Governor Crittenden played in aiding the cause of Frank James before and during the trial will never be known. However, his decision after the trial not to grant Liddil a pardon, which practically guaranteed James's eventual freedom, suggests that the governor's feelings toward the notorious bandit were hardly neutral.

Crittenden and defense counsel John Philips were longtime acquaintances. Their close personal ties started in college and continued during the war, as the two rode and fought side by side for three years. Afterwards, Philips and George Vest established a law partnership at Sedalia, as did Crittenden and Francis Cockrell, a former Confederate general, at Warrensburg. The professional reunion of ex-Union officers Philips and Crittenden, and the ex-Confederates Vest and Cockrell created a center of legal and political power (they were called the "Big Four") that greatly influenced Democratic rule of the state of Missouri for many years during the post-Reconstruction period.

It was not by chance that Major Edwards and General Shelby recruited the legal services of Philips for their client Frank James. Philips was far more than just an able defense attorney. By bringing the well-connected lawyer into their camp, Edwards and Shelby had tapped a direct line to the governor, which also made it easier to interest other big-name attorneys in their case. It is not too far-fetched to imagine Crittenden doing everything in his power to help Frank James as a personal favor to his old friend John Philips, who was acting on behalf of Edwards and Shelby. Perhaps this was one of the many secrets surrounding the Frank and Jesse James affairs that the governor once admitted were so sensitive and politically damaging that he could never divulge them to the public.

Just how much public distrust of the railroad companies influenced the Gallatin jury will also never be known. Their role was significant, however, for it was the rich and powerful train moguls who ponied up the reward money that indirectly brought down Jesse James and caused Frank to come in. Many rural citizens in western Missouri felt far more hatred for the railroad owners than for the popular local boy gone wrong. Whatever its final effect on the outcome of the trial, the defense team reaped incalculable dividends, even before the trial began, by calling the Frank James trial a "railroad prosecution." It was a classic spreading of disinformation.

5 FINAL JUSTICE

> Laws are the spider's webs which, if anything small falls into
> them, they ensnare it, but large things break through and escape.
>
> Solon

Last Irony

In his lifetime, Frank James was never found guilty of any crime,
fulfilling the prophecy of many observers at the trial at Gallatin. An
unexpected event dashed any further hopes of prosecuting Frank
James: the invalidation of Dick Liddil's right to bear witness. It was
another example of the serendipitous good fortune that seemed to befall the unrepentant outlaw.

In early winter 1883, the wheels of justice turned once again to
bring Frank James before the law, this time for the outlaw's complicity in the Blue Cut train robbery of 1881. William Wallace, still pur-
suing James with the tenacity of a bulldog, was scheduled to read
criminal indictments against James and Charles Ford on February 11
in the circuit court of Jackson County. But his prosecution was interrupted by a decision of the Missouri Supreme Court.

On December 17, 1883, the high court, in a lengthy opinion ren-
dered in an unrelated appeal case involving a black man named
George Grant, clarified the state laws of 1879 that addressed the issuing of pardons by the governor. These original laws contained much
complex and ambiguous language that had led to considerable argument in court whenever the subject of pardons came up.

The Frank James trial was a good example. When Liddil first took
the stand at Gallatin, both sides hotly contested these laws. The same
laws were reviewed and interpreted by Judge Goodman to mean that
Liddil's pardon was indeed valid, and allowed the judge to legally
qualify Liddil as a competent witness for the remainder of the trial.

The Supreme Court's findings were terrible news for prosecutor
Wallace. The justices started off by stating that the pertinent statutes
of 1879 were never intended to remove "disabilities" that attached

themselves to persons convicted of crimes prior to the enactment of said laws, (meaning, among other things, citizenship and the right to bear witness at a trial). The Court further emphasized that the power to pardon was solely vested in the governor. In support of its decision, the court cited a number of decisions from other states with laws like Missouri's—affecting pardons similar to, and in some cases broader, than Liddil's—which, in their opinion, *did not* restore competency to the convicted criminal. The bottom line was that releasing a prisoner under the "three-quarter rule" did not constitute a pardon.

Wallace was stunned. Based on the high court's decision, there was little doubt that Judge Goodman had ruled improperly in allowing Dick Liddil to speak at Gallatin. The bitter irony of it all was that even if Wallace had succeeded in convicting Frank James with Liddil's testimony, a new trial without Liddil almost certainly would have been ordered if the case had been appealed to the Supreme Court—something Frank's attorneys had planned to do if they lost the case. Without Liddil all further attempts to prosecute Frank James in the state of Missouri offered scant hope for success. The state's indispensable witness was silenced forever.

But there remained one glimmer of hope. The determined public prosecutor read and reread the Court's complicated declaration, going over each word. Perhaps he had missed something or misinterpreted a point of law. Wallace submitted Liddil's old pardon and the Grant decision to some of the brightest legal minds in Kansas City and around the state, asking their opinion. To his astonishment, they unanimously declared Liddil's pardon an exception to the Supreme Court's ruling.

Bolstered in confidence, the Jackson County prosecutor forwarded a copy of the Grant decision to Governor Crittenden in late December and asked him to grant Liddil a full and complete pardon, to assure Liddil's testimony at Frank James's subsequent trial on charges pending in Jackson County. To Wallace's great surprise and frustration, however, the governor stubbornly refused to grant the pardon, offering the weak excuse that to do so might embarrass Lieutenant Governor Brockmeyer, who had signed Liddil's document.

Wallace could not go forward with a trial knowing that the court would ultimately disqualify Liddil as a witness. It would not only be a waste of taxpayers' money, but Wallace would suffer enormous personal and professional embarrassment. For the first time since he had launched his personal crusade to put the James gang behind bars, over three years ago, the battling prosecutor had to admit he was beaten.

In the circuit court of Jackson County on February 11, 1884, a visibly shaken Wallace (described by the *New York Times* as "pale as a ghost") announced with great regret that the state was dismissing charges against Frank James and Charles Ford for the Blue Cut train robbery in 1881. Also dropped were other charges pending against James in the Winston robbery. It wasn't long before the remaining cases against James, fast gaining fame as a man above the law, quickly unraveled. The vaunted bandit now stood on the verge of freedom.

Later that month Frank James was transported to Huntsville, Alabama, to stand trial for robbing federal paymaster Alexander G. Smith in Muscle Shoals in 1881. The handwritten indictment, handed down by a grand jury in the U.S. District of Northern Alabama, accused Frank James "and with divers other evil disposed persons" of conspiracy to rob Smith "of a large sum on money to wit, five thousand dollars" composed of "treasury notes of the United States, gold and silver coin and national bank notes."

Frank James, handcuffed and accompanied by two U. S. marshals, arrived at Huntsville on February 20, 1884, and was taken to the old Calhoun house on Eustis Street, a former residence that was serving as a federal courthouse and jail. While awaiting trial, James entertained a seemingly endless parade of visitors and reporters clamoring for interviews which James gladly granted.

Riding the momentum of his astonishing victory at Gallatin, the defendant wasted no time trying to pull off a repeat performance, the odds of winning suddenly jacked up by a trial venue right in the heart of Dixie. To gather local support for the proceedings, Major Edwards entered the scene and helped engage the legal services of a prominent local attorney and esteemed citizen of Huntsville, Leroy Pope Walker. Edwards had chosen well. Walker, during the "late unpleasantness," had served the Confederate States as an army general and Secretary of War in Jefferson Davis's cabinet. He was the same darling of the South who, after the shelling of Fort Sumter, which launched the war, had proudly predicted that the flag of the Confederacy would fly from the dome of the capitol in Washington, D.C.—words that sent the partisan crowd into wild cheering.

Assisting the elderly sixty-seven-year-old Walker in the defense of Frank James were: Richard W. Walker (no relation), a former justice of the Alabama Supreme Court; Raymond B. Sloan of Nashville, longtime acquaintance of James who had testified for the defense at Gallatin; and James W. Newman of Winchester, Tennessee, an expert at cross-examination. Leading the government's prosecution was U. S. District Attorney William H. Smith, former governor of Alabama, and his special assistant, district attorney L. W. Day. Presiding over the trial was federal judge Henry Bruce. Both Bruce and William Smith had participated in Dick Liddil's trial the year before.

Sloan reportedly busied himself with all the "little work" of the trial. Walker was in constant communication with William Rush, Frank James's industrious behind-the-scenes counsel at the Gallatin trial, for purposes that are unclear but no doubt involved supplying advice on jury selection or conduct of the case.

Given an enthusiastic reception upon his arrival at Huntsville, James was in a buoyant, almost euphoric mood. This was revealed in a letter he wrote to Rush from jail on April 4, 1884, thirteen days before the trial started. James wrote: "I have not an enemy in town so far as I have heard. Everyone is talking for me, especially the ex-confederates and southern Methodists . . . I am in high spirits and feel as I will be acquitted."

Frank's premonition was right. The trial in the U. S. Circuit Court unfolded in a series of familiar scenarios that made it a virtual carbon copy of the one at Gallatin, including the verdict.

The trial began on April 16 and ran for ten days. The prosecution sent to the stand a steady parade of eyewitnesses who gave testimony against James. District attorney Day's last witness was a surprise—Dick Liddil. The antagonist of the defendant swore to overhearing Frank and Jesse plot the Muscle Shoals robbery and afterwards hearing them admit that they had pulled the job. Liddil's testimony, however, fared badly. A writer of the *St. Louis Globe-Democrat* declared him "unworthy of belief."

The long-suffering Liddil was pilloried before the jury by the defense and his testimony lampooned at one point by attorney Sloan who, in a dramatic highlight, uttered the caustic barb: "If Liddil had been present at Besworth field when Richard III cried: 'A horse, a horse! My kingdom for a horse,' Liddil would have replied, 'Don't be troubled, o King, I will steal one in just a minute!'"

After all the evidence had been given, Frank's wife and young son entered the courtroom and joined the defendant seated behind the defense bench. The event was deliberately staged and the timing couldn't have been better. The tender scene provoked a not-unexpected reaction from a reporter: "The sympathy of the public is most heartily bestowed upon the true, faithful and loving wife and the innocent little boy; and an earnest desire is manifested that the husband and father, if innocent, may be set free to his wife and child."[1]

Judge Bruce instructed attorneys to limit their summations to thirty minutes. His plea for brevity, though, was ignored by General Walker. In an oration that lasted well over three hours, the unrestrained counsel attacked the credibility of the government's witnesses, creating as much "reasonable doubt" as possible. Predictably, Walker extolled Frank's Confederate war record and portrayed him as a victim of "Yankee injustice," themes that struck responsive chords in a jury composed entirely of rebel veterans who appeared to sit at military attention as Walker paced up and down in front of them.

Finally, on April 26, Frank James rose in his chair to hear the jury foreman announce, "We, the jury, find the defendant not guilty." The foreman's words were almost drowned out by a loud cheer from the audience.

While the acquittal came as welcome news to the many James supporters, the local press condemned it, believing the defendant guilty and lamenting the government's failure to prove it. The outburst of applause particularly rankled one newsman who saw in it evil portent. He commented: ". . . applause that gives worship to such heroes as Frank James . . . may plant in the mind of the boy a seed that may afterwards grow and lead him into a similar life to end on the gallows, or in a felons' cell."[2]

News of the verdict created little excitement in Missouri. From a Kansas City newspaper came this cynical comment: "It appears from the evidence introduced in the Frank James trial at Huntsville, Ala., that Mr. James never belonged to the James gang, but that he is an innocent, much abused personage who has been sadly misunderstood by the world. It is certainly unfortunate that such an excellent, irreproachable gentleman as Mr. James' witnesses prove him to be, should have been the victim of such cruel suspicions" [3].

But Frank's troubles weren't quite over. As soon as the verdict was read in Huntsville, Sheriff Rogers of Cooper County, Missouri, purposefully seated behind the defendant, immediately arrested James on an old indictment for his complicity in robbing a train near Boonville in 1876 and hustled the defendant back to Missouri [4]. This case, however, never came to trial. In Boonville, on February 23, 1885, prosecuting attorney Shackleford, at the end of a circuit court session, stated to the court that his main

FRANK IS FREE.

A Triumph for Gov. Crittenden's Famous Policy.

The Cases Against James Dismissed by the State

Because Dick Liddil Can Not
Testify.

What James Thinks of the
Result.

Poor, old Missouri. Frank James is discharged for his many violations of the laws of Missouri and will be molested no longer. For which which he is indebted to Gov. Crittenden. Without Liddil's testimony it was folly for the state to further prosecute the case for all other testimony was only corroborative in character. Liddil many years ago was convicted of horse stealing and afterwards pardoned, except as to his disfranchisement. This disfranchisement follows him through life and disqualifies him as a witness in Missouri until the disqualification is removed by the governor. Prosecutor Wallace petitioned Gov. Crittenden to restore Liddil to citizenship that he might use his testimony. The governor

Facsimile portion of an article that ran in the *Kansas City Evening Star* February 11, 1884.

witness, Mr. R. P. Stapp of Kansas, had died and that other evidence was missing. He had no choice but to dismiss the charges against Frank James: one for obstructing a railroad, the other for robbery. No further indictments were brought forward and with this action the last criminal charge against James in the state of Missouri was vacated.

The state of Minnesota made the last legal effort to bring Frank James to justice, for the murder of cashier Heywood during the Northfield bank raid of 1876. A warrant for the robber's arrest was issued previously in 1883 by Minnesota governor Hubbard but, at the time, James was still awaiting

From the balcony of the Calhoun house in Huntsville, Frank James waves to a street crowd busy celebrating his courtroom victory, the last legal obstacle on his way to freedom. (Woodcut, source unknown.)

trials in Missouri [5]. Governor Crittenden, nearing the end of his term, refused to extradite the prisoner as long as cases were pending against James in Missouri. When James was finally freed of indictments in his home state, public prosecutors in Rice County, Minnesota, renewed attempts to bring the outlaw north to trial.

Their efforts, however, were stymied by James's old friend and ally, General Shelby, who circulated a petition in Butler, Missouri, asking the governor not to honor the request. If this failed, a series of trumped-up legal cases against James would be announced in each session of the legislature, thereby ensuring the continued presence of "Colonel James" in the state of Missouri [6]. The official foot-dragging and backroom political conniving finally wore down authorities in Minnesota, and the case against James, by all accounts, was dropped from the books. At long last, legally absolved of any criminal wrongdoing, Frank James, the outlaw king of Missouri and hero to legions of admirers, walked out of jail a free man.

Home Free

In his new life, the public spotlight followed Frank James everywhere he went, even long after he had become assimilated into society as a normal person providing for his family. Wealth never accrued to Frank James in his new life; he appeared to shun it. Somewhere along the way, he had discovered that money didn't mean that much to him; other things seemed to hold far greater value. He tried to explain this in the letter he wrote to Governor Crittenden prior to his surrender. Frank James had truly become a different sort of man.

That is not to say, however, that Frank James, the retired outlaw, did not have opportunities to get rich. Entrepreneurs and fast-buck artists saw in Frank James's name golden opportunities for exploitation, and the former outlaw was besieged with all sorts of business deals and schemes. Immediately following the trial at Gallatin, for example, James was offered $100,000 for a three-year contract to star in a stage production based on his life. He refused, as he did another tender of $10,000 for an exclusive photograph of himself. When the theatrical offer was boosted to $125,000, with all his expenses included, the publicity-shy celebrity still could not be induced to accept. James apologetically explained that he simply wanted to retire from public life and spend the rest of his days in peace and quiet with his family.

Another lucrative deal was dangled in front of him in 1891. On the eve of the World's Fair in Chicago, known as the Columbian Exposition, Frank was offered $25,000 for his home in Nevada, Missouri, a plain, modest, one-story wooden cottage worth perhaps $750. [7]. The plan was to move the house to the fairgrounds in Chicago, where it would be set up as a display, and visitors (for a nominal fee, of course) would be allowed to tour the premises. James turned the idea down, as he did all other offers.

Gone were the wild and lawless ambitions of his youth. They were replaced by a concern for home and family and the pursuit of an honest and peaceful life. As praiseworthy as these changes were, they could not undo the terrible wrongs he had committed and the suffering he had inflicted on so many innocent victims. Not much was written about Frank James in his new life as a free man for the simple reason that there was little to report. He had also proclaimed a vow of silence to the press and, with the exception of periodic stints of employment, shunned publicity in general.

The normally taciturn James spoke out publicly on occasion when he felt a need to do so as in January 1886 when he went to the aid of Thomas Crittenden, his former benefactor. The ex-governor had become embroiled in a flare-up of the never-ending controversy surrounding his role in the assassination of Jesse James, specifically, the charge that he had hired Bob Ford to kill Jesse for his own political aggrandizement. James supported statements already given to the press by Crittenden, who had denied the charge. Frank held the ex-governor blameless for the death of his brother, explaining that "there were hundreds of men who were ready to take our lives for the sake of the reward."

James worked at a number of menial jobs in various places over the years, acting as a drawing card. He sold shoes in Nevada, Missouri, and in Dallas, Texas. He was also was a doorman at Ed Butler's theater in St. Louis and, later, because of his love of horses, an assistant starter at the Fair Grounds racetrack in St. Louis.

For a while James was in business with his old friend, fellow gang crony and Quantrill raider Cole Younger, who had be^ recently released from prison in Minnesota. The two men put together a traveling Wild West show in the tradition of Wild Bill Cody, complete with bronco riding, rifle shooting, and the usual circus sideshows of snake-eaters, sword swallowers, and freaks of nature. The show went on tour in 1903. While it achieved moderate success, Frank's heart just didn't seem to be in it and he pulled out.

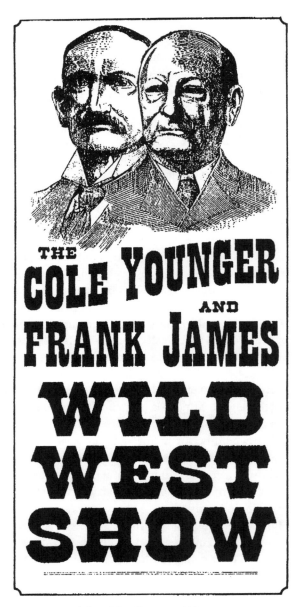

Advertising flyer, ca 1903.

Formal portrait of Frank James at the age of 55. Dated 1898 and copyrighted, the photograph was probably used as a money-making scheme. (Courtesy Jesse James Farm & Museum, Kearney, Missouri. Reprinted with permission.)

★ ★ ★

Of all the lives to change following the trial at Gallatin, none did so more profoundly than Dick Liddil's. The habitual petty crook who had managed to escape serving jail time in Alabama for the Muscle Shoals robber remained a free man after the Frank James trial. It was a precarious freedom, however. No longer protected by a pardon, Liddil was subject to arrest on a stack of old criminal charges in Missouri ranging from train robbery to murder.

From his hard experiences in life, Liddil wisely decided to go straight. He bounced around Jackson County for a year or so after the Gallatin trial, but amazingly no attempt was ever made to arrest him. He ventured to New Mexico around 1887 and ran a saloon there for a while. Eventually, Liddil decided to seek a better-paying profession. Like all the riders who followed Frank and Jesse, he was a good judge of horseflesh and, in the late 1880s, put together a string of race horses. He went East and cleaned up on the all-winter tracks in New Jersey, reportedly winning $30,000 in prize money over a two-year period.

Liddil returned to Kansas City in 1891 and made the mistake of visiting friends in Ray County. There he was surprised when authorities with a long memory finally arrested him for the murder of Wood Hite in 1882. The trail of history runs out on Liddil at this point, but it is quite likely that the charge never stuck and the man who snitched on Frank James–and lived–never went to trial. [8]

★ ★ ★

For years, Frank James spurned a fortune by not appearing on the stage. But whether he needed the money or finally succumbed to an irresistible urge, the man who was a walking encyclopedia of Shakespearean prose took his superb acting talents from the witness chair in a courtroom to the theater.

In November 1904, a Kansas City newspaper carried the news that Frank James had just appeared in a light-hearted theatrical farce put on in Chillicothe, Missouri, titled *The Fatal Scar*. James played the lead role and afterwards was given such a tumultuous applause that he came out on the stage and made a short speech to the audience. It was one of those extraordinarily rare occasions when Frank James publicly discussed his inner feelings.

> There are many in this audience tonight who think I am better fitted for a tragedy. I hope I may be indulged to say that this play does not illustrate the fact that there is a vast difference between reputation and character. While my unenviable reputation may be the cause of my being here tonight, there is as little truth in it as there is the quality of a good actor in me. If I have one ambition paramount to a desire to earn a competency for my wife and child, it is the yearning to live long enough to prove to the world that I am not as bad as I have been painted.
>
> Beneath the caricatures unjustly given of me by the public press there beats a heart full of love and tenderness and kindliness for my fellow man and loyalty to society. There was a scene back of these curtains tonight that did my soul good. A minister of the gospel, the Reverend Mr. Gee, came on the stage and extended his hand to me and said: "Mr. James, I want to pray for you."
>
> That is religion. That man is following the steps of our Savior–seeking souls to save. How different from that other minister of this city. I don't remember his name and I don't want to.
>
> When I was invited four years ago by the citizens of Livingstone County to start the races there, that other minister said it was a shame that a man like Frank James should be asked to start the races. I broke no law when I came here. How far behind our meek and lowly Savior that man was! You remember how our Savior, stooping over the fallen woman, said: "Let him who is among you and without sin, cast the first stone," and when he raised up, they were gone? Therefore I say that minister who tried to blacken me is far behind the teachings of the Savior.
>
> (*Kansas City Star,* November 22, 1904)

It was a short and impassioned speech, full of religious eyewash and heartfelt pleading, but really nothing more than a generous wallow in self-pity. Nevertheless, it touched the hearts of a roomful of Missouri rustics, and was as close as Frank James would ever come to making any sort of public apology for his evil past. Repentance, as far as Frank James was concerned, was for weak-willed and cowardly men. His words that night reflected the same arrogant attitude he had shown in the letter written to Governor Crittenden on the eve of his surrender.

The impromptu monologue also revealed pent-up anger and frustration with those who still refused to accept him as a fully rehabilitated member

Frank James and his dog Jerry in a buggy pulled by a sulky pacer named Dan, c. 1910. (Courtesy M. C. Russell, Stockton, Missouri.)

of society. Public detractors were finally getting to Frank James. Another thing was also clear. Ever since he had been freed from jail, James continued to labor under the notion that leading a law-abiding life was enough to atone for his crimes.

Before Frank James had his stint on the theatrical stage, he petitioned the Missouri legislature, in 1901, to appoint him official doorkeeper of the state House of Representatives. His request was promptly denied. Various reasons were given. U.S. Senator William Hamilton, one of Frank James's prosecutors at Gallatin, held no personal grudge against James but was against the idea because the election of a former outlaw to the body of the legislature might be an embarrassment to the Democratic party [9].

Another person who was instrumental in thwarting James's plan, however, did bear ill will toward the former outlaw. A. W. Dockery was one of the principal owners of the Gallatin bank robbed by the James gang in 1869. Dockery had entered politics and was governor of Missouri at the time of James's petition. Dockery was one of many who never forgot or forgave Frank James for his role in the bank heist that led to the death of William Sheets. Thirty-one years after the fact, he was able to take some retribution against James [10].

On the family farm at Fletcher, Oklahoma in 1909. Left to right: Frank James, his son Robert, and wife Ann. (Courtesy Jesse James Farm & Museum, Kearney, Missouri. Reprinted with permission.)

Frank James never lost the ability to be made a public spectacle if he wished, to be put on display in dime museums and on the stage (as in Chillicothe), to stand before leering throngs like a wild circus animal and be forced to answer an endless barrage of stupid questions relating to his lurid and sensational past. Even the mundane, run-of-the-mill jobs he was able to land were not based on any special skill he possessed, but solely on the former outlaw's ability to draw a crowd, nothing more. These experiences were demeaning and degrading.

Eventually, the name of Frank James lost much of its magical allure. People's expectations were dashed when they laid their eyes on the stoop-shouldered and homely-looking man wearing shabby and ill-fitting clothes. Ever since he had come out of hiding and rejoined society, James failed to live up to the image of Missouri's fearless and intrepid robber of banks and trains. For the romantically inclined, it was far better to read about Frank James rather than see him.

An 1882 view of the James family homestead near Kearney, Missouri. (Courtesy Library of Congress, Prints and Photographs Division.)

All Debts Paid

On the morning of February 18, 1915, following a protracted winter illness, the famous gunslinger suffered a stroke and passed away that afternoon. A few days later, a simple funeral was held near Kearney at the James family homestead. There, in the tiny parlor of the ramshackle, yellow-clapboard house where he had spent his youth, the body of Frank James was laid out in a plain black casket.

Early on the morning of the funeral, a long and slow-moving cortege of neighbors and family friends wound its way along the country roads that led to the James farmhouse. By two o'clock, horses, buggies, and automobiles lined the dirt road to the James house for a quarter of a mile. On a little plot of ground beside the old coffee-bean tree, where for many years Jesse's body had lain, the mourners gathered to pay their last respects to Frank James. In back of the house stood a solitary apple tree, now gnarled and bent with age. It was the one Frank and Jesse used to tether their horses to when they came home for one of their infrequent visits. The boys always made sure that their horses were kept ready for a quick getaway.

John Finis Philips in later years.
(Courtesy State Historical Society of
Missouri, Columbia. Reprinted with
permission.)

Colonel John F. Philips, well into his eighties, journeyed from Kansas
City to say a few words at the service, fulfilling a promise he had made to
the man he had defended in court over thirty years before. In a husky voice
bordering on tears, Philips recollected that promise: "The last time I saw
Frank James was about a year ago at the Hotel Baltimore in Kansas City.
He took me to one side and said, 'You and I are getting old and soon both of
us will go. I know no other man I prefer to speak such words as your heart
will prompt at my death. I want you to promise to make my oration.'" Philips then recalled his first meeting with Frank James in the company of
John Edwards. Impressed by the outlaw's sincerity, the attorney had
agreed to defend the former bandit without taking a single penny in pay-
ment. "Take your wife and little boy and acquit yourself, as I believe you
can, and I'll have my reward," Philips remembered assuring James.

The ex-Union officer continued to reminiscence about Frank James
before the attentive audience. Before long his old courtroom passion surfaced: "Now he is gone and his ashes and dust will find the surcease that

the world would not give, but which it cannot take away. . . . Had he had the advantages and his lines cast on the right paths, he would have been one of the strongest and most brilliant men of his state.

"Things change our reputation and character. Here back in the fifties was a pale, nervous, black-eyed young man, leading the life of a farm boy. . . . Then war's lurid lightning played along the western border. Riders and men came on the quiet home. They did things that outraged the James brothers. It sent the red blood madly through their veins. It spurred the tiger and he became a rider and a raider. One false step led to another and on and on he went, spurred by many causes.

"Thus we see the mortal of Frank James. He has endured the scoff of the world and by fortitude and courage has succeeded at the end of a tragic life. As I look on his inanimate face, I think of what Shakespeare said: 'He that died, pays all debts.'"

The funeral of Frank James was not a religious service. There were no preachers, no hymns, no prayers. It was an informal affair. As such, it made a stark contrast to Jesse's funeral. Few people in Clay County were still around to remember the comical circumstances of that occasion.

Mrs. Zerelda Samuel, despite her many faults, was a deeply religious woman and a regular attendee at the New Hope Baptist church in Kearney. The trouble started soon after Jesse's assassination, when she requested that a formal church service be conducted for her recently departed son. Since few people in the state of Missouri at that time had been sorry to see Jesse go, finding a minister for the service proved difficult. To eulogize Jesse James in a house of the Lord seemed highly inappropriate, if not sacrilegious.

The first to decline was Reverend William Harris of St. Joseph, who feared adverse publicity for the Baptist church. He was quick to wash his hands of the entire affair by stating to the press that Baptists everywhere "look upon the removal of Jesse James, the notorious bandit, with a blessing," and added that Jesse James did not belong to any church. The indomitable Mrs. Samuel, however, applied enough pressure on the church that finally Reverend J. M. P. Martin, minister of the local Baptist church in Kearney, volunteered to conduct the service. Reverend Martin, having composed the most carefully and tactfully worded sermon of his life, gave the eulogy for Jesse James without once mentioning the bandit's name or making any reference to the kind of life he led. Instead, he dwelled on the subjects of soul and salvation and made a fervent appeal to all those present to prepare to meet their Maker [11].

For Colonel Philips, on the other hand, it was appropriate to speak well of Frank James. Years earlier, in 1897, he had paid a similar tribute to another principal of the Gallatin trial and close friend of James, General Shelby. As at Shelby's funeral, Philips was speaking to friends of the deceased. Of those who came to Kearney that day, it is safe to say that not one of them had ever suffered at the hands of Frank or Jesse James. Many were old colleagues of Frank James from Quantrill's band, now aged but still able to serve as pallbearers.

The former comrades shared stories of their wartime experiences together. Among them was George Wiggington, who had been in Kentucky when Quantrill was shot down in his last stand. He told of seeing the Federals charge upon Quantrill, who headed his horse toward the brush, stooping low in the saddle to escape the deadly fusillade, but was felled by a bullet in his neck.

Another veteran was George Shepherd. He remembered Frank James as the quickest man with a revolver in Quantrill's band. "He was the biggest-hearted man I ever knew, but when he did get started, he would do tolerable execution," Shepherd was recorded as saying. The old soldier was referring to the men's participation in two of the most ruthless raids of the Civil War, at Lawrence, Kansas, and a year later at, Centralia, Missouri. Morgan Mattox was there, too. "Morg" had come all the way from his home in Bartlesville, Oklahoma, to say good-bye to Frank James. At sixty-nine he was the youngest of the old war veterans in Kearney that day. Mattox had enlisted with Quantrill when he was only thirteen.

Captain Bill Gregg was the fourth pallbearer. He had commanded the rear guard when Quantrill retreated from Lawrence. The fifth and sixth men were John Wortman, who came from Independence, and Ben Morrow, of eastern Jackson County.

The seventh pallbearer, not a Quantrill veteran, was Thomas T. Crittenden Jr., former mayor of Kansas City and son of the former Missouri governor, whom Frank James had good reason to regard with special fondness and eternal gratitude.

Another story told that day brought a chilling comment from one of the veterans. In sight of the old James homestead was another farmhouse, where Pinkerton agent Whicher had found a job as a farmhand in order to spy on the James place. A few months after the bombing raid on the James

Frank and Annie James's headstone, Hill Park Cemetery, Independence, Mo. (Courtesy Marjorie Vossenkemper. Reprinted with permission.)

house and the mysterious shooting death of Whicher, the owner of the neighboring farm was called to his front door one night and received a bullet in the chest. "He died rather sudden," drawled an old Quantrill guerrilla, with seeming firsthand knowledge of the incident.

One man was conspicuous by his absence that day at Kearney. Cole Younger, Frank James's best friend and the last surviving member of the James gang, was living out his remaining years on a farm near Lees Summit. He sent word to Jesse's son that he would be unable to attend the funeral because he was sick in bed with a bad cold.

Finally, forty buggies, farm wagons fitted with chairs, and a number of automobiles followed the hearse into the town of Kearney. The mourners crowded into the freight room of the train station with bared heads as the casket was placed in a pine box and loaded aboard a train. The sons of Jesse and Frank James accompanied the body of the deceased to its final destination, St. Louis.

(As a side note, a representative of the *Pathé Weekly News* asked permission of Jesse James Jr. to film the James homestead and Frank's funeral. He was refused. To ensure compliance, guards were posted on all roads leading to the James farm who stood watch the entire day of the funeral; as a result, the movie operator left town without his pictures [12]. "Frank wouldn't have liked it," explained Jesse's son.)

Frank James's will contained strict instructions for his cremation. Ever since Jesse's death the former outlaw lived in the morbid fear that doctors would try to use his brain for medical research after he died. This was not a paranoid concern. An autopsy had been performed on Jesse James before he was buried so that his brain could be examined by physicians. (A well-publicized exhumation of Jesse's body in 1995 showed that the top of Jesse's skull had been circumferentially sawn off for this purpose.) The notion that the brain of a criminal might be anatomically different from a "normal" brain was quite commonplace in the medical community at the time. As an added precaution, Frank James insisted in his will that family members remain with his body until the cremation was completed. He also stipulated that his ashes be stored in a safe-deposit vault in Kansas City until his wife's death.

Frank James's estate, which was divided equally between his son, Robert, and his wife, consisted of the James family property near Kearney and a 160-acre farm in Oklahoma. He had nothing more, relatives stated, quickly adding that he was free of debt [13].

Ann survived Frank by almost thirty years. She died frail and blind in a sanitarium in Excelsior Springs, Missouri, on July 6, 1944, at the age of 91, and fulfilled to the end her solemn vow to never reveal the "true story" of her fabled husband. She was cremated and Frank's ashes were removed from storage and mixed with hers, then placed in a small metal box. In a brief graveside ceremony held on the morning of July 26, their remains were buried in Hill Park cemetery in Independence, Missouri, by park superintendent Noel C. Russell. Russell admitted afterwards that, per family instructions, he placed certain things in the little mausoleum, but he was sworn to secrecy to never reveal what they were.

Epilogue

For any trial by jury to end in a just and proper verdict, it must be conducted without bias or prejudice. This process is facilitated by established rules and principles known as due process. The jury's responsibility is to hear the evidence, determine the truth, and make a decision of guilt or innocence based on that evidence. If the case is a criminal prosecution, a presumption of innocence is conferred upon the defendant, and no one accused of a crime can be judged guilty unless that guilt is determined beyond a reasonable doubt.

The American system of justice is not perfect. Indeed, no legal system on earth works flawlessly to ensure that the guilty are always punished and the innocent go free. While jury members are charged with the obligation to be fair and impartial, they are human beings and, as such, can and do make errors in judgment that interfere with the judicial process. However, we have come to regard these errors as acceptable risks in a system that otherwise seems to function satisfactorily.

It is naive to believe that every juror summoned for duty at a criminal trial does not harbor hidden prejudices that may affect his or her opinion of the defendant. Nonetheless, the cause of justice is preserved because jurors, even prejudiced ones, have the capacity to temporarily set aside deep personal opinions when judging a defendant's guilt or innocence. This is what happens most of the time, but sometimes extraordinary circumstances arise during a criminal trial when the law, or the jury's sworn obligation to apply it, simply does not mesh with the jurors' own ideas about justice.

The potential for conflict and impasse in these situations has been averted by granting the jury the privilege of ignoring the law, the evidence, and the judge's instructions in order to make a decision that satisfies its concept of what is right and what is wrong. This special veto power is called nullification. It allows jurors to render a verdict on those rare occasions when they believe that the defendant by strict definition of the law should be convicted, but by a liberal interpretation of justice should be acquitted.

While strong emotional issues are likely to trigger an anomalous verdict, historically the refusal to uphold unpopular laws has been the most common reason of utilizing this safeguard. But jury nullification is a sword that cuts two ways, and on even rarer occasions it permits the guilty to be acquitted. This result generally occurs when the jury comes to a trial with preconceived notions of the defendant's innocence and overlooks over-whelming evidence to the contrary.

Excessive pretrail publicity surrounding a well-known public figure is the usual scenario. Whereas today this publicity tends to get the defendant convicted, it had the opposite effect in the case of Frank James, whose reputation preceded him at Gallatin. Many observers have concluded that the not-guilty verdict in James's case was due to jury nullification, and on this issue the Frank James trial left an important legacy in the field of American jurisprudence.

A modern example of justice going awry in this fashion is the acquittal of celebrity O. J. Simpson in his double-murder trial of 1994. Its cataclysmic aftermath caused legal experts and media critics to immediately condemn the jury system and call for reform. Do away with the presumption of innocence, they cried, and eliminate peremptory challenges and the need for a jury's unanimous verdict. Change the burden of proof so that prosecutors are held to a lesser standard than proof beyond a reasonable doubt. Best yet, get rid of lawyers and juries altogether and let cases be tried by a panel of judges, as they are in France, so that justice is never trampled again.

These controversial suggestions, typically the result of an enraged public bent on revenge, offer scant hope of improving the delivery of justice. The uproar usually dies away, and nothing is said or done about the American jury system until the next cause célèbre comes along.

Over one hundred years later, the Frank James trial of 1883 remains a classic among criminal prosecutions in demonstrating how persuasive argument can undermine the strongest cases and emotional responses can override hard evidence. The masterful and moving closing speech given by William Wallace in a losing cause was not wasted; law professors still use it as a teaching aid in discussing criminal defense.

Bibliography and Note References

1   Frank and Jesse—The Robbing and Killing Years

Books

Breihan, Carl W. *Saga of Jesse James*. Caldwell, Ida., 1991.
Jesse James: The Life and Daring Adventures of This Bold Highwayman and Bank Robber. Philadelphia, 1883.
Settle, James. *Jesse James Was His Name*. Columbia, Mo., 1966.

Newspapers

[1] *Kansas City Evening Star*, May 2, 1882.
[2] *Atchison Daily Globe*, April 4, 1882.
[3] *Kansas City Evening Star*, July 18, 1897.
[4] *Kansas Chief (Troy, Kans.)*, April 13, 1882.
[5] *Louisville Courier Journal*, July 27, 1909.
[6] *St. Joseph Gazette*, April 12, 1882.
[7] *Atchison Daily Globe*, April 20, 1882.
[8] *Topeka Daily Capital*, April 15, 1882.
[9] *Kansas Chief (Troy, Kans.)*, April 6, 1882.
[10] *New York Times*, January 30, 1886.
[11] *Atchison Daily Globe*, October 20, 1882.

2   Return of the Outlaw

Details of the surrender of Frank James to Governor Crittenden were extracted from news items printed during October 1882 in the *Atchison Daily Champion, Atchison Daily Globe, Denver Daily Times,* and *Kansas City Evening Star.*

Books

Crittenden, H. H., ed. *The Crittenden Memoirs*. New York, 1936.

Newspapers

[1] *Atchison Daily Globe*, April 6, 1882.
[2] *Atchison Daily Globe*, April 17, 1882.
[3] *Atchison Daily Globe*, May 18, 1882.
[4] *St. Louis Globe-Democrat*, April 24, 1882.
[5] *Atchison Daily Globe*, April 27, 1882.
[6] *New York Times*, April 8, 1882.
[7] *Kansas City Evening Star*, October 6, 1882.
[8] *Denver Daily News*, October 10, 1882.

[9] *Independence Sentinel,* October 9, 1882.
[10] *Atchison Daily Globe,* October 10, 1882.
[11] *Kansas City Daily Journal,* April 13, 1882.
[12] *Topeka Daily Capital,* April 13, 1882.
[13] *Atchison Daily Globe,* May 1, 1882.
[14] *Atchison Daily Globe,* April 17, 1882.
[15] *Atchison Daily Globe,* May 31, 1882.
[16] *Atchison Daily Globe,* June 5, 1882.
[17] *Atchison Daily Globe,* June 6, 1882.
[18] *Kansas City Evening Star,* April 25, 1882.
[19] *Atchison Daily Globe,* October 10, 1882.

3   The Trial at Gallatin

The only known documentation of the dialogue spoken at the Gallatin trial is contained in *The Trial of Frank James for Murder,* an obscure little book published in Kansas City in 1898 by George Miller Jr., William Wallace's nephew, and reprinted in 1954 by Jingle Bob/Crown Publishers. Miller's account, although unquestionably genuine and accurate, is not, and was not intended to be, a complete and official transcript of the trial. No such transcript exists. While Miller's book records who said what throughout the proceedings, its most glaring omissions are the summary arguments given by all but two of the attorneys involved in the trial. Newspaper articles remain the only source for these speeches and they give only summaries. However, the complete text of Colonel Shanklin's closing argument was discovered in the Daviess County prosecutor's office, where it had lain hidden for well over a century.

Practically all daily and weekly newspapers in Kansas and Missouri covered the trial to some extent and stand, for the most part, as fairly reliable sources of information. Not only do articles about the trial corroborate Miller's text, but they also contain snippets of unofficial courtroom dialogue, such as comments among judge, attorneys, and witnesses, that added much flavor to the otherwise long and tedious interrogations.

Of particular interest are the news reporters' personal impressions of the trial and personalities involved. Oddly, the size and prestige of the paper was no guarantee of high-quality reporting. Some of the most insightful commentaries and illuminating vignettes, for instance, came from small Kansas newspapers.

Books

Campbell, Robert A. *Campbell's Gazetteer of Missouri.* St. Louis, 1875.
Conard, Howard L. *Encyclopedia of the History of Missouri.* New York, 1901.
Jackson, William R. *Missouri Democracy: A History of the Party and Its Representative Members, Past and Present.* Chicago, 1936.

Larsen, Lawrence H. *Federal Justice in Western Missouri: The Judges, The Cases, The Times.* Columbia, Mo., 1994.

McDougal, Henry Clay. *Recollections (1844–1909).* Kansas City, 1910.

Miller, George, Jr. *The Trial of Frank James for Murder.* Kansas City, 1898.

O'Flaherty, Daniel. *General Jo Shelby: Undefeated Rebel.* Chapel Hill, 1954.

Wallace, William H. *Speeches and Writings of Wm. H. Wallace.* Kansas City, 1914.

Whitney, Carrie Westlake. *The History of Kansas City and Its People.* Vol. 3, *1800–1908.* Kansas City, 1908.

Williams, Walter. *A History of Northwest Missouri.* Vol. 1. Chicago, 1915.

Newspapers

Details of the trial were compiled from the following newspapers, generally the issues between August 10, 1883, and September 8, 1883:

Atchison Daily Champion
Atchison Daily Globe
Cameron (Mo.) Citizen Observer
Denver Daily News
Denver Daily Tribune
Gallatin (Mo.) Democrat
Gallatin (Mo.) North American
Inland Tribune (Great Bend, Kans.)
Kansas Chief (Troy, Kans.)
Kansas City Daily Journal
Kansas City Evening Star
Kansas City Times
Leavenworth (Kans.) Times
New York Times
St. Joseph Daily Gazette
St. Louis Globe-Democrat
Saline (Kans.) County Journal
Topeka (Kans.) Daily Capital

[1] *New York Times,* January 24, 1883.
[2] *Atchison Daily Globe,* April 6, 1882.
[3] *St. Louis Post-Dispatch,* May 27, 1882.
[4] *Kansas Chief (Troy, Kans.),* August 30, 1882.
[5] *Kansas City Star,* September 9, 1906.
[6] *Kansas City Times,* February 9, 1912.
[7] *Kansas City Star,* October 2, 1938.
[8] *Kansas City Star,* May 29, 1942.

[9] *Kansas City Star*, August 4, 1915.
[10] *Kansas City Star*, October 23, 1910.

4 Redemption and Recrimination

Newspapers

[1] *Atchison Daily Champion*, September 8, 1883.
[2] *Kansas City Evening Star*, September 7, 1883.
[3] *Inland Tribune (Great Bend, Kans.)*, September 14, 1883.
[4] Article originally printed in *St. Louis Chronicle;* reprinted in *Kansas City Evening Star*, February 23, 1884.
[5] *Atchison Daily Champion*, September 12, 1883.
[6] "Society and the James Boys", article originally printed in *New York Tribune*, reprinted in *Denver Daily News*, Sept. 27, 1883.

5 Final Justice

Newspapers

[1] *Huntsville Advocate*, April 23, 1884.
[2] *Huntsville Mercury*, April 30, 1884.
[3] *Kansas City Evening Star*, April 27, 1884.
[4] *Topeka Daily Capital*, April 24, 1884.
[5] *St. Louis Globe-Democrat*, March 5, 1885.
[6] *New York Times*, February 28, 1885.
[7] *Washington Post*, August 8, 1891.
[8] *Kansas City Evening Star*, April 23, 1891.
[9] *New York Times*, January 2, 1901.
[10] *Des Moines Register*, February 8, 1901.
[11] *New York Herald*, June 10, 1882.
[12] *Kansas City Post*, February 21, 1916.
[13] *St. Louis Republic*, February 20, 1915.

Index

123-4, 126-8, 130-4, 144-7, 150-6,
164-6, 172, 180, 189-90, 192, 200;
pardon from Gov. Crittenden, 16;
conviction for horse stealing, 56;
trial at Huntsville (Ala.) and Alabama pardon, 56-7; Missouri pardon, 97-8; summary of Gallatin trial
testimony, 98-100; open letter to
Gen. Shelby, 154
Lincoln, Pres. Abraham, 174
Love, Robertus, xvi
Low, Marcus A., 71

M
Magruder, Gen., 138
Mallory, James, 110-1
Marmaduke, Gen. John S., 107
Martin, Rev. J. M. P., 206-7
Matchett, Rev. Jamin, 111, 166, 186
Matthews, J. P., 182
Matthews, Mr. (witness), 116
Mattox, Morgan, 207
Maximilian, Emperor, 139
McCraw, George, 115
McDougal, Henry Clay, 71, 170, 185
McGee, Maj., 165
McGrath, Secretary of State (Mo.), 21
McIntyre, Attorney General, 156
McKinley, William, xvi
McMillan, Frank, 55, 58, 60, 86, 88-9,
94, 100-1, 119, 121, 144-5, 152, 156,
162-3, 167; murder of, 63
Merritt, William R., 83
Miller, Ed, 41
Miller, Clell, 6, 41
Millstead, John, 129
Mimms, Thomas M., 128
Missouri State Legislature, amnesty of-
fer to James gang, 10
Moffat, James, 91
Montgomery, Elizabeth, 123
Montgomery, Missouri, 123

Morehead, Gov., 138
Morrow, Ben, 207
Murphy, Marshal, 37, 49
Murrah, Gov., 138

N
Nance, Charles R., 83
Newman, James W., 192
Nicholson, William, 129
Norris, Silas, 92, 140
Norwalk, Mr., 129

O
O'Neil, Frank R., 78, 112-3, 116-7,
121-2, 134

P
Parmer, Allen, 124, 131
Parmer, Susan, 132-4
Philips, Col. John F., 27, 71, 74 (photo),
91, 96-7, 102-4, 113, 125-7, 129,
141-2, 144, 146-7, 148-9, 156, 158,
161, 166, 173, 176, 179, 186, photo of
205; member of Missouri State Su-
preme Court Commission, 74-5; ac-
tions in Civil War, 125-6;
biographical sketch, 148; summary
speech, 150-3; eulogy at Frank
James's funeral, 205-7
Pinkerton detective agency, xvi, 10, 15,
24
Pleasanton, Gen. Alfred, 126, 137
Polk, Gov. Trusten, 138
Poole, William (Bill), 120, 176
Poole, Dave, 124
Potts, Jonas, 110-1, 123-4
Prentiss, Noble, 69-70
Price, Gen. Sterling, 5, 125, 138-9, 167

Q
Quantrill, William C., 4, 5-8, 39, 174,
176, 207